An English Ro:

Judy Opitz

Judy Opitz. June 2009.

Judy Opitz (born June Rowley) the photographer,
c. 1950.

Edited and published by David M. Welch 2009

An English Rose in Kakadu

Copyright © Judy Opitz, 2009

www.englishroseinkakadu.com

Edited and Published by David M. Welch

Box 503, CMB 19

Virginia

Northern Territory, 0822

Australia

Fax. (61) (8) 8983 1145

National Library of Australia Cataloguing-in-Publication entry:

Author:	Opitz, Judy
Title:	An English rose in Kakadu / Judy Opitz ; editor: David M. Welch.
Edition:	1st ed.
ISBN:	9780977503551 (pbk.)

Subjects: Opitz, Judy.

Hotelkeepers – Northern Territory – Cooinda – Biography.

Immigrants – Northern Territory – Cooinda – Biography.

English – Northern Territory – Cooinda – Biography.

Other Authors/Contributors:

Welch, David M. (Maxwell)

Dewy Number: 647.94092

Designed and typeset in 11.5pt Times Roman by Bruce Welch

Printed on 115gsm Lumi Silk artpaper, section sewn

Printed in China by Everbest Printing

Cover: Judy Opitz astride a freshly shot crocodile, before it is skinned. Nourlangie Safari, Western Arnhem Land (now Kakadu National Park), 1961.

For my sister, Julia, and her husband, Anthony

Judy and Tom Opitz named and established Cooinda. An early view folder, 1970s.

Jim Jim 'Ideal for park'

The Jim Jim area had some unique features that made it ideally suited as a national park, Mrs Judy Opitz said yesterday.

She was giving further support to the Government's plan to establish a national park in the Jim Jim area.

The plan has been opposed by safari operator, Mr Tom Atkinson who says the park should be in the Woolner area.

Mrs Opitz said that among the unique features of the Jim Jim area was a handsome rock feature on a spur of the rugged escarpment country which runs into Arnhem Land.

It was the home of the shy rock wallaby (an animal possibly not found in the Woolner area) and certain rare birds.

"Nourlangie Rock is an Aboriginal burial ground and to the sincere traveller offers an unusual find," she said.

"But it is a pity that some of these burial caves have recently been desecrated by someone and skulls and certain burial paraphernalia pilfered.

"Oh for rangers and national park to protect them."

She said that although the wildlife was not as prolific as it was a few years ago it was still an area of "wondrous delight" to the serious connoisseur of wildlife.

MRS JUDY OPITZ

There could be found the chestnut quilled rock pigeon, the spotted kuku-taw, Aboriginal lore and scenery to delight the discerning photographer.

Conservationist Mr Graham McMahon also recommends the Jim Jim area as a national park.

He said the escarpment area of the proposed park was considered by botanists as being important for its unusual flora, not found anywhere else in Australia.

Discussions prior to the establishment of Kakadu National Park. Northern Territory News, 1970s.

~ iv ~

Contents

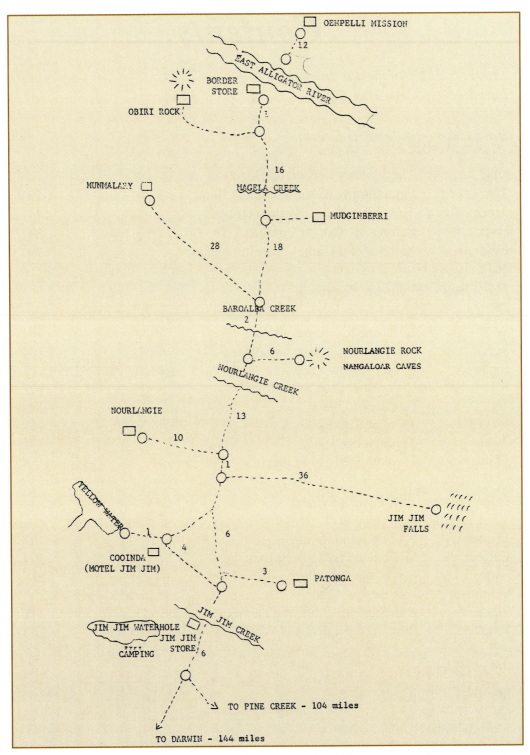

One of my mud maps given to Cooinda visitors, late 1960s. At first, access to the area was only from Pine Creek. Later, access was across the Marrakai plain (to cross the Adelaide River) and the Old Jim Jim Road (to cross the South Alligator River).

Introduction

A Remarkable Human Adventure

One of the wonderful things about living in the Northern Territory is that, when you walk down any street in Darwin, you are quite likely to meet history and history makers walking toward you. That happened to me when I first met Judy Opitz, nearly thirty years ago. I already knew something of her amazing life story and then I learned more and more about important parts of our history as I got to know her better.

I listened and laughed as she told me about her journey from the footlights of the Empire Theatre in Liverpool, England, to Cooinda, in Kakadu. That's a long trip, but it needs an even longer stretch of the imagination to believe that an English chorus girl might start one of the Territory's best known tourist ventures. It's further still from Cooinda to a university graduation ceremony where Judy was awarded a Doctorate of Philosophy at the age of 84 years. But that is the true and remarkable story of Judy Opitz, a woman whose whole life has been an amazing and hugely entertaining journey through adventure to achievement.

Her journey certainly defied all the expectations that might have been held for Judy when she was born into comfortable and well-settled privileged English circumstances. Why should she seek a different life in a far-off place? After all, it would have been thought, she already had the best that life could possibly offer.

But that was not enough for Judy. After adventures in England, she still yearned for experience and achievement that she could call her own. That yearning finally brought her to Australia, when she migrated as a "ten pound Pom" under a post-war assistance scheme that brought Britons to Australia. Certainly, Australia has got more than its ten quid's worth from her.

Judy came to Darwin and almost immediately met Tom Opitz. Together, they pioneered Cooinda and made history. Tom died and later Judy began yet another career, this time as a student of anthropology and archaeology.

Judy was just as successful in academe as she had been in Kakadu. She is now Dr. Opitz, while Cooinda, now known as Gagudju Lodge Cooinda and owned by the Gagudju people, is one of the world's best known tourist resorts with its Yellow Waters boat cruises.

So our history is made, the names of places are put on our maps, we come to be what we are today. The best part of Judy's adventure is that it has now been written down and captured as a permanent record of important episodes in our past. Judy, for that, I thank you most sincerely. So will everyone else who reads this most engaging, enthralling and good-humoured story, a story that emphatically proves that truth can be stranger and much more interesting than fiction.

Peter Forrest
Historian and Writer
Darwin, December 2008

Part One – Towards a Dream

CHAPTER ONE

The Journey to Kakadu Begins

I suppose you could say my journey to Kakadu began in England in 1958. One dank, foggy afternoon in November I boarded the P & O liner *Orontes*, berthed at Tilbury, striding boldly up the gangplank with somewhat mixed emotions, not knowing whether my decision to emigrate was the right one. I was 34 years old, with memories of fun and adventure behind me and still, in between time spent at home in Norfolk, a useless wanderer over the face of the earth.

Just a year previously, in November, 1957, I had returned from a trip on a bus to India, suffering from an attack of jaundice which left me so weak and depressed that I had had to change my hoped for plan of travelling on from Bombay to Australia for the next adventure. I had probably picked up the disease on the outward journey through sharing the contents of a goatskin water bottle and handfuls of chicken mash with some Persian truckies, after a dust storm hurtling over the piece of desert we were crossing had temporarily halted all traffic. Safely home in Norfolk once more, and attended by the family doctor, I lay in civilised fashion between crisp white sheets and luxuriated in hot water bottles to stave off the wintry chill. At Christmas I was allowed up to join in the festivities but warned not to drink anything alcoholic. Guests came in for the usual Boxing Day dinner, an event when all family members would try and get together. I had always so enjoyed those dinners in earlier days when my mother was alive and had presided over her end of the table. An apple log fire glowed and sparked in the grate under the marble mantelpiece at one end of the long gracious room. Holly would be stuck coyly behind my stepfather's family portraits which adorned the walls. The walnut table gleamed with highly polished silver, and we would be served by the staff with Windsor soup, turkey, Christmas pudding and brandy sauce, mince pies and all the trimmings. The repast over, vintage port from my stepfather's cellar, perhaps Taylor's '24 or Cockburn '27, would be sent clockwise in the ritual manner round the table, and woe betide anyone who "sat" on the port. The wines were apparently fine and precious but my palate had never learnt to appreciate them as fully as they deserved and I only ever drank a "splash" for fear of "wasting" them. Crackers would be pulled and the enclosed jokes bandied about before the ladies would retire, followed shortly by the gentlemen, to the chandelier-hung drawing room where we would all play charades and paper games in between roasting chestnuts. This time the Boxing Day dinner was a rather more low key affair with less guests and family members able to attend, not to mention less staff, but the customary dining room setting was almost the same. It was in somewhat stark contrast to the chicken mash repast in the desert with all-comers' hands digging into a communal bowl!

I remembered how the enforced idleness and returning cheerfulness had given me time to consider my next moves. If I wanted it, the atmosphere augured well for a future civilised country life in the Norfolk I loved so fiercely. "Stay as long as you like. It's your home," said my stepfather. As I convalesced, I considered the future and the idea of getting a job in King's Lynn and living at the Hall. But would such a life hold my wild, roaming nature for long? I found, however, I had no need to worry about any decision in that respect as the Hall itself had other ideas for me.

That it was haunted there was no doubt. In the 400 years since it had been built, several murders and suicides were known to have occurred, and from time to time evil emanations had been felt, with guests reporting odd feelings. It did not worry my stepfather when bedclothes were mysteriously pulled off him in the old panelled room in which he slept. "Ghosts are just as entitled to live here as we are," he said, "after all, they were here first." I could not feel the same. I had had to change my bedroom years before when I had felt an evil presence there. Catlike feet had landed on my bed one night, but we had no cats and the door was closed. I put my head under the blankets in a lather of fright while the feet or hands crept up towards my head till I felt I was choking. Then a gurgling sound and the feeling passed. "I forget the whole story," said my stepfather when I had told him about it later, "but someone or other got strangled in that room."

Narborough Hall, where I spent later childhood years, in Norfolk, England. Photographed in 1993.

The bedroom I slept in on my return from the bus venture – the same room I had moved into after the "cat" experience and which had accepted me then – now seemed to be systematically trying to oust me. I was frequently awakened by a strange feeling. Although putting on the bedside light seemed to send away whatever it was that was causing the feeling, it kept recurring. Sometimes I was too frightened even to put out my hand and turn on the light. The bedroom door rattled for hours and the windows thumped though there was no wind to make them move. And on occasion "something" would come into the room – no definable shape or even cold breath of air – but the back of my neck would prickle and a feeling of fear and horror would threaten to engulf me. Overwrought imagination! Maybe! But it was strong enough to send me from the Hall, and Norfolk.

My bedroom held many wartime relics. When there was a crash landing on the aerodrome, from which the crew walked away, I'd tear away the "skin" with the plane's serial number. The "MM22.." at the top is from a crashed Mosquito bomber. Against the wall I have placed a flag of the Union Jack. In front of this, the large propeller is off a Sopwith Camel retrieved from a First World War crash. I'm sitting on the couch in front and the dog looks miserable.

When I had finally recovered from the jaundice, I returned to London, found some unhaunted digs and got back an earlier job I had had driving for J. Davy Self Drive Car Hire firm. Geoff, a wavy-haired, blue-eyed young Australian joined the firm about the same time and I became an avid audience when he talked about Australia. As a J. Davy driver, Geoff saw more of England in a short while than many other Aussies who spent most of their time in Kangaroo Valley at Earl's Court, often running down the English. Geoff was enjoying his visit but was also getting vaguely homesick for the sound of the surf and wanted to get back to the girl he'd left behind. He booked his passage home. "Lucky you," I said, "see you out there one day."

Australia was still calling me to go there but I could not afford the full fare. The fare was only ten pounds for a migrant assisted passage, but there was a two year wait. "If you like," Geoff volunteered, "I'll ask my parents if they'll nominate you and you may be able to get there sooner." Geoff's parents kindly wrote back agreeing to this plan and I went through medical tests at Australia House and filled in numerous forms. Geoff was sailing on the Orient liner *Orontes* in November. Five days before the ship was due to leave, the authorities asked me if I'd like to go on the same boat as there'd been a cancellation. My fate was sealed. Would it lead me to that gentle dreamer, yet withal a hardened bushman with a liking for sleeping under the stars in the wide, open whispering spaces, that I yearned for? Well, I thought, as I strode up the gangplank of the *Orontes*, I was about to find out.

No-one in the family could get down to Tilbury to see me off, for which I was thankful as I cannot bear last minute goodbyes. It was bad enough watching other people give a last brief hug to their loved ones and stand disconsolately at the rails as the gangplanks were withdrawn. Those still ashore fluttered their handkerchiefs and indulged in furtive eye-dabbings. I wandered down to my two-berth cabin on "G" Deck which had been allotted me and found I was sharing it with a red-haired Australian girl called Mary Green. She was already ensconced on the lower bunk. Having been away from her native land for over five years, Mary was able to return home under the ten pound migration scheme. We exchanged brief histories. "You going to settle in Australia?" asked Mary. "Too right," I said. "Not a bad place," she said. "Fair dinkum," I said. "You'll like it there," she ventured. "My oath," I cried. She burst into laughter. "I'd say you've been reading Nevil Shute."

I couldn't deny it. I had read every book he had written about Australia. "You'll find not too many Aussies talk like that," Mary went on, "Just what are you expecting Australia to be like?" "Oh, wide open spaces, starry skies, he-men," I murmured vaguely. "Ah, you're thinking of the outback," said Mary, as though it were another country. "It's not every Aussie who knows about the real bush. They talk about going bush sometimes when all they mean is taking a picnic ten miles out of the city. We're actually a very civilised country, you know." I did know. As well as novels, I had devoured every history, travel book, picture book or impressions about Australia I could lay my hands on. But I didn't want to live in a glossy city. I wanted to live in the outback.

The engines had been going for some time and darkness had fallen before we slid imperceptibly away from the quay. The fog had more or less cleared as, with scarcely any movement beyond the slight vibrations of the engines, the ship set course down the Thames for the open sea. I watched the lights of Southend standing out clearly on the port bow and then we had passed them and a hundred winking lights seemed to be beckoning us through the indicated channels, saying: "This way, Australia." Some three weeks later, after crossing the Equator with none of the customary dunking in the swimming pool because of a serious accident on a previous voyage, we sighted Australia. Slowly out of the dawn mist the coastline took shape, gazed at with eager eyes by homecoming Australians. No less eagerly did I strain my eyes to see the Aussie equivalent of the White Cliffs of Dover. I was a little disappointed and could not see anything very dramatic about the dunes that trailed forlornly into the sea. As we neared Fremantle, I met up with Geoff again. I hadn't seen much of him on the voyage as he had been enjoying himself with new shipboard friends and visiting the various ports en route – visits which, as a migrant, were denied me. Perhaps it was thought migrants might not return to the ship if let ashore.

Geoff now suggested I look at my first dingo. "Look, over there," he said, and he handed me his binoculars for a better view. I scanned green patches in a general line with his pointing finger where I thought a wild dog might possibly be lurking, little knowing that dingoes hardly inhabited those parts any longer. It turned out to be an enormous black dog painted on the yellow wall of a factory that I was supposed to look at. The cleanness and neatness of Fremantle Docks contrasted greatly with the rather grim and untidy boatyards of Liverpool and Tilbury back in England. Formalities completed on board, it didn't take long to clear Customs in the light and airy shed. "Well, I've arrived," I thought, "Now what?" I had twenty-five pounds in my pocket to start a new life. The whole vast continent of Australia was before me. I stayed awhile with Geoff's parents, Mr. and Mrs. Chandler, in Scarborough, before settling in at the Y.W.C.A., near King's Park in Perth. In the New Year, 1959, I found myself an office job at Winterbottom's, a car firm.

Sometimes, before bedtime, I would walk along the fringe of King's Park where I could look over the wide and peaceful Swan River, to the twinkling lights of the city. The white bark of the gumtrees glistened in the moonlight and the heady eucalyptus scent of their leaves filled the air. By day, King's Park look rather drab, although I knew in the wildflower season, which I had just missed, it was riot of colour. I heard the magpie sing his beautiful melodious song and could hardly believe he went under the same name as his raucous-voiced English counterpart. But everything was so brown. "Oh, for a tinge of English green," I sighed at work one day. "Does it get you like that?" asked a workmate. "Funny – when I visited England I got so fed up with seeing nothing but green fields that I pined for some good old harsh, brown scenery."

At weekends, newfound friends took me on the rounds of Places of Interest to Show the Newcomer. I was taken crabbing at Bunbury, to see the caves and koalas at Yanchep, and down to Pemberton to look at the Gloucester Tree and the magnificent kauri forests. The Gloucester Tree – so called, I learnt, after the Duke of Gloucester visited it in 1946 when it was first prepared as a fire post – was 200 feet high. Stakes stuck into its trunk curved round like a circular staircase to the small hut built into the topmost branches. The hut is manned night and day for any signs of fire breaking out in the surrounding country. Visitors may climb to the top if they wish but, having no head for heights, it certainly wasn't my wish.

After three months in Perth, I decided to venture over to the Eastern States, and boarded a train bound for Kalgoorlie, famous gold town of Western Australia. There I changed trains on to the *Overlander* diesel train which travelled over the Nullarbor Plain. It was extremely comfortable with soft seats – made up into beds at night for the three day crossing – radio, air-conditioning, hot water showers and good food. The rail track ran on straight for 300 miles through flat saltbush desert. We drew up at various halts for fuel and to offload provisions. Children scampered about barefoot while their elders attended to the business of sending the train on its way again. It cannot have been much of a life for the families living out there in the yellow dust of a treeless waste. If that was the outback, I wasn't sure if I'd like to live in it.

I stayed a week in Adelaide, and took day tours around the Ranges, visited the wineries in the Barossa Valley, went out to the old whaling station at Victor Harbour, and viewed the lights of the city at night from Mount Lofty. Gorged on sightseeing I finally boarded a Pioneer coach for Melbourne where I thought I'd work for a while.

The journey took fifteen hours, the road winding over the rolling Mount Lofty Ranges outside Adelaide into flatter country which gradually became greener as we travelled eastward. Then over the border of South Australia and into Victoria. The inevitable gum forest and unchanging bush gave way at one point to some deciduous English trees lining the road, just turning to autumnal colouring. No doubt they had been planted by homesick English migrants many, many years ago. I started to feel homesick myself! Up till then, this new country I was in had meant nothing very much to me. I'd seen a lot and loved what I'd seen but only as an interesting new experience. Now it sunk in that I was here to stay and I started to compare everything with England.

Those silly one-storeyed houses Australians lived in which we'd call a bungalow back home – except our bungalows didn't have tin roofs. Their ridiculous meal hours! Whoever heard of dinner as the mid-day meal – that was called lunch in England. And tea at 6.30 pm, which was really a meal that the English would call dinner, except we'd never have it at such an early hour. Tea should be thinly sliced cucumber sandwiches and cake at 4.30 pm, but there seemed to be no such meal in Australia. And how could they say that their bare, brown hills were beautiful. Now take the glorious rolling green hills of Devonshire if you want to call a hill beautiful. And all the Australians could say was "Australia is the MOST BEAUTIFUL COUNTRY IN THE WORLD, THE MOST HOSPITABLE . . . THE MOST THIS, THE MOST THAT."

I arrived in Melbourne and hated it at once. The overpowering homesickness reaction had quite made me take leave of my senses! I booked in at the Y.W.C.A. in Footscray, found myself a job in a wool firm in the city, and walked to work every day. My shoes soon went into holes and I stuffed them with paper. I was saving every penny I could for my fare back to England! How could I stay in this terrible place. Why, even the weather was worse in Melbourne than England. What monstrous temperature fluctuations there were. One would stagger to work in the thinnest of dresses with the temperature nearly 100 degrees and by mid-day it would be cold enough for an overcoat. If one bounded to work in woollies against a cool day, by mid-day one was likely to expire from heat exhaustion. And the wind! It didn't just blow you over like a good, solid English wind. It blew upwards in gusts from the ground so that one needed half a dozen hands to wipe the grit from one's eyes, hold down one's skirt which threatened to tie itself about one's neck, and hang on to the nearest lamppost to prevent being blown clean across the street.

The superiority of many Melbournians, boosting up their city to equal any in the world, stuck in my throat. "Just look at Collins Street," they said, "isn't it the most beautiful street in the world?" At one end of the street, tables are put out in summer for one to sit out over one's coffee and it is called the Paris end of Collins Street. But where was the old world gaiety, the atmosphere or charm of Paris? I asked myself. And their river, the Yarra! A nasty, dirty, little stream! Sydney says that Melbourne has the only river that flows upside down with all the mud floating at the top. Melbourne says that Sydney spoiled a beautiful harbour while they enhanced a poor one. Little love seemed to be lost between New South Wales and Victoria. It was all the same to me. I had no love for Victoria and no interest in seeing New South Wales. All I wanted was to get back to England. I was a typical whinging Pom.

One day in Myers Emporium, I ran into petite, rosy-cheeked, silver-haired Rhona Bird. She and her tall, bespectacled husband, Bob, and their dark-haired, magnolia-skinned daughter, Margery, had travelled back to Australia after a world tour on the same ship, the *Orontes*, that had brought me out. I had often chatted with them on board. They were both qualified chemists and owned two chemist shops. Rhona had qualified as a chemist long after the age when new careers are usually started, and had studied for her pharmaceutical exams while looking after her husband and three growing children. I greatly admired her, and was glad to see her again. "Do give us a ring and come out and see us," said Rhona, and she gave me their phone number. I suddenly remembered I hated Australia and Australians. I grunted "Love to" as politely as I could and said I'd have to dash as my lunch hour was nearly up. I thought no more of her kind invitation, wallowing as I was in homesickness for England.

A fortnight later, the Birds called at the Y.W.C.A. I was spending the Saturday afternoon going through shipping schedules and trying to work out sums to find out which ship I could sail home on. If I left under two years from the date of my arrival, it meant I had to repay the Government for the fare they had paid out for me. "You're coming with us," said Bob Bird, and they stood by firmly while I packed my few bits and pieces and settled my account. An hour or so later, they drove me out of the city and up the winding Dandenong Hills, through the autumnal glow of red, yellow and russet trees planted by settlers years ago, to Sassafras, deep in the heart of a gum forest. Whipbirds and bellbirds vied with each other in their song, and bright blue and red mountain parrots scolded raucously as they flew by.

Bob Bird had only recently finished building the house at Sassafras himself, while Rhona had started the garden. The house was luxuriously furnished and had wall to wall carpeting. A huge plate glass window ran round two sides of the lounge, giving an uninterrupted view of the garden and the surrounding gum forests. The trees were shedding their bark which festooned in long strips from the trunks. The garden had built-up rockeries filled with sweet-smelling boronia and many shrubs unfamiliar to me. A flame tree was in full glory, its leaves lighting the garden like a torch.

"Let's have a cup of tea," said Rhona, after we had taken my gear inside. "Well, and what do you think of Sassafras?" asked Bob, over the teacups. "Quite pretty," I said, half-heartedly. I didn't want to admit I thought it was a lovely spot. After all, I hated Australia! "It's the most beautiful place in the world," said Bob. I put down my teacup carefully. I wished I hadn't come. How awful if I said something impolite. I wanted to say "You and your darn beautiful country. England's beautiful too. And I think England's the most beautiful country in the world. And what's more I'm going back there just as soon as I can." Instead, I gripped my cup tighter, took a long drink and said nothing. "Will you settle in Melbourne, do you think?" asked Rhona. "No," I said, "actually I'm saving hard to go back to England – and there I'll stay." "And do you think you'll be able to settle down there after all the travelling you've done?" asked Bob, quietly. "Goodness knows," I shrugged. I didn't want to think about it.

We had a film show that evening of all the pictures Bob had taken on their world tour. It was wonderful to see the old familiar beauty spots of England and to hear the Bird's commentaries about them. "Now, there's a lovely spot," said Bob, flashing a picture of a riot of flowers in London's Kensington Gardens. I had to have a little dig. "So Australians do find places other than their own country beautiful?" I asked. "Of course," said Bob, surprised. "There are beautiful places all over the world. But naturally the most beautiful place of all is home where one's heart is. What's the matter," he laughed, "are you getting sick of us Aussies raving on about our country. Why shouldn't we. We're proud of it. We made it."

Suddenly I thought I saw the light. Naturally the Aussies were proud of everything in their country. After all, hadn't they built it up from the dregs of convict humanity and a handful of free settlers. It was now a country reaching a maturity that had old English diehards, who still thought of it as a colonial possession under the rule of the Crown, gasping at the effrontery in making such headway. The Aussies were so proud of it that they could see beauty, as applied to their country, with different eyes. I thought of the corrugated iron roofs and wrought iron balconies, supported by spindly pillars, of so many of their older houses, which I had considered so ugly compared with the gracious lines of a row of Georgian terraced villas back in England. Then I thought about them again through the eyes of an Australian and began to also to see a beauty in them from the fact of the wealth of love that must have gone into their building. Perhaps the settlers who built them had thoughts of home and easier times, but they hadn't got up and run when the going got tough. They'd stuck it out and built with what materials they could get in designs best suited to the climate and the circumstances, and fashioned a country for their children and their children's children, who now – quite rightly – raved over it.

A deeper admiration of Australia and the Aussies stole over me. I may have appreciated their efforts in my mind from all the books I had read, but now I was getting an understanding with my heart also. I also began to realise why I had rejected Australia when the first natural pangs of homesickness had struck. Perhaps it was a feeling that I would be disloyal to the country where I had been born, and where I'd been brought up to believe that there was no country of any value other than England. It was a feeling that had made me close my mind to the delights of a new country and the advantages it could offer me if I would let it. Until I got rid of that feeling, I could never settle anywhere outside England. I decided that just because I might love another country, need not mean I loved England less.

With an unshackled heart that was now free to wander till it found its own "home," I asked: "Have you got any scenes of the outback?" "We've some pictures of a farm in Gippsland. Is that outback enough for you for a start? And we'll take you there tomorrow if you like," suggested Rhona. Later, I was taken to see the Cumberland Forest near Marysville with its stately 300 foot high mountain ash trees, Mount Buffalo, the Victorian ski resort, the tobacco plantation of the fertile Ovens Valley, Tarra Valley Park with its splendour of tree ferns and waterfalls, and various weirs and dams. And so I began living in Australia as opposed to merely existing. I don't suppose the Birds will ever know quite what they did for me, either consciously or unconsciously, but without their timely rescue from my pit of misery, I might have returned to England, another migrant misfit. They offered me accommodation in rooms over one of their chemist shops, and I changed jobs from the rather dreary wool firm to an exciting Travel Office. With doors opening to fresh adventures, I began to regain my equilibrium. Life was taking on meaning again.

One evening I accompanied an office girlfriend, Sonia, to the Tivoli Theatre. We saw a most colourful revue-type show, resplendent with lavishly costumed showgirls. With memories of my stint on the boards in England, for a moment I wished I were up on stage too. Afterwards we went backstage as Sonia had thoughts of being a showgirl herself. "Come back tomorrow morning for an audition," she was told. Next day I took time off work and went with her. The backstage atmosphere stirred me even more than the night before. Making a sudden decision to try and get back into show business, I ventured to enquire if they wanted any more showgirls. But they only needed one replacement at that time and Sonia got the job. "But we do need some models," they said to me, "show us your legs, dear." I obligingly hauled up my skirts as I had absolutely no objection to showing off my legs. What I didn't realise was that I would be required to show much more than that. "Fine, dear," they said, after a cursory view at my legs, "that's O.K. Now go and see the Wardrobe Mistress and she'll see to the rest."

I didn't feel quite the same excitement as I had when I'd got into the chorus of "Annie Get Your Gun," back in my stage days in England, but I sought out the Wardrobe Mistress as I had been bidden, wondering what I might be letting myself in for. The Wardrobe Mistress sized me up and down. "Take off your blouse, dear, would you, and your bra too, if you wear one," she added. She seemed satisfied with what she saw. "Right, here are your costumes," she said, handing me several pairs of fishnet tights and some glamorous headgear. "Go out front tonight and see what the girl you will be replacing does, and then come back for rehearsal in the morning."

Meantime, my friend Sonia was being fitted for the costumes in which she would parade around the stage with graceful movements. I was told my actions were to be entirely static as decreed by the Lord Chamberlain at that time. I now realised what I was letting myself in for. As I wasn't really sure if I wanted to be seen on stage in all my naked glory, static or not, I decided that, rather than give in my notice at my office job, it might be more circumspect to take another couple of days off. Then I could re-assess the situation.

For two matinee and evening performances I quite enjoyed being onstage again, and racing up steep steps to the draughty dressing rooms, and joining in backstage chat while the scenery was being changed. I told the girls how incredibly diminished I felt standing there in my pose on stage with bared bosom for all and sundry to see. The girls assured me that they had all felt like that at first and one soon got used to it. But the most unnerving part of all for me came in the finale, when we had to pose on a foot-wide catwalk swinging fifteen feet above the stage. Stagehands placed ladders in position for the girls to race up nimbly and assume their poses, but I was clumsy and fearful of the height and delayed the stagehands in getting on with their next job. And then, once I was safely on the catwalk, I didn't dare look down but semi-crawled to my allotted position before levering myself up one of the narrow poles from which the catwalk hung. Finally there, instead of nonchalantly leaning against the pole, all I could do was cling to it as though it were a lifeline. I'm sure the stage hands were very pleased when I decided I wasn't cut out to be a model at the Tivoli and resumed my office life before the management could fire me.

I'd been nearly eighteen months in Australia when Michael, a very English boyfriend with whom I used to frequent the motor race tracks to watch drivers like Stirling Moss, Mike Hawthorne and the matchless Fangio perform, wrote to say he was coming to the "Antipodes," as he put it. He'd been studying for his exams when I first knew him, but was now a fully fledged architect. His firm in England was sending him to Melbourne on a short contract. I met him at the Airport. How strange to hear the English "actually's" and the "jolly's" again. I showed him round the Melbourne I now loved, with a feeling of pride. "Quite a jolly little spot, what," he commented, dampeningly, "but, of course, actually it's not quite London, I mean, is it, old girl?"

When he managed to wangle a few days off to visit Sydney, I took time off too and went as co-driver in the second-hand car he had bought for the duration of his stay. We drove straight through the night and saw the Sydney Harbour Bridge through bleary driving eyes at dawn. "Oh, what a wonderful bridge," I cried. "Yes, we've got one just like it over the Tyne at Newcastle," said Michael, "though ours would be a bit smaller, I suppose." We headed for Cremorne where we were to stay with friends of Michael's Australian boss. Sydney's central streets confused me with their square layout, but I found no difficulty in driving round the outer maze of winding streets and narrow lanes, which reminded me of London.

Later we drove through Wooloomooloo, a name that had always fascinated me, and out to Bondi Beach – the golden sanded surfing beach I'd heard so much about. But it wasn't the season for surf. Not a soul was in evidence and the sea was as calm as a millpond. We took a trip by launch into innumerable bays, where architect designed houses had been built into the hillsides, and then up a wild creek which had not yet been cleared of trees for its future building programme.

"What a modern and lovely city Sydney is," I remarked, as we headed back to Melbourne. "Oh, it's all right, but a bit second-rate after London though, you must admit, old thing," said Michael. Clearly I was fast becoming Australianised while Michael still suffered from his English superiority that could not admit anything outside England was worthy of his attention. I was ashamed that I had once talked about Australia as he was now doing. His contract completed some months later, Michael flew back to England. "Have you enjoyed yourself? How did you like the Aussies," I asked him, as we were saying goodbye. "Oh, quite nice people, frightfully hospitable and all that. But really, I mean, they're not quite English, not quite one of us, are they," he said, with his genteel giggle. "How much longer are you going to stand it out here?" I said nothing. He would have been quite incapable of understanding that I was no longer one of whatever he thought I was.

At the end of my two years, I weighed up the pros and cons of settling in Australia like a good migrant. I had had a marvellous time, and made many friends. I had lived

My brother was a keen photographer and practised with me as his model. Late 1940s.

with families and got to know the Aussie way of life as it was in the late 1950s, with the wife at home caring for the children while hubby was out at work. Then at weekends the car would be loaded up with food and masses of home-baked cookies and a round of visiting relatives went on. I loved the people and I loved the country. But not enough! Perhaps I'd come back and settle one day, maybe in the outback, maybe in one of the cities – zinging Perth, dignified Adelaide, gracious Melbourne, sophisticated Sydney or spacious Brisbane. But not yet! I was still a rolling stone and there were more countries to see, one of which might say: "This is your country, this is where you can live and never want to roam again."

Wild buffalo near Cooinda. Photo by Eric Brandl

CHAPTER TWO

On Safari in Western Arnhem Land

Me with one of the crocodiles, prior to its being skinned. Nourlangie Safari camp.

I saved hard and did a lot of overtime in the Travel Office. My passage back to England was booked for March, 1961. From England, I would set off again for other outposts of what had once been the pride of the British Empire – perhaps Canada, Jamaica, or Kenya. When the time came round for an office holiday in July, 1960, I decided to splurge some of the saved-up pennies seeing Queensland and the Northern Territory. This decision met with a mixed reaction from my friends at the Travel Office. "See Queensland by all means," they said, "but there's not much of interest in the Northern Territory, apart from Alice Springs and Ayers Rock."

I flew to Brisbane, enjoyed a few days in that city and then took a coach tour to Mackay. I was rather disappointed. The tropical heat I was expecting at that time of the year was not apparent in the icy cold winds that rushed down the main street.

The lush vegetation I had mistakenly supposed to surround Mackay was not in evidence, and I learnt I would have to travel several hundreds of miles further north to Townsville or Cairns before I struck such scenery. I toyed with the idea of cancelling my trip to Darwin which everyone said would be such a waste of time, and going up to Townsville instead, but in the end left the arrangements as they were and flew to Darwin. I got off the plane at Darwin Airport as dusk was descending. The air was balmy and enveloped one with a peaceful warmth. By the time the airline bus had delivered me to the Darwin Hotel where I'd booked in, darkness had fallen, so I had to wait

The "pill box" near Lee Point, an old World War Two bunker on the beach.

until next morning to see what manner of town it was I'd landed in that no-one thought worth visiting. I was up for an early breakfast served in the hotel dining-room which opened out to a smooth lawn dotted with palm trees and shrubs. A blue sea shone invitingly from the other side of a grassy esplanade.

Darwin railway station, 1960.

It was true there wasn't much of a town to see. Five minutes up one side of the main street with its few tin-roofed shops and five down the other side and that was about it. But I hadn't come to Darwin to go shopping. I went into a milkbar to have a coffee. "Is there anything to see in Darwin?" I asked the girl behind the counter. "Well, there's the Chinese Joss House and the Botanical Gardens, and the old wrecks down at the wharf – you know, from when it was bombed in 1942 – and, er, well, I think that's about all," she said. "Unless," she added, "you've got a car and then there's the swimming hole at Howard Springs 16 miles out." Not having a car I had to give Howard Springs a miss, but I wandered down to the wharf and the Gardens and inspected the Joss House. There was an air of friendliness and informality everywhere. In the late afternoon I sat in the hotel lounge and had a reviving brandy and dry. I wondered how I'd fill in the week I had allowed myself in Darwin; probably just relax on the beach and let the sun soak into me. Perhaps there wasn't much to do in Darwin, but what a wonderful place to do not much in!

I met Tom in Darwin and joined him at Allan Stewart's hunting camp at Nourlangie.

Tom Opitz, 1963.

Two men standing at the bar held my attention rather longer than was polite. I saw a tall, big-boned man with a florid outdoor face, dressed in immaculate cream moleskin trousers and safari jacket, and elastic-sided boots. He was in earnest conversation with a shorter man in well-pressed khaki trousers and shirt. I thought at first this man was the Australian actor, Peter Finch. The film of Nevil Shute's book *A Town like Alice*, starring Peter Finch and Virginia McKenna, had been one incentive, I remembered, in becoming a migrant. Perhaps I stared overlong. When their conversation came to an end they looked over and caught me staring. Picking up their glasses they headed in my direction. The blue eyes of "Peter Finch" were twinkling merrily. "Are you just visiting Darwin?" asked the tall man. "You look new in town. May we join you for a moment?" I indicated my willingness for their company. "I'm Allan Stewart of Nourlangie Safari," said the tall man as he drew up a chair beside me, "and this is my guide, Tom Opitz." Tom, the man I had thought was Peter Finch, sat on my other side.

What was all this? Safari? Guides? "My name is June Rowley," I said, "and I didn't know there were lions and tigers and things up here." Allan Stewart laughed. "Well, no. But we've got buffalo and crocodile …" "What," I cried, "and you take people out and shoot them, just like they do in Africa?" "We've never actually shot any people yet," said Allan, gravely, trying to keep a straight face. "Now, how would you like to come out to Nourlangie and give it a try? Tom here will look after you." I wasn't sure whether the idea of hunting a buffalo or having Tom look after me appealed the most. "Oh, what fun," I said, "When do we start?" "We'll be leaving in half-an-hour," said Allan, "Do you think you can make it?" "But I haven't any safari clothes," I wailed. "Never mind about that. Barbara, my hostess, can fix you up with something," said Allan.

In ten minutes I had packed my bags and booked out of the hotel. I dashed round to the milk bar where I'd had a coffee earlier. The girl who had served me then had just come off duty and was sitting over a milk shake. I bought a sandwich and joined her. Recognising me, she said, "Did you get down to the wharf?" "Yes, it was a wonderful day, and now I'm off to Nourlangie on safari with Allan Stewart." "Oh, I never thought to tell you about that," said the girl, "hunting being more in a man's line. Allan Stewart's a great character. Everyone knows him up here. We call him our Big White Hunter. You'll have a good time at Nourlangie. You'll need to, too," she added, "it costs twenty pounds a day." I didn't care. What was twenty pounds a day against the fun of going on safari. It just meant I'd have that much less to take back to England with me when I returned there next March.

A smart blue Peugeot Station Wagon with *Nourlangie Safari* painted on its sides, was drawn up at the kerb outside the Darwin Hotel. Tom was at the wheel and got out when he saw me. "All set, Judy?" he asked, as he took my case. So he's forgotten my name already, I thought. I turned the name, Judy, over on my tongue. I liked it. It had more bite than June. I decided not to correct him. Allan appeared, briefcase in hand. "Well, I think that just about completes business for this trip," he said, casting his eye into the back of the vehicle loaded with stores. "Let's go." We headed off down the Bitumen. In the Northern Territory the strip of road which runs between Darwin and Alice Springs is known simply as the Bitumen I was told. I was full of questions.

Part of a brochure for big game hunting at Nourlangie camp.

Alan Stewart.
39 Great Western H'Way
Kingswood

WHITEHUNTER SAFARIS
ARNHEM LAND, NORTHERN TERRITORY
AUSTRALIA

Extract from the Whitehunter's Visitors' Book:

R.F.W., Santa Ana, Calif., USA: "This is the best—the *grooving type*—the staff tops . . ."

.... regon, USA: "Fabulous".

C.C., W. Hartford, Conn., USA: "Undoubtedly my best days in Australia—what I will remember most about this fine country."

G.F.McL., Bank of England, London, UK: "A wonderful time".

O.M. Van D.G., Hamburg, Germany: "Most beautiful place of wilderness".

R. Wilson, Dunedin, NZ: "Best hunting of my life—be back first chance".

F. Van D., Antwerp, Belgium: "Sorry I could not stay longer".

M.S. Journalist, Sweden: "Enjoyed every minute".

The cover of a later brochure (about 1973) for Allan Stewart's safari camp.

"What's that for?" I asked when we passed piles of some bright yellow substance several miles out of Darwin. "That's sulphur used in processing uranium," said Tom. "You ought to go out and see the mines at Rum Jungle before you leave the North." A little further on, a few old tin buildings caught my eye. I was told they were for milling the rice from a new venture at Humpty Doo. The venture wasn't proving too lucrative as geese were eating the crops.

About 27 miles from Darwin, just as it was getting dark, I noticed the foundations of a small building at the side of the road. "What's that going to be?" I wanted to know. Tom supplied the information. "A Mrs. Clare Best is building it herself. Yes, by herself," he repeated, sensing my query. "She makes the bricks out of cement in a two-brick making machine and does all the bricklaying on her own. It's going to be the Noonamah Store." "Why doesn't her husband help her?" I asked, stupidly. "Oh, he's away earning money to buy the material to build the store," explained Tom. By the time we reached Adelaide River it was quite dark. Rows of coloured lights shone through the trees and Tom turned off the road towards them. "Come and have a beer and meet Mrs. Myrtle Fawcett," said Allan. "She owns the pub here and she's quite an identity. She's a fourth generation Territorian." A further 80 odd miles brought us to Pine Creek. "This is where we turn off the Bitumen," said Allan, "so we'd better have a last one for the road. Come in and meet Mrs. Mayse Young. She owns the pub here and . . ." "Don't tell me," I interrupted, "she's a fourth generation Territorian and an identity?" "That's right," laughed Allan, "and a mighty fine woman." Mrs. Young, a natural blonde and a still beautiful woman with kind, soft, blue eyes, stood behind the bar. She greeted Allan and Tom warmly. I was so tongue-tied with shyness and awestruck in the presence of yet another real pioneer, that I could hardly say a word.

Several beers later, we were on the road again. Allan took the wheel as we turned on to a dirt track. "We've got 120 miles of this," he said. After some miles of smooth, wide, dirt road, we turned left again. "The El Sherana uranium mines are straight on. That's why that bit of road is so good. They keep it graded for the ore trucks," explained Allan. The track we were now on didn't look as though it had ever seen a grader. We bumped over stones, through sand and across dry creek beds, but the Peugeot never faltered. At the Mary River, we stopped with the headlights shining on a shallow, rippling stretch of water overhung with large-leaved green trees and long, brown sticks of dead bamboo. Here I was introduced to the ritual of rum and river water. Allan produced three tin mugs and filled them from the creek. "Is the water all right to drink just like that? I asked, remembering my English training of testing all water from river sources for purity before drinking. "Safe as houses," said Allan. "Of course, there might be a few old dead jaundiced pigs floating upstream, but they'll give it a good flavour." He poured a dollop of rum from the crinkly Beenleigh bottle into each mug. I enjoyed it so much that I held out my mug for another dose but Allan put the cork firmly back in the bottle. "Next rum at the South Alligator," he said.

We jolted on through the darkness. "Hm, won't be long now before it's quite dry," commented Allan, as we pulled up by a trickle of water in a very wide creek bed. The steep approaches were deeply fissured, making it a test of skill to drive in and out of them without disappearing down the holes. "Can you drive through these creeks all year round?" I asked. "If we were standing right here in, say, February," said Allan, "we'd be under about 40 feet of water. He laughed at the look of astonishment on my face. "Yes. People find it very hard to believe that this country can get flooded when they see it so arid and brown at this time of year. But you must have heard about the Wet and Dry Seasons up here? Roughly, the Dry is from April to November, and the Wet the other months. We get no rain, or very little, in the Dry and around 60 inches in the Wet. And that makes the rivers flow in no uncertain manner, I can tell you." "Well, how do

Nourlangie Camp from the air.

you get to Nourlangie in the Wet, then?" I asked. "Fly," said Allan, laconically, "we've got our own all-weather airstrip." "It sounds awfully isolated," I said. "Suppose you get ill?" "No worries," said Allan. "We've got a two-way radio and we're in contact with Darwin 24 hours a day. If there were an emergency you'd probably get a plane out and be in hospital quicker than if an ambulance collected you from a town house."

One rum and river water later we drove on. Pale moonlight shone down on the track. Kangaroos jumped out of the way and wallabies bounced along in front of us. Curlews, a bird looking like a miniature ostrich and as reluctant to fly, ran this way and that when caught in the glare of the headlights. Once a huge buffalo stood in the middle of the track, but a blast of the horn made him amble off into the bush. "That didn't look much like an African Buffalo," I said, rather disappointed. "The buffalo here are not the Cape Buffalo of Africa," explained Allan, "these are water buffalo from the Philippines. They were brought over as domestic beasts early last century when a settlement was started at Port Essington on the Coburg Peninsula a couple of hundred miles from here. When the settlement closed down a few years later, the buff just wandered off and these are their progeny." "But if they are domestic animals there can't be much fun in shooting them for sport, is there? I asked. "I mean, they can't be very dangerous or anything." "Well, now, said Allan, "suppose you're a trophy hunter and you see a buffalo with a fine spread of horns you fancy hanging on your wall. You stalk him out on the plains and shoot him. But your first shot doesn't kill him and then you're in

Parched grasslands in the Dry Season.

trouble. Just like the African buffalo, his system takes the shock and gives him a bit of a boost. He's roaring mad. He paws the ground and puts his head down. He comes straight at you, a ton of greased lightning. What do you do?" "Scream," I said. Allan ignored me. The question was rhetorical. "You've got to kill him before he kills you, and you've got to keep a cool head and shoot true this time. Now, does that sound a dangerous enough sport for you?" "Yes," I said, humbly. Perhaps I wouldn't be doing any buffalo hunting after all. My head wasn't that cool.

As we drove on, I learnt a bit about how Allan's venture had started. He had opened up his camp in 1958 when safaris had started to be the in thing for the adventurous, although Australia obviously could not offer quite the same big game thrills that were to be found in South Africa. Nevertheless buffalo and crocodile were presented as a lure, with Nourlangie Safaris catering for the hunter after slightly different game. Allan explained that he first got the white hunter bug in 1939 when he was a member of the Darwin Mobile Force. When his unit was training in the Darwin area prior to World War II, troops were taken out bush every weekend where platoon commanders taught them "natural" shooting, as there was no rifle range. As a twenty-year old and a romantic, he said, he had an urge to start up a safari business there and then, but with the intervention of the war and later interests he was not able to fulfil his ambition until some twenty years later.

Allan was not to be the first safari operator in the area. Jerry Randall, from Kapalga and Mudginberry Stations, although mainly making a living shooting for buffalo hides, also took out hunting parties. In this Alligator Rivers region, up until the 1960s, said Allan, individuals

A guest with his bag and young guides.
Nourlangie, 1960.

Aboriginal staff line up to greet us.

Staff at the Nourlangie Safari displaying a crocodile trophy skin. 1960.

Allan, Jackie and fish, Nourlangie. 1960.   *Pudney and baby pig, Nourlangie Camp.*

took advantage of whatever income producing opportunities presented themselves. These included shooting buffaloes for hides or meat, breaking in brumbies, shooting horses for horse-hair, prospecting for minerals, timber-getting, gardening, mustering, crocodile shooting for skins as well as safari operations.

Allan told me Europeans dominated the area, rather than the original inhabitants. He estimated the number of Aborigines living between Maningrida and Nourlangie in the early 1960s to be only about 1,200. But, for the few Aborigines still around, Allan described Nourlangie as being one of the richest hunting areas in the Top End. It was a regular meeting place for the coastal and rock country tribes of Western Arnhem Land. Those tribes would use each other's camps for certain periods each year, varying their diet with "swamp tucker" and "rock country tucker". Swamp tucker was file snakes, mullet, barramundi, goose, turtle, goanna, bandicoot, possum, pig, dove, wallaby, buffalo and salt water crocodile. Rock country tucker was rock wallaby, berries, wild plums, pigeon, python and freshwater crocodile.

The camp area of Nourlangie itself, situated in a large stand of native pine, was not known as Nourlangie to the tribespeople, but *Unlaar* or the Camp of Pine Trees. Around the turn of the century, explained Allan, Chinese from Darwin had started up a timber camp. They dragged the timber by sixteen-horse team from *Unlaar* to the tidal mouth of the Nourlangie Creek, which enters the South Alligator River about 20 kilometres west of the camp. The timber was then loaded on to scows and towed to Darwin, a sea and river journey of about 400 kilometres. Pine used in the original building of the Vic

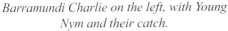

*Barramundi Charlie on the left, with Young
Nym and their catch.*

Me holding a python at Nourlangie, 1960.

Hotel in Darwin is supposed to have come from Nourlangie. After World War II ended,
the camp was run as a timber mill owned by the Arnhem Land Timber Company, but it
was fast running out of millable timber. In 1958, the owner, Russ Jones, was glad to sell
the camp to Allan who saw the potential of the place as a base from which to start his
long held dream of a safari venture. When he took over Nourlangie, the camp consisted
of a combination kitchen-mess-room-store and a few small cabins, mill and machine
shed. Several more cabins were added but otherwise it was little changed. It may not
have been 5-star accommodation but, in those days, it was quite in keeping with a safari
venture in the middle of the wilds.

As we drove the last few miles into Nourlangie Camp, Allan said that section of
the track was known as Boozer's Boulevard because of its many twists and turns. These
were the work of Russ Jones when he was blazing a new route through the scrub in his
old wartime Blitz truck, a large all-terrain vehicle.

We finally reached Nourlangie Camp in the small hours. The place was in darkness
but Barbara, the hostess, must have heard the motor approaching because as we drew
up at the door of a large wooden hut, oil lamps suddenly flickered on inside. "Welcome
back," she said to Allan and Tom, and "welcome to Nourlangie," to me. "There's stew
keeping hot on the range." An appetising aroma drifted across the room and I realised
I was very hungry. "That was delicious," I said, sopping up the last mouthful of gravy
on a forkful of home-baked bread, "what sort of meat was it?" "Buffalo," said Barbara,
"not bad tucker, is it?" She showed me to a mosquito-proofed cabin, one of nine in a

Cement mixing and construction at Nourlangie camp, 1960.

Nourlangie staff members, holding their skinning knives. 1960.

In later years, this 5.1 metre (17 foot) male crocodile, named "Sweetheart" by wildlife ranger Dave Lindner, attacked about ten boats on the Finniss River south of Darwin. While being caught in 1979, seen here, Sweetheart accidentally drowned and is now on permanent display at the Darwin Museum. Photo by Dave Lindner.

Displaying a large set of crocodile jaws, sometimes kept as a trophy.

Tom beside a large termite mound.

large compound, and I rolled between the sheets to dream of snakes and crocodiles and charging buffaloes.

I awoke to the discordant cackling of the kookaburras and the rising sun streaming between the wooden louvres of the windows. Odd gruntings erupted from under the floor of the cabin which was built on short steel-capped stilts to protect it from the depredations of white ants (termites). I wondered if a buffalo were resting there but it turned out to be large, friendly black pig which roamed the compound, always wanting his back scratched. I took a shower in the roofless shower-room, hoping that an overhanging tree did not hold any snakes likely to drop down my neck. Savoury smells of bacon and eggs cooking wafted over from the kitchen. Tom and short, grey-haired Fred Hunter, another of Allan's guides, had finished breakfast by the time I got there. I sat down to breakfast with Barbara who, it turned out, was cook as well as hostess.

Guide Freddie Hunter cools off.

Barbara Worthington, a tall, tousle-haired New Zealander with a zany sense of humour, had only lately flown over to Australia after Allan had chosen her on the strength of an amusing letter out of a hundred applicants for the position.

When I'd done justice to the bacon and eggs, Tom took me off to be initiated into the gentle art of fishing for barramundi, the finest eating fish in the Northern Territory. I followed him along a path edged with long grass and through a glade of paperbark trees, to the arm of a lagoon. A small boat snuggled into the mud at the base of a tree whose roots stretched out into the deeper water, and we clambered aboard. Tom squatted in the bows and carefully pushed under the seat the sharp knife and fishing reel he had been carrying. Taking up a paddle he threaded his way through a maze of tangled branches and semi-submerged logs. Liquid bird calls accompanied the plash-plash of the single oar he was using. Red petals lay scattered thickly under the freshwater mangrove trees, the leafy recesses of which looked just the place to hide a snoring crocodile. The narrow waterway presently opened out to a vast expanse of sparkling lagoon with white-armed gum trees reaching down its length.

I took up the reel and unwound about 30 feet of the stout nylon line, with its wicked looking triple-jag hook, weighted with a .303 cartridge case. I flung the line far out in the water as I was instructed. The first cast nearly ended in disaster. The line lodged itself under my heel and the hook curved round and went perilously near Tom's nose before landing in the boat at his feet. "The idea is to throw the line in the water," said Tom, handing me back the hook end. Feeling very much in disgrace, I gathered the line, made sure it was clear of all obstructions and cast again. This time it sailed well out into the lagoon. No bait is attached to the hook as the fish seem to be sufficiently dazzled by the shining cartridge case being pulled through the water and imagine it must be a choice morsel.

Feeling the unmistakable nibble of a fish on the end of the line, I let out a chortle of joy, and with encouragement and advice, hauled it to the side of the boat in a frenzy lest the first fish I had ever caught should get away. He was a lively customer and resented being brought on board, and who could blame it. With a mighty heave I succeeded in landing it in the boat, where it kicked and squirmed and tied itself up in the loose line which I had forgotten to wind up in my excitement. Tom came to the rescue, unhooking the sharp barbs from its gaping mouth, before untangling it and throwing it into the corner of the boat. My first barramundi! It measured about 18 inches long and weighed around 12 lbs. After catching two more in quick succession, I became blasé. It proved my undoing. The fish jumped out of the water, they threshed about, and they threw the hook. They fought as only barramundi can, and I was unequal to the occasion.

By mid-day, when the heat of the sun was almost unbearable on the open water, and the fish had gone off the bite, we returned to camp for lunch and a siesta. "If you want to bag your buff tomorrow," said Allan, "we'd better have a spot of target practice." He led me to where a practice range had been set up and gave me a brief grounding in the use of a .303 rifle. He knew his subject inside out. A regular Army man, he'd seen plenty of action in the Middle East at the time of the Desert Rats. His quarry was somewhat different now. When he was satisfied I was as proficient as was

Allan Stewart and guest with a catch of barramundi, Nourlangie Safari, 1960s. Photo by Don McCann, courtesy of William Collins

After one fishing trip, Tom and Jackie show off their catches. I stand in the middle holding out my empty hands!

One of my later catches of barramundi, while working for Allan Stewart at Nourlangie.

possible after the short instruction – and my shoulder was too black and blue to take any more practice shots – we felt a cold beer would be in order. A party of people in a Land Rover, exploring the country, had dropped in and a most convivial evening followed. As a raconteur, Allan would have few equals and his fund of stories was something to listen to. He later included many of his yarns in his book *The Green Eyes are Buffaloes*.

Old Nym entertains the guests at Nourlangie. 1960.

The Aborigines were also having a party, though without alcoholic stimulant. Allan employed about a dozen Aborigines, the girls helping with the washing up and cleaning and the men on hand to chop firewood or do any of the hundred odd jobs which must be done to keep a safari camp running smoothly. They were a happy crowd. The chanting of their voices that night, from their own camp about half-a-mile from the compound, the beat of the singing sticks and the zuzza-da-zuzz of the didgeridoos was a wonderful lullaby for sleep and a totally new experience.

Early next morning, guns, ammunition, lunch boxes and, most important of all in this climate, the portable ice-box full of beer and soft drink, were loaded into the Peugeot. Fred was at the wheel and I sat beside him. Tom and a number of Aborigines piled into the back, and we set out for the haunts of the buffalo. There were certain areas they liked and others they avoided and Fred seemed aware of all their movements. It was not long before we came across a bull buffalo with a fine spread of horns, standing glowering at us about 50 yards from the track. The .303 rifle was pushed into my hands, and I was muttered at to "have a go". I slid out of the car, trying not to make too much noise, and crouched up to a handy tree which could support the weight of a rifle in a convenient branch. From movements behind me I realised Tom had also got out of the car and was standing nearby, his rifle in hand. I took aim and fired. Since, in a most unhuntsmanlike fashion, my thoughts were more on whether I could shin up the tree quickly enough if the buff charged, my aim was poor. The buffalo wheeled about at the report and made off unharmed into the deeper bush.

"Let's find another," said the patient Fred, and we drove on across a wide, grassy plain where brolgas danced, and through the grey-green scrub, avoiding the denser vegetation of marshy ground where big, black boars with evil-looking tusks snuffled about. Presently Fred's keen eyes spotted another bull buffalo half hidden behind a pandanus palm. This time I took more deliberate aim at the vital spot behind the shoulder but was dismayed to see I had hit him in the stomach. He had no fight in him. Perhaps he'd been dreaming of the days of his progenitors when children rode on his back and tickled his ears and led him as he pulled the plough. Pathetically now he tried to lurch off to safety. I was so stricken by what I'd done when my second shot hit him in the hind leg, that I couldn't bring myself to fire again lest I caused the animal more suffering without killing it. Tom fired four more shots but they seemed to have no effect although seen to hit in the right place. The poor beast just stood there his head drooping. Then he fell to the ground and lay motionless. Tom went forward and put a last shot into him at close quarters. Buffalo have been known to look very dead and yet find some last reserve of strength to charge the hunter. I pondered on the surely dubious joys of killing for fun in the name of sport. What thrill had I expected to get out of it? A feeling of power, perhaps that would boost the ego. But there must be other ways of ego boosting than taking the life of an animal. Was killing for a trophy different from killing for fun? The genuine trophy hunter didn't just kill for the sake of killing. He searched for the finest example of the species he was seeking, killed swiftly and cleanly and perhaps with a feeling of reverence, and later had his trophy mounted, a perpetual reminder not to his bravery but of the living glories to be found on earth. Could I then condone the hunter? After all, it was all the same to the unfortunate quarry whether his life had been taken in fun or not. Round and round

Buffalo near Nourlangie.

A buffalo shot on the plains by a guest, Wilf Farran.

in my head went Robert Browning's poem *The Lost Leader*, except that I found I was putting different words to the metre.

> Just for a feeling of glory they downed him,
> Just for a trophy to hang on the wall,
> Deep in the heart of the bush where they found him,
> Gleefully pranced the safari men all.
> They with their guns on high, sought to do battle,
> Nothing like killing for having some fun,
> What is a buffalo, who cares about him,
> Why not enjoy bubbling blood in the sun.
> We, who had loved him so, saw him hit, staggering,
> Looked at his wild and so terrified eye,
> Helpless to stop them, those splendid brave hunters,
> Watched him roll over, and noisily die.
> Why must they kill him; how has he hurt them?
> Far rather would he be a friend of a child,
> Pulling a plough like illustrious forebears,
> Or quietly at peace with the rest of the wild.

Was I being too sentimentally squeamish about it all? I didn't know, but I knew that I could never again take an active part in a hunt. The buffalo which I had shot so aimlessly was not, however, wasted, as beef was needed back at camp. The beast was butchered and great joints of meat laid on green branches on the floor of the Peugeot, before we hurried back to camp to get the meat stowed in the kerosene refrigerator away from flies. Then Allan joined us and we all set off again to have a picnic lunch at Dreaming Water, a magnificent stretch of water not far from Nourlangie. "You can go for 40 miles on these waterways, even at the height of the Dry Season," commented Allan. It seemed incredible. How many people in the south knew of this fantastic country. What was it the travel people had told me? It's only desert up there, nothing to see really, the Territory is not a holiday place at all, no shops, bright lights or mod-cons,

Pushing out the boat at Dreaming Water.

Dreaming Water.

they said. Maybe not, but here was a country bursting with wildlife and scenery such as I'd seen nowhere else in Australia. There was an invigorating magic in the air. There was everything to soothe a heart lost in the intricacies of civilised living.

We left the car at the water's edge and, armed with the picnic gear, thrust our way through the pandanus to a tree-shaded sandy beach. Fred waded off to catch a fish for lunch while Tom hollowed out the sand and made a fire to get some coals. The rest of us plunged fully clothed into the cool waters and floated idly around as we awaited the results of Fred's expedition. His successful catch was wrapped in paperbark, placed on the glowing coals and sand shovelled on top of it. We sat under a tree, a cool breeze blowing on our clothes still wet from swimming. Several beers later, the fish was unearthed, or rather, unsanded and we all forked into the easily broken off flesh, before drifting off into a nap.

Aboriginal painting of a lugger at Nangaloar, which later became known as "ship cave," after this boat. 1960.

When the sun had lost its afternoon bite and we had sufficiently woken up, we drove to Nourlangie Rock to see the cave paintings at Nangaloar. We cut through the scrub, on no defined track, until a rocky escarpment some six hundred feet high towered above us. Leaving the car, we scrambled over big boulders until we reached the base of the mountain. Allan called on us to halt under an overhanging slab of rock. "I can't see any caves," I said, expectantly, peering about for holes which I thought would lead down subterranean passages. "This is what we call a cave up here, more of an overhanging rock to you, perhaps" said Allan. "But look about you. Look at what they contain." I looked and realised there were most unusual designs of people and animals painted on the rock face in red, white and yellow ochre colours. Some of the figures appeared to be almost grotesque in proportion with pencil-like bodies and outsize limbs, and

Aboriginal rock art at Nangaloar, showing an elongated spirit figure.

Aboriginal paintings of fish, incorporating blue pigment from Washing Blue. Nangaloar, 1960.

More spirit figures at Nangaloar. 1960.

some were painted in extraordinary detail, rather like an X-ray picture. I was absolutely intrigued and I realised that to understand it all I would have to read a book about Aboriginal rock paintings. It was too big a subject for Allan to explain to me in five minutes. He did his best all the way back to camp, but my mind was only half listening as I was trying to work out how the pictures were painted so high up on the walls of the cave, far out of normal reach.

Crossing the South Alligator River at low tide, before the bridge was built. We could cross at low tide, but needed to carry a rifle in case of crocodiles. Allan Stewart shouts to me to hurry up.

Me crossing the South Alligator River, rifle in hand.

Late that night, under the thin sickle of a moon and diamond bright stars, Fred rowed us silently up the lagoon whilst Tom cast a powerful torchlight beam across the water to each bank. The only sounds were the honking of geese flying over, the slap of a fish as it came to the surface and the trampling of buffalo on the nearby plains. This time, we were after crocodile. Our quarry showed itself at last as two red pinpoints of light moving slowly across the water. I was told the crocodile swims with only the top half of his head visible, but it is easy to catch his eyes which shine so red in the beam of a torch. Tom raised his rifle to shoot between the eyes but the croc had submerged before he could fire. The length of his snout multiplied eight times is apparently a rough guide to the size of the reptile. "That was a nice lot of inches, that was," said Fred. With croc skins at that time fetching a pound an inch, measured across the widest part of the belly skin, he would have been worth quite a few pounds. We rowed around, spotlighting, for another hour but the croc did not reappear.

Croc hunting was much in favour with the many big game hunters who visited from the United States, keen to add a somewhat different style of Australian safari to their experiences. Taking home a treated crocodile head would be a trophy to later grace their homes. Shooting, retrieving, and skinning them was all part of the excitement in which I occasionally joined. Whilst I never shot a crocodile, I did help with skinning. But first catch your croc! Crocodile hunting had it moments of the "now you have it," "now you don't" variety. One method used by Tom's nephew, Ken, who joined the staff for a while, was to shoot them when they surfaced. The croc would then sink and

1. Tom's nephew, Ken Couzens, has shot a crocodile and it has sunk to the bottom. Here, he stands in his dinghy and uses an oar to "pole" (feel) for the croc. Nourlangie area, 1960.

2. Ken dives overboard and down to grab the dead croc and lifts its head, seen here just above water level.

3. Ken drags its head and upper body and hauls it into his boat.

4. Towing the croc to shore.

have to be poled for. When it was located, Ken would dive overboard and heave its head over the back of the boat, where it was roped and then towed to shore. Willing hands ashore took over and pulled it up the bank for a dry spot for skinning.

Breaking ropes were one of the various hazards when trying to get crocs safely to shore. This happened on one of the croc hunts nearer to the mouth of the South Alligator River and it took a team of willing helpers in the party to wade in and manhandle it to shore. There could also be a problem of the tidal bore which could come racing down the river when the tide came in. One croc was too big to get on board so the boat had to come ashore without it. Skinners then waded out to work in the water and were fortunately able to finish their task before the bore came down with a rush, which could well

Yorky Billy and guest with a file snake, 1960.

Yorky Billy and riders.

1. This large crocodile was shot and killed in the river, and an attempt is made to bring it to shore by boat. South Alligator River.

2. Too heavy for the boat, instead it is dragged in by rope.

1. Another crocodile, too large to bring to shore, is being skinned in the water, the skinners working hurriedly before the tide comes in. South Alligator River.

2. The skin is saved before the tide rushes in. Here, the tidal bore (or "tidal wave") is seen coming down.

EVERYBODY'S Oct. 1963

IT'S MOVING DAY FOR YORKY BILLY

VERY soon the best-known bushman in the north will round up his huge family, his string of ancient horses, and his new, young aboriginal wife and set off to find a new home.

Civilisation is catching up at last with the secluded little world of Yorky Billy, buffalo, crocodile, and dingo hunter, horse-breaker, and old-time bushman.

The Government plans to build a road from Humpty Doo east to Oenpelli, spanning the coastal flood plains which form one of the last really "wild" corners left in the Northern Territory.

And the alarmed Yorky has been told this road will go right past the front door of his shanty at Spring Peak, a few miles from Jim-Jim Billabong.

Though he shuns cities and hates strangers, Yorky has achieved fame several times in his long life.

A short time ago, a film on buffalo hunting was made in the Jim-Jim area and Yorky was called in as expert adviser, with his string of 13 buffalo ponies.

Yorky has shot crocodiles professionally. He's tried his hand at cattle raising and has found and lost several mineral claims.

Officially, Yorky is now a dingo hunter, but he doesn't make much at it.

Not that he worries. Each month he collects his old-age pension, with which he buys sugar, tea, salt, and an occasional bottle of rum.

He can see the advantages of the new road. His children will be able to travel to school at Pine Creek, for one thing.

"But I'll have to move deeper into the bush," he says.

"With all those cars and trucks going past the front gate, a man won't be able to sleep at night."

— Keith Willey

have carried them all away. After skinning and drying any shot crocs, the skins were rolled up and later taken to the relevant dealers in Darwin, making them a valuable cash asset for the camp.

Lesser excitements at camp were more likely to be my lot. One morning I went out riding on one of the dozen or so horses kept at the camp. They were an alternative means of transport for hunting for food in the Wet when the movements of vehicles were restricted. They belonged to an Aboriginal called Yorky Billy, whose knowledge of the bush was endless.

In his younger days, Yorky had made a living shooting buffalo for their hides, from horseback – a pastime not recommended for the faint-hearted. Now he tended the garden and was at hand when necessary for guiding work.

Full of confidence, though my horsemanship was of a poor order, I was hoisted into the saddle of one of Yorky's rather splay-footed mares and, in the company of Tom, headed up a bush track. Rashly I urged my steed to a trot, getting ready to rise at the correct point as had been drummed into me during my few riding lessons in England. But it seemed that brumbies – wild bush horses – are not taught how to trot when they are broken in, and my mount started hastening along the track at a most uneven and alarming pace. "Hold her back," yelled Tom from way behind me. But this was a lot easier to say than do. The horse had a mouth like iron and I was so busy trying to hang on to its neck that I didn't have enough hands to gather the reins in. Slithering sideways and bouncing madly in the saddle, I finally managed to haul the wretched creature to a stop. Shaking at the knees, I skidded to the ground. Tom came racing up, howling with laughter, and saying it was the best circus performance he'd ever seen, and would I do it again, please.

The days flew by. We drove up to the sombre brooding escarpment country of the East Alligator River and watched the barramundi jumping over the rock causeway when the brown, foaming tidal water came rushing in from the sea. Long-limbed Aborigines, their ebony skin gleaming like satin in the sun, walked down from Oenpelli Mission to spear the fish as they leapt in the rushing torrent. We drove down to the Jim Jim Waterhole which had a reputation for being the finest fishing hole in the Territory, and gorged ourselves on fresh grilled fish. The track from Pine Creek to Oenpelli ran over the Jim Jim Crossing and the billabong by the crossing was a favourite spot for campers in the know. What a place for a little store, I thought idly. Not that there would be much business, with vehicles only averaging about four a week, but one day, perhaps, when the country became better known … But of what interest was that to me when I was due to return to England very shortly and leave this wonderful country behind.

The highlight of the safari for me was a visit to the Goose Camp, a particularly marshy area where thousands of wild geese congregated. Their murmuring chatter could be heard for miles. Sitting in the water, with their necks so close together, they looked like a solid wall. When alarmed, the geese would take off with a whoosh of wings and blacken the sky as they circled, before dropping back to the water after the danger had passed. To see them flighting in the evening, honking mournfully as they wheeled against the backdrop of a blue sky, so quickly turning through the pink and gold of dusk to darkness, was a sight to remember. It touched a chord from the past when, as a mixed-up teenager, I had felt that where the wild geese flew, there also would I find my happiness. Was I going to be haunted by memories of the sight in the years to come, or could I be a part of it?

"I'm booked to catch my plane to Melbourne the day after tomorrow and I don't think I want to go," I said to the Big White Hunter, Allan, as my stay at Nourlangie drew to a close. "Do you mean you'd like a few more days here?" said Allan. "Perhaps you could get another flight." "Few more days be blowed," I said, inelegantly, "I want to stay in this country forever." Allan sighed. "It gets a lot of people like that," he said, "but what about England? I thought you were all set to go home." "I rather think this country is my home," I said. Allan considered a moment before suggesting that he

On safari.

Thousands of geese at Red Lily.

Another time: bogged and winching.

could use a secretary for a few months. "That would give you a chance to see a bit more of the country and then you could make a less hasty decision to stay, or go back to England as you'd planned. How would you like to be my secretary?" How would I? I could have hugged the man for the opportunity he was giving me. But first I had to return to Melbourne. Tom drove me back over the long, winding bush track to Pine Creek and then up the bitumen to Darwin. "See you next week," he said, as he put me on the plane.

Goose Camp.

CHAPTER THREE

Towards a Yellow Waters Dream

David M. Welch

Yellow Waters at sunset in November.

There was plenty of time to think on the flight back to Melbourne. Had I been carried away by the magic country of Arnhem Land? I thought about Tom and liked what I thought. Born on a farm in South Australia, one of five children, Tom had set out to hump his bluey when he was fifteen and the Depression days were making life difficult. He worked on sheep stations, dug for opals, learnt the welding trade, got married, and saw war service in New Guinea and Borneo. In the trying period of settling back into civilian life he found himself part of the beginning of a story of imagination and endeavour. It was an endeavour which resulted in the million dollar company now known as Hills Hoists. In 1946, a young man in Adelaide called Lance Hill designed a laundry hoist for his wife. His brother-in-law, Harold Ling, with a fantastic business

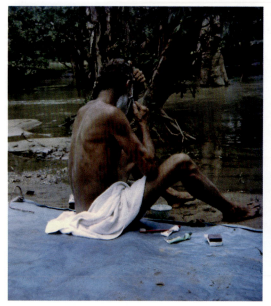

Tom's ablutions by the creek

Washing up in the creek.

brain, realised the potential and a little workshop was set up. Tom heard they needed a welder and went to see if he could help. Four men toiled in the workshop under the organisation of Harold Ling, while twenty hoists a week were turned out and trundled round in wheelbarrows for delivery and setting up. The potential was there; the money for wages and material was not. The men went on short wages yet worked with a will; no clock watching, no slackening off. The business grew and flourished exceedingly. It could not do otherwise. It was ably run and provided a commodity which the housewife was finding such a blessing. A company was formed and those who had been on short wages were given shares in lieu. Business activities expanded, new premises sought, and staff increased. Tom found himself no longer in the workshop but in an office, directing his side of operations.

He had a wife, two boys, a beautiful house, and an enormous car, but happiness eluded him. City life and business worries were not for him; he hankered for a life in the bush. Incompatibility in marriage is no crime and it is often a better solution for two people to go their different ways than make each other miserable trying to live against the grain of their hearts. Anyone with a sense of responsibility, however, cannot just up, up and away, and it was many years before the final break could be made and satisfactory settlement effected. Tom had come north, alone, to the land of his choice, with ideas of getting a piece of land and producing fruit and vegetables for market. It was unfortunate that he should get mixed up with a man who promised this and that, and that and this – there were many plausible fellows in the Territory. The outcome was that when the man disappeared into the limbo, Tom no longer had the wherewithal to start any venture. It didn't really worry him. His only responsibility was now to himself and he was quite happy so long as he was in the bush and had enough money for tobacco. Crocodile hunting and guiding work for him at Nourlangie was an ideal existence. His soul was free, his mind unfettered, his heart could sing. With a romantic effusiveness more suited to a first love, I felt our hearts could sing in tune together.

Tom dragging a crocodile up the bank. This is the one I sat on for a photo, now on the book cover.

When I went back to work at the Travel Office, I said "I'd like to give a week's notice, please, and I want to cancel my passage back to England next March. I'm getting married." I was somewhat premature in my statement of impending marriage as I hadn't yet been asked but at that moment I wasn't going to let a little thing like that bother me. Melbourne was cold and grey and drizzly as I boarded the plane a week later. I stepped out into the sunshine at Darwin Airport and Tom was there to meet me. "Welcome home," he said. Tom and I returned to Nourlangie and, as the days went by, I knew I'd made no mistake in cancelling my ticket to England. This bush life was for me – particularly with Tom by my side.

I did a little secretarial work, I helped with cooking and cleaning, and Barbara and I often went out on safaris with the guests. We did not always acquit ourselves very well. On one occasion Allan was due to take an important fishing guest out on the billabong. The other boats were already out and the only one left was a rather ancient wooden one, called the *Lady B.*, that was not renowned for its waterworthiness. Barbara and I found her tucked away safely out of sight on the mud under some low freshwater mangrove branches and, forgetting she had purposely been hidden, we pulled her to a more accessible boarding point further along the bank. Allan followed the guest into the boat and we shoved off the *Lady B.* with a concerted heave. The boat groaned and gurgled and, unnoticed by the guest, water trickled ominously through her bottom planking. The guest seized the oars with a flourish and dipped them in the water. He was, however, evidently unaccustomed to shallow water rowing. With an incredible splashing of mud and water, waterlily roots suddenly shot into the air and at the next dip one oar got affectionately entwined round an especially long root and would not move. Meanwhile, the *Lady B.* started sinking slowly at the stern. By this time, Barbara and I on the bank were doubled up with laughter. Desperately, we tried to hide behind a tree and control our almost hysterical behaviour, for it is really unpardonable to laugh on such an occasion, but we were too late. "You stupid half-witted girls," bellowed Allan, "don't just stand there giggling. Do something." His face was red from fury at our lack of tact and we expected our notice at any moment. He threw the painter towards us and Barbara, quicker in the uptake than I was, plunged nearly waist deep into the mud and dragged the boat to the safety of the shore.

Crossing a swamp with guests.

After this episode, the *Lady B.* was beached and repairs effected. She remained waterworthy for some time until two young guests, John and Ross, took her out to fetch some geese they had shot down over the water. Four other guests whom I had driven out, and myself, were assembled at vantage points along the bank, waiting for whistle duck to fly over, when we heard the cry "We're sinking." About 100 yards from shore, the *Lady B.* was slowly disappearing under the water. Ross could be seen saluting as the water reached his neck and John was holding his shotgun high above his head out of harm's way. The dead geese which they had collected, floated all around them. "Good as the pictures any day," I shouted at them. "Seen any crocs lately?" they shouted back. Taking it all as a huge joke, they seized the rope and as many geese as they could muster and started swimming through the waterlilies to the shore, trailing the semi-sunken craft behind them. They waded the last few yards through mud, crying, "We're the *African Queen*," and "Is this the way to the safari camp?"

The days passed all too quickly. The Wet came and rivers rose making entry by road impossible. Business was slack. Hunting was not a pursuit one could follow in the Wet Season as the area of movement is so restricted. Nevertheless a few people flew in to enjoy the beauty of the surroundings. There was plenty of work to be done. Barbara and I were kept busy painting the cabins, gardening, and doing other small chores. Tom and Fred pulled down the old kitchen whilst building a new one round it. It was a pity the old kitchen with its great character had to go but the white ants had undermined it and it was no longer safe. March, 1961, came and went and I still had no regrets about cancelling my passage to England. I had no wish to leave Nourlangie and Tom. But at the end of that Dry Season, force of circumstances made it impossible to stay at Nourlangie. The safari business was having a patch of the doldrums. There was little guiding work for Tom, and Allan could no longer afford to employ us. We'd have to go to Darwin and find work. Before we left the area, Tom and I spent a couple of days camping at the Jim Jim Crossing. When the time came to pack up camp, I ventured the thought I had had about putting up some sort of a store there. The track from Pine Creek to Oenpelli ran over the crossing and the billabong nearby was a favourite spot for campers in the know. "Oh, nonsense," said Tom, emphatically, "there wouldn't be a living in it." "There may not be much money," I argued, "but if there's just enough return to exist on, it would mean we could live at the Jim Jim for ever and ever ...."

Tom laughed. "O.K. I get your point. Now, let me see," and he began to think aloud. "Suppose the store was right on the track by the crossing, you'd get all the traffic – not that there's much of it – passing through to Nourlangie and Oenpelli, but we couldn't stay in the Wet because the store would be under water when the river rose. Perhaps if we built on the higher ground we could one day expand to a year round guesthouse or even a motel. But the high ground is too far away from the track crossing and a lot of people wouldn't bother to call." "Well, what about two areas of land?" I offered. "Ye-es, it's possible," said Tom, scratching his chin thoughtfully.

In those days, one square mile Special Purpose Leases were granted for approved projects and we planned to split this permitted square mile into two areas – a small one of five acres which would contain the store site, and a much larger area as close to Yellow Water as was reasonable. One portion of this larger motel site area would run in one direction right to the edge of Yellow Water where land was exposed in the Dry Season but submerged in the Wet. In the other direction, the lease would narrow down in the middle of some swamp country and widen out again to run to the edge of a blue, deepwater billabong. This area would include enough high ground so that an airstrip could eventually be graded. The Lands Branch surveyors who pegged out the area would have very odd shapes to deal with, but we believed it to be necessary so that guests could always be assured of access to Yellow Water.

The name Yellow Water is prosaically believed to have sprung naturally to the minds of the few earlier visitors who saw the sometimes muddy, murky appearance it presented at the end of the Dry Season. After the water had completely receded back off the flooded plains into the billabong, buffaloes would churn up the mud at the water's edge, and then traverse the waterway at narrow points leaving a muddy base to spread. The hue is also more romantically attributed to the golden glow the water achieves during some of the spectacular seasonal sunsets. It is further said to be the result of a form of yellow algae growing below the surface of the water, or even the host of tiny yellow snowflake lilies sometimes to be seen. We felt Yellow Water billabong contained many treasures of nature. The surroundings did not have the striking rugged beauty of the escarpment country but they had a gentle beauty all of their own, capable of engendering a sense of space and freedom and a closeness to nature with its wildlife.

And we would be able to enjoy all this on our leased land! "Just think," I said, "the Jim Jim for ever and …" "Yes, yes, you've said that before," Tom interrupted. "Now do just keep quiet a moment and let me think. First, we've got to get the money to build such a store and then we've got to get the leases. I don't know which will be the most difficult. Righto, Jim Jim, here we come." So saying, we headed away from the Jim Jim to Darwin, as the first step towards fulfilling the dream we had in mind.

There was plenty of work available in Darwin. I soon got a job with a Government Department where the material advantages for me were excellent. Short hours, good pay, subsidised hostel accommodation, and five weeks' holiday a year with fare paid to a southern city every two years. Actual working conditions perhaps were not the best. The offices of the Lands Department for whom I worked, were overcrowded and antiquated, but foundations were being laid for air-conditioned buildings. Tom also found a job. A Melbourne syndicate was starting up a fishing venture and needed a crew for their boat – a converted ex-RAAF rescue launch – and Tom joined them as crewhand, fisherman and croc hunter.

After six months with the Government I was granted a couple of weeks' leave and went with Tom on one of the combined fishing and crocodile expeditions to the mouth of the Daly River. The skipper of the boat, sandy-haired Norm Harper, as salty as they come, and what he didn't know about the sea wasn't worth knowing, was to take us out and leave the croc hunting party for a week or so while he carried on fishing. Tom warned me I'd be left alone a good part of the time and was afraid I might be lonely. He needn't have worried. During the day I had no time to feel lonely as I turned out dampers to feed the crew, the way I had learnt under Tom's tuition at Nourlangie, then made roo meat stews, brewed tea and yet more tea. Men get very hungry, skinning and salting croc hides.

But on my first night alone I did feel a little lonely, and nervous too, as the men headed off in the dinghy for croc-infested creeks further down the river, leaving me to keep the camp fire burning so that they would know in which direction to head back. I lay on my camp stretcher under the mosquito net extremely conscious of slithering noises in the trees (python about to drop on me), squelchy sounds in the mud where the tide had gone out (croc coming to chew me up), and heavy stomping in the bush that grew thickly to the beach (buffalo getting ready to charge). And whatever was that noise like a hundred sheep pulling away at grass? I shone the torch around and saw the sand covered with hermit crabs munching steadily away at succulent grains of sand.

Ken Couzens displaying a crocodile skin against a paperbark tree. August 1962.

Wide awake then until the small hours, I stoked the fire and watched the Southern Cross turn over and the tide come creeping back over the mud, glad at last to hear the chug chug of the outboard that heralded the return of the men with the night's booty.

After the men had slept but before the skinning of the catch began, I insisted on having a "house" of corrugated iron rigged up for me around my camp bed. The iron, which we had collected from a derelict Air Force post on the Perron Islands on our way out, would be used to make a proper shelter later. But even though the iron leaning over my bed perhaps solved the problem of being eaten by a crocodile, it didn't help sleep because the hermit crabs made a Luna Park of it, laboriously crawling to the top of the sloping iron, and rolling down again. It was soon discarded.

What I felt I needed was a watchdog to keep me company and when a dingo appeared in the light of our campfire one evening, I decided he would do the job nicely. Tom had other ideas for dingoes and fired a shot which made the dingo disappear as quickly and silently as he had come. He came again the following evening but once more faded into the shadows when another shot was fired at him. I pleaded for his life if he should come again and said I wanted to make him my friend for the night watches. I was snorted at with derision and told it was quite impossible to tame a wild dingo. I wasn't so sure. Anyway, I didn't want to tame him, I just wanted him to be a friend in passing.

The dingo came to the beach soon after sun-up next morning and stood looking at us from a hundred yards away. It was plain to me he wanted to be a friend of man but wasn't sure of the best way to go about it. I took a chunk of meat from its hook on the tree and advanced slowly towards him. The dingo, a rather mangy but fine-headed specimen, wavered on his feet, but I kept up a long and meaningless one-sided conversation with him and he stood his ground. When I reached him he gently took the offering of meat while I bent over and ruffled his ears. He dropped the meat quite unconcernedly and seemed far more interested in the attention he was getting. Then suddenly his lips curled back and he jumped up at me. For a fraction of a second I

Meeting a dingo on the beach.

Red Boy and Grey Mother, two wild dingos that befriended me, on a beach near the Daly River mouth.

Tom with a large crab at Snake Bay, Melville Island. These are boiled and make excellent eating.

Visiting Tom at Snake Bay, Melville Island. 1963.

thought he was going for my throat but he was only "laughing" and prancing in play, and I joined him in the game he seemed to want like any pet dog.

Later that day, Red Boy, as I called him, brought his girl friend along for my inspection. I called her Grey Mother, on account of her grizzled chops which made her look older than she probably was. She was rather timid and would not come too near me although Red Boy ran from one to the other of us encouragingly. I didn't try to force the friendship on her as I knew she would

Boys playing in the sea, Snake Bay, Melville Island.

come eventually, and a few days later she tired of hanging around in the background while Red Boy enjoyed the privileges of camp life, and allowed me to hand feed her. Most of the day Red Boy and Grey Mother rested under a large shady tree, or cooled off by lying at the water's edge when the tide was in and letting the waves break over them. At night, although making occasional excursions into the bush from which they would return after an hour or two, they would curl up in the soft sand by my bed. If, on their return from foraging, they found me asleep, they would tug at the mosquito net

Children playing on Pukamani poles, Melville Island, 1963.

Tiwi Islander with his carvings, 1963.

Tiwi carving, 1963.

My Volkswagen crossing a creek.

Meeting a stockman along the way.

Testing the height of an ant hill (termite mound).

and snuffle at me until I was awake enough to put an arm out and pat them. Sometimes a dingo in the distance would start its mournful yowl and Red Boy and Grey Mother would fling back their heads and answer. I wondered if I would wind up with a pack of dingoes but no more showed up. Perhaps Red Boy warned them away in case he lost any of the favours bestowed upon him. He was inclined to be jealous and did not even like more attention to be shown to Grey Mother than to him. When the time came to return to Darwin, I wished that I could bring my two companions of the night watches with me, but of course that was out of the question and they would have been very unhappy out of their own territory.

Shortly after this trip the syndicate folded and Tom had to look around for another job. He joined the Forestry Branch of the Wildlife Department and was sent to Melville Island, about 45 miles north of Darwin, where he supervised the planting of cypress pine plantations. With Tom away, I felt lost. As consolation I bought a Volkswagen car and spent every available weekend driving down to the Jim Jim. Grace Pratt, a blonde Englishwoman with whom I shared a table at the Government Hostel, was a useful passenger on these trips. With unfailing humour, she would push me out of sand-bogs and boil the billy when required. She never seemed to tire of me raving on about the store to be at the crossing, and I never tired of hearing all about her two daughters and their children in far off countries, to whom she wrote every week.

Grace worked for the Department of Works, which occupied one of the large new air-conditioned buildings, and spoke of the happy atmosphere there. Feeling like a change from the Lands Department, I applied for a job there as typist, and soon found myself working in the Typing Pool under Beth Campbell. I couldn't have found a more congenial job. Beth, pretty, auburn-haired, a complexion as fresh as her two teenage daughters, and with the sweetest smile, was a good person to work under. Cherry Campbell, one of Beth's lovely daughters, was shortly to marry a good-looking young man called Marshall Perron. Marshall was destined to play a leading role in the Northern Territory Government when he became Chief Minister of the Northern Territory, while Cherry later began a fish-feeding tourist attraction called "Aquascene," located at Doctor's Gully off the Darwin Esplanade.

Government working hours in Darwin are not arduous – 8.00 a.m. to 4.21 p.m., five days a week – so with Tom away in Melville Island I had plenty of time outside working hours to study a bookkeeping course. Too many small businesses fail for lack of properly kept books and we were determined ours (when we got it) was at least not going to fail from that cause. When Tom had announced that he was going to be the "outside man" and it would be up to me to do the paperwork, I panicked. How could I do bookkeeping? I was such a dunce at school, particularly anything to do with figures. I wrote to the Director of the International Correspondence Schools in Sydney, and through his encouragement, embarked on a correspondence course in bookkeeping. I was thrilled to find it was all so clearly and simply explained that I not only understood it but thoroughly enjoyed all the exercises.

There was also some general excitement that year, when Her Majesty Queen Elizabeth and Prince Philip visited Darwin on the Royal Yacht *Britannia,* and toured the streets in their limousine to much flag waving. Needless to say, I was a most loyal flagwaver in the front row of the gathered crowd. I hoped my excitement was noticed and that one of the gentle waves in reply to the all round homage was directed at me.

I forged ahead in my studies but the issue of the leases was not doing so well. We had applied for two leases at the Jim Jim, but there was a covenant attached to them. The land would have to be improved to a certain value by such and such a date and, before the leases could be issued to us, we had to show evidence that we had the finance to do this. The Director of Lands had a figure in mind that made it quite impossible for us for a long time. Our savings were not exactly mounting astronomically. And then we were advised that if we could not find the money soon, our application would be withdrawn and we would lose our chance altogether.

I wrote to Mr. Roger Nott, the Administrator of the Northern Territory, outlining our plans in detail, the various stages in the project and explained how we'd build up as we went along if we could just start off with what we had. One afternoon, when the phone rang in the Typing Pool, Beth called me over. She held the phone towards me. "Mr. Nott wants to talk to you," she said. "Hello, sir, yes, sir, Mr. Nott, sir," I stammered into the mouthpiece. It wasn't every day an Administrator rang up a common or garden typist.

Our first home together – a shack near the Elizabeth River – was a bit different to Narborough Hall.

"I've just read your letter, Judy," said His Honour. "Can you come over to my office and we'll have a chat about it?" Beth gave me time off and I scuttled over to the Administration Buildings next door. Kind-faced, grey-haired, bespectacled Mr. Nott bade me be seated. "I like your plans," he said, encouragingly. "They appear to have been well thought out. Money's the bugbear, isn't it? Now, how much can you and Tom muster?" "About five hundred pounds right now," I said. "Hm, not really enough, is it? The minimum requirement before we can let you have these leases should be five thousand and you're not going to be able to get that in time, are you?" "No," I agreed, miserably. "Well, I'm going to give you and Tom a chance to start on less. If you can raise a thousand pounds by the end of the month, you can go ahead with your plans."

I bounced back to Beth and told her the good news. I was sure we could get the money. That night I wrote to my stepfather in England, asking if he could loan us five hundred pounds. He wrote by return saying he wouldn't loan the money but as it had been his intention to leave me that amount in his will, he saw no reason why I shouldn't have it now as a wedding present. He would cable it at once. We had our thousand pounds and, true to his word, Mr. Nott saw that the leases were issued to us. That hurdle over, Tom and I were married in the Registry Office in Darwin on Christmas Eve, 1963. But there was yet another delay to starting the building of our store. The Wet Season. We had to wait until the following May before the tracks had dried up enough to reach the Jim Jim.

In the meantime, Tom left Forestry and Melville Island and found a job 24 miles outside Darwin with Ben Havlik. Stocky, silver-haired, rugged-faced Ben, from Czechoslovakia, owned a piece of land near the Elizabeth River, on which he wanted to grow cypress pine. He, himself, grew the seedlings at Batchelor where he worked in the Rum Jungle Uranium Mines, and then brought batches of them to Tom to plant out. We lived in a draughty, corrugated iron shack on the plantation, together with the Golden Labrador puppy I had given Tom as a wedding present and a tabby cat of uncertain parentage that Tom had given me. It was our first home as a married couple. Primitive living, perhaps, but I loved it. The hard-tamped earth floor remained comparatively dry while channels for water dug round the outside of the shack took away the heavy Wet Season rains. We had a bed, two camp chairs, and several rough bush tables. Tilley (kerosene) lamps, a kerosene fridge and a Primus cooker completed the necessities. Our clothes were kept in a couple of suitcases and I had to remember to keep them shut, after finding a tree snake coiled up in my underwear one day. A native cat took up residence under the roof which was supported only by rough bush timber, and bush rats enjoyed the crumbs from our table, after we had gone to bed.

Our bath was a forty-four gallon petrol drum cut in half and laid on its side – hardly the right shape in which to lie back and enjoy the pleasures of bathing in soft rainwater out in the open. The compensations were in listening to the liquid notes of the butcherbird in the tree above, and feeling soft breezes caress one's skin, as one soaped down. A small amount of water usually remained in the bath after we had tipped it out, and at night frogs made full use of this residue, croaking away at full blast. Frogs and dog, rats and cat. Songbirds. Spiders, snakes and scorpions. Living with wildlife. It all added up to a style of life I had dreamed of with a man such as Tom by my side, and I revelled in every moment. I couldn't wait to get to the Jim Jim, and the wider opportunities it would offer for living with the wildlife that I loved.

Tom with Weasel, our Golden Labrador puppy.

CHAPTER FOUR

Setting up Shop at Cooinda

With Tom at the Cooinda Trading Post. At first, only four cars a week passed through. 1964.

At the beginning of May, 1964, Tom and I cleared our belongings from the 24 mile shack and set off down the bitumen to Pine Creek. Tom led the way at sun-up in a green Ford truck we had bought with part of our precious £1,000 at a recent Department of Works auction. Weasel, the Golden Labrador puppy, sat by his side. The back of the truck was piled high with tents and beddings, odd furniture, stores, tools, a kerosene fridge, a boat, a brick-making machine, cement and a wheelbarrow. I followed him in the Volkswagen carrying the last minute oddments and the cat. We reached the Jim Jim Crossing with enough daylight left to make camp. "This is the place for a store," I sang out, waving my arms about. "Who do you think you are, John Batman?" asked Tom. "No, John Superman," I giggled. It was that sort of an evening. "One day we'll live somewhere round here in a little white house with a red front door," I told Tom confidently. "Don't count any chickens before they're hatched," warned Tom. "Better just keep it in the back of your mind as a fairy story. And if you can bring yourself down from the clouds for a moment and would like to boil the billy, I'll get the tent up."

In a dream I gathered sticks and made a fire. Rainbow birds flitted in the blossoming trees and water gurgled merrily over the crossing. Leisurely we sat back as darkness fell and sipped our tea out of chipped enamel mugs. Perhaps if we'd known all the heartaches and headaches that were to come our way in the next few years we would not have felt so carefree. We had no thought of failure. We wanted to live at the Jim Jim and this seemed to be the only way to do what we wanted. People said we were crazy to try it; there weren't enough tourists; we'd bitten off more than we could chew; what did we know about running a business? etc. They were right. They were wise men. We were fools and fools are apt to rush in regardless. But at least one wise man thought we could do it and that was Mr. Roger Nott, the Administrator.

The first Cooinda / Jim Jim store at the Jim Jim Creek crossing. June 1964.

Our first task was to set up the store tent with its kerosene fridge for soft drinks, and a lean-to shelter of slatted blinds for customers to sit under. We opened for business on D-Day, the 6th of June, 1964, and found travellers only too pleased to stop and break their journey to the fishing holes, and have a yarn. But it seemed that these few passers by for the initial weeks of the Dry Season also expected the hospitality of the bush to be laid on for them, with free cups of tea and bickies. Since the setting was so informal, it was really not surprising that they didn't consider themselves customers. As the season progressed, however, we began to make a few sales of tinned goods and other items, particularly fishing lures.

While I looked after the few customers who called, Tom fetched sand and gravel from the creek bed and made cement bricks, two at a time, in the tiny brick-making machine. It was the same machine that Clare Best had used to make her bricks for the Noonamah Store, and which we had bought from her. The brick-making was slow but the pile of bricks grew in spite of constant interruptions to serve petrol. This was not a job I was very good at. It meant sucking petrol, by means of a piece of hosepipe, out of 44 gallon drums into 4 gallon jerry cans. The contents of the jerry cans were then poured into the customer's vehicle. Sometimes Tom had to be storekeeper when I went to Darwin for more stores. We had taken out the back and front passenger seats in the Volkswagen and put a roof rack on top, and the gallant little car came back over the rough track with loads she was never designed to carry.

Soon after we opened and while I was away in Darwin on a stores run, Tom had a visit from a man staggering in from a nearby camp set-up. His wife had apparently just shot him in the stomach. It was clear he needed urgent medical attention but we had no radio and the nearest one was owned by Frank Muir at Muirella Park. Tom was able to transport the critically injured man there, where help was requested over the radio and the man flown to Darwin. Tom was later called as a witness in an attempted murder trail at which the wife was sentenced to a few years in prison. The man made a complete recovery.

DARWIN: FRIDAY, JUNE 19, 1964   Price: 8d.

BADLY HURT CROC HUNTER SHOT — WIFE IS CHARGED

▓▓▓▓▓▓▓▓▓▓▓▓▓▓▓▓▓▓▓▓▓ about 40, was this morning remanded to appear in the Darwin Police Court in two weeks time on a charge of the attempted murder of her husband, crocodile shooter ▓▓▓▓▓▓.

This afternoon ▓▓▓▓▓▓▓▓▓▓▓▓ was still listed as "dangerously ill" in Darwin hospital following an operation to repair bullet damage to his abdomen.

Today the story was told of a dramatic night-long overland dash by a Katherine Hospital nurse that saved ▓▓▓▓▓▓ life.

It has been alleged that ▓▓▓▓▓▓▓ shot her husband in the stomach at their safari camp near Jim Jim Creek on the South Alligator River on Wednesday.

An unknown man at the camp drove 22 rough, bush miles to Muirella Camp, owned by Mr. Frank Muir, to call for help.

There is no radio at ▓▓▓▓▓'s camp, about 150 miles south east of Darwin.

It was too late for a plane to make the Muirella airstrip before dark Wednesday night, so Katherine's Sister Shirley Madex left by road with Welfare Officer Trevor Millikins in a jeep.

▓▓▓▓ who appeared in Katherine Police Court yesterday afternoon and again this morning. She was remanded to appear in Darwin.

Mrs. ▓▓▓▓▓, an attractive blonde woman, was once a receptionist at one of Darwin's leading hotels.

She and ▓▓▓▓▓ started a safari camp about a year ago. Last week an article by ▓▓▓▓▓ about her safari honeymoon appeared in a leading national woman's magazine.

CROC shooter ▓▓▓▓ ▓▓▓▓▓ who was rushed to Katherine hospital with a gun ▓

I, too, was involved in a drama of the snake kind when Freddie Hunter, Allan Stewart's erstwhile safari guide now working at Muirella Park, got bitten one evening by a death adder. He drove himself down to us in an ancient Toyota of uncertain mechanical reliability, and sought assistance in taking him on to the First Aid Post at Moline Mining Company base. The base had already been advised by radio that a snake bite victim was on the way. Speed was of the essence and, since I knew every wash-out and tight detour round the trees, I volunteered to do the needful in my trusty Volkswagen. A visiting Judge from Adelaide suggested he accompany us for moral support. Happily the patient survived and the main sufferer was the unfortunate Judge who bit his nails to the quick during the somewhat hair-raising drive. Freddie was mainly oblivious of

Tom with an unwelcome visitor.

SEPT 19 1969

DESTROYERS RUN FREE IN ARNHEM LAND

..."But they won't appoint safari men as rangers"

Arnhem Land safari man Allan Stewart said yesterday that people were blowing fishing holes with dynamite and poaching barramundi with nets in the East Alligator country.

And at the same time offers by men living in the area to become honorary wildlife rangers had been rejected.

The situation had become intolerable and the people in the area were angry, he declared.

The appointment of wildlife rangers in the area was the only way to combat the serious situation.

Mr Stewart said that **he personally knew of four cases of blowing lagoons during the past six weeks.**

Laughs

There had been use of dynamite and poaching at Dreaming Waters, Goose Camp and Bingie Water.

"Yet the Administration laughs at us when we offer our services as rangers," he said.

Mr Stewart, the Top End Great White Hunter of Nourlangie Safari Camp, Mr Tom Opitz of the Jim Jim and Mr Don McGregor of Patonga Safari Camp have offered to become rangers.

"Each time, some one on the Administrator's Council blocks our offers," said Mr Stewart.

"This is not funny while our wildlife is being destroyed without thought for the future."

Mr Stewart said that at the moment they had no power to stop what was going on.

They could only take action against the poachers if they were given the powers of wardens.

In his case, his base at Nourlangie was in the middle of a wildlife reserve "by a Government mistake," he said.

10 years

He had lived there for more than 10 years, knew the area well and intended to stay there.

It was reasonable that he at Woolwonga, Tom Opitz at Jim Jim and Don McGregor at Patonga should be the honorary wildlife rangers.

"We want to help as rangers, but we do not want to be honorary pimps to sneak about", he said.

Mr Stewart said that he supported a move announced by the Minister for Aboriginal Affairs, Mr Wentworth, that Aboriginals would be appointed as rangers.

But he said Aboriginals should not be given preferential treatment.

A fair chance should be given to Europeans living in the area, which at the moment was being badly hit.

Mr Stewart said that it was the bitter bit that it was he who proposed the original plan to appoint rangers to conserve wildlife in the NT.

His plan largely had been implemented.

But his offer and those of other "battlers" in the Alligator country to help in the work had been rejected.

Mr Stewart said that the Minister for the Interior, Mr Peter Nixon, should look into the reasons why the Administrator's Council had rejected their offers.

ALLAN STEWART

what was going on, having had the foresight to arm himself with a bottle of "crinkly" rum. I was fast becoming aware of this term used in the bush for a particular rum put out by the Beenleigh distillery at that time. The "crinkly" attribute actually referred to the furrowed shape of the bottle, not the liquor!

We were lucky if we saw more than ten cars a week at first, but occasionally at weekends an undesirable element would come out in battered old vehicles, with iceboxes, guns and nets. Indiscriminate shooting and illegal netting in the waterholes around the Jim Jim, so famous for its barramundi fishing, made us wonder how we could protect the wildlife and the fish. In the hope of deterring the despoilers, we tried putting a gate across the track which went through our lease to the waterhole, and charging a fee. But some smug, self-righteous citizen wrote to the Lands Department that his rights of access to wherever he chose to go were being denied him. We were officially rapped over the knuckles by the Director of Lands, and told to take down the gate, and stop charging a fee. Since the area was then completely open to vandalism, we thought a ranger might have some good effect and Tom applied to the appropriate branch to be appointed an honorary ranger. The Department showed little interest beyond saying one of their Wildlife Officers would be with us shortly to discuss the problem. The Officer duly visited us, agreed a ranger in the area would be a Very Good Thing, and that appeared to be the end of the matter.

Tom (centre) in city garb off to town on business, during Nourlangie days.

Dynamiting was added to the netting and the fish dwindled. We made repeated complaints and Tom continued his pleas to be made an honorary ranger. We knew when the law-breakers came and where they went, but had no power to stop them. Four years later Tom was to receive the official reply to his request. The Department regretted having to refuse, but explained that it was against their policy to appoint anyone in the tourist business to such a position. It felt a conflict of loyalties would be suffered – whatever that meant. What did the Department think we were going to do? A little quiet netting and selling? There may have been a quick quid to be made that way, but an abundance of fish was what attracted the tourist. We catered for the tourist, so it was hardly likely we would queer our own pitch. But perhaps the Department didn't want

ARLUNGA
COOINDA ✓ 1
COORANGA
DANGUNYA
DULKARA
GANNAWARRA
GINGANUP
KANAGRA
KARAWATHA
MURRUM BONG
YARALLA 2.

The original list, written in about 1962, of possible Aboriginal names for our tourist venture.

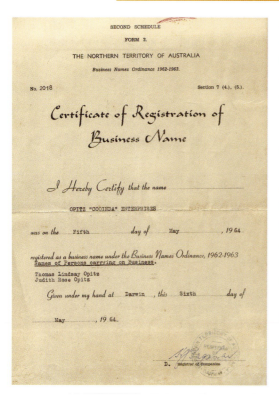

SECOND SCHEDULE

FORM 2.

THE NORTHERN TERRITORY OF AUSTRALIA

Business Names Ordinance 1962-1963.

No. 2018   Section 7 (4.), (5.).

Certificate of Registration of
Business Name

I Hereby Certify that the name

OPITZ "COOINDA" ENTERPRISES

was on the   Fifth   *day of*   May   , 19 64

registered as a business name under the Business Names Ordinance, 1962-1963
Names of Persons carrying on Business.

Thomas Lindsay Opitz
Judith Rose Opitz

Given under my hand at   Darwin , *this*   Sixth   *day of*

May   , 19 64.

D.   Registrar of Companies

us to provide an attraction for the tourist. Or then again, perhaps they couldn't be bothered with all the ensuing fuss if any netters were caught. Or what was the real reason? It was certainly odd that the law which made it illegal to net, also seemed to protect the interests of the few law-breakers who were able to go about their lucrative operations unhampered by competition, and also apparently let alone by those in authority. And who is to say that those in authority may not have felt a conflict of loyalty and been persuaded in the time-honoured custom to stay away from the sphere of action?

It could hardly be said that our first Dry Season of business showed a rip-roaring profit. Turnover was in the region of six hundred pounds, and the balance sheet I drew up the way I'd learnt in my correspondence course, showed a loss. This was aggravated by the fact that many of our customers had become regulars and liked to stock up on credit. They usually paid up on their next visit or the one after, but that didn't help a steady cash flow. At the end of the season, we were left owing suppliers ourselves and were in quite a parlous state. Underfunded, undercapitalised and under no illusions that we were tottering on a razor's edge of failure in our first season, I had to undergo the humiliating experience of writing to ask for time to pay. Yet, almost without exception, our pleas were heard and understood and it was agreed the balances of the accounts due could be held over until after the Wet, when an income would start again. Through their magnanimity, various firms and people like Keith Kemp and Ted Davies of Davies Sports Store, Messrs. Burns Philp, and Thomas Brown and Co., enabled us to remain in business.

But it had been a happy few months. The store became a place for people to stop at for a chat over a cup of tea, fill up with fuel and buy some immediate necessity. We chose to call it *COOINDA,* which is Aboriginal for "Happy Meeting Place". "Why don't you just call it the Jim Jim Store?" visitors asked. "The name Cooinda will never catch on, and people won't know where you are." "We might call this the Jim Jim Store," said Tom, "but we'll put the name *Cooinda* on the map and Cooinda Motel will become known world-wide." It was one of our biggest thrills, later, when we actually saw the name Cooinda starting to appear on official maps of the area.

Our first season's business came to a hasty close in mid-October. Unusually heavy rains fell and our tents were not sufficiently waterproof. Tom hurried over to the eventual motel site on the high ground some five miles from the store, and in nine

After the tent, our next store was at ground level, made from Sand Palms (Livistona humilis), *1965.*

days erected a three-sided 40 foot by 40 foot bush timber and corrugated iron shed. We pulled down the sopping tents and vacated our store site just before the Jim Jim Creek rose in early November, cutting off our access to Darwin. And for four months we saw not a soul and had no contact with the world outside the Jim Jim.

Six months' supplies of stores had been obtained and drums of flour, small sacks of sugar and rice, and tins of corned beef and such were lined up on

ABSOLUTE MINIMUM STORES FOR US TWO (WET SEASON 66/67)
(IF STAYING OPEN DURING NOVEMBER)

FLOUR	4 DRUMS
TEA	20 × ½ lbs.
SUGAR	1 × 70 lbs.
CORN BEEF	1 CARTON (48)
DRY - BALM	6 TINS
BAKING PDR	4 × 8 oz TINS
SPUDS	AS HAVE
PROTO	1 × 12 lbs.
ONIONS	AS HAVE

My original list of stores needed for the 1966/1967 Wet Season, when Tom and I would be cut off for at least four months. The rest of the list includes: Milk – 6 cartons; Butter – 30 tins; Dripping – 30 tins; Porridge – 16 tins; Cornies – 20 packets; Rice – 10 lbs; Herrings – 20 tins; Camp pie – 48 tins; Baked beans – 24 tins; Spaghetti – 24 tins; Green peas – carton Biddys 36; Golden syrup – 3 tins; Jam – 8 large tins; Tomato sauce – 6 large; Hot sauce – 3 large; Cheese; Steak and Veg – 30 tins; Custard powder – 4 lbs; Curry powder – 2 large or 4 small Plus Army; Tinned fruit – 20 fruit salad; Matches – 20 packets, 1 gross (12 packets) green, and 8 packets red; Tobacco – 12lbs; Papers – 1 box; Rinsos – 5 boxes large; Wash soap – 5 boxes; Sweet soap – 5 bags; Nescafe; Ovaltine; Kokoda – 15; Salines – 6; Tooth paste; Toothbrush – 2; Toilet rolls – 10 rolls; Beetroot – 24 (1 carton); Vegemite; Wettex pax; Scourers; Kleenex tissues.

raised planks above the earth floor of the new shack which would undoubtedly get damp underfoot at times. To the foodstuffs, supplies of tobacco for Tom were added and further supplies of cement for more bricks for the piers at the store site. The rain came spasmodically at first but enough to bring the rivers up and cut us off from all human companionship. We had no two-way radio or any other contact with the outside world. Our nearest neighbours across what soon would be flooded country, were Allan

Tom crosses the Jim Jim Creek at the end of the Dry Season.

The same creek at the end of the Wet Season – start of the Dry.

Stewart at Nourlangie and Frank Muir at Muirella Park, both over 30 kilometres away.

We busied ourselves measuring out a suitable site for the motel and Tom began clearing the ground by chopping down trees. I did some lighter clearing work, preparing the ground for a garden of snake beans – a prolific grower in the Wet. The beans became quite a staple diet added to the bully beef and damper made in the camp oven. We also wanted to grow pineapples and pawpaw and were getting a nice little crop of pawpaw seedlings to flourish until a fairly friendly buffalo decided the soft cleared ground made a comfortable bed for him.

Since one day was much like another, it was hard to keep track of days passing. I would ritually cross off a day on the calendar on rising each morning, but I was always plagued later on in the day with the thought I might have forgotten to cross it off. When we thought it was Christmas Day, we celebrated by sharing a can of Vic Bitter. Thinking of finances

Me cuddling Bosie, our pet wallaby, at the store. About 1965.

and the necessity to limit luxuries, our liquor supplies for the Wet consisted of one carton of beer only. Yet without mates to drink with him, Tom in no way seemed to miss it.

Tree chopping, land clearing and brickmaking kept Tom very busy whilst I, when not outside, buried my head in a bookkeeping course and a journalism course supplied

Playing with Bosie and our dog.

by the International Correspondence Schools. I'd arranged to have more material supplied than is usual at one time, because there was no means of getting lessons in and out for at least five months. It just meant I had to carry on with several lessons without knowing the result of previous ones. The accumulated pile of lessons would be posted in due course at the start of the Dry Season. The time came in early March, however, when I ran out of correspondence course

Tom feeding Bosie, our pet wallaby, which we reared after its mother was killed.
Photo by Michael Jensen, 1973.

material, and had also read all the books we had with us, not to mention all the jam tin and other food labels a hundred times or so. Not a very brain stimulating exercise.

Our pet wallaby was a comfort and kept us amused with her growing-up antics. She would race to the top of a pile of sand and take off into space; she rushed around in circles, stopping suddenly and changing direction – practising escaping from dingoes we supposed; and she loved batting at an old thong hanging from a piece of string. Tom had found her earlier in the season, a mere scrap of fur, beside her dead mother who had been knocked over by some vehicle on the track. We had reared her successfully on strong sweet milk and glucose. She had got over the scours and consequent weakness from which so many hand-raised wallabies apparently succumb. Just in time to save her, a visiting zoo-man from Adelaide had told us there was some element in wallaby droppings that it was necessary for the youngsters to ingest. It was important that they should either graze over ground where other wallabies have grazed, or have dried wallaby droppings mixed in the milk. She was getting a big wallaby now but still liked the warmth of our double bed, and would curl up between us at night, taking her time to settle and slapping each of us heartily in the face with her long tail as she did so.

The billabong which lay some 100 yards from the shed, rose and rose. From my days working for Allan Stewart at Nourlangie Safari Camp I knew the extent to which the floodwaters of the Wet Season rains could rise. An interesting sight always pointed out to visitors was the coffin in a tree. There had been a death at Oenpelli

Mission just before the Wet Season had set in and a Mission truck was trying to take an empty coffin from Darwin to Oenpelli. Unfortunately the coffin had to be abandoned when the truck got bogged in rising waters between Nourlangie and Oenpelli. The truck turned around and was able to return to Nourlangie Camp but the coffin was left by the side of the track, there to await the return of the Dry and its collection. However, after the Wet Season it was found to be high up in a tree where the flood waters had evidently lifted it. All I could think of now was how could we possibly survive, marooned up a tree for several months.

"Hadn't we better get a boat ready?" I asked nervously. Tom assured me we wouldn't be flooded out but I wasn't so hopeful. I'd also read about the Polishuks at Daly River in the Doug Lockwood's book, *Life on the Daly River*, published

This coffin was left up a tree after high waters from the Wet Season.

in 1961, and how the Polishuks had had to swim for their lives. We had no two-way radio and no airstrip. What had at first been a rather exciting isolation became for me a nightmare. What if one of us were to get ill? We'd simply die there, nobody knowing or caring until our bones were found next Dry Season. Illness preyed on my mind. Tom had had his appendix out and I suddenly wondered what would happen if mine played up. And then! I felt a twinge in my right side. I doubled up in pain. It seemed to disappear, then recurred. It went on for a few days. Was it a grumbling appendix? Then the pain went up to my chest. I read the medical dictionary I had, trying to diagnose the symptoms. The symptoms pointed to a certain horrible disease but as yet I didn't have the difficulty in swallowing that went with it.

Next day, I had difficulty in swallowing! But what could be done about it? Absolutely nothing! The nearest airstrip was Muirella Park and how were we to reach it over flooded plains and fast flowing creeks? I tried to turn my mind to other things. But I'd run out of lessons in the correspondence courses and there were no more books. Neither was there much work I could do outside – perhaps if I'd been a real Aussie pioneering woman, I should have taken up an axe and helped Tom grub trees – except we only had one axe! I'd just have to grin and bear it.

One evening, over a supper of buffalo stew, we saw what we thought was the tail of our pet wallaby draped over the bumper bar of the Volkswagen which was garaged in the shed, near our bed. But no wallaby's tail was six foot long. A king brown snake had decided to take up residence with us. A shot from a safe distance would have peppered the tyres, so gingerly we pushed the car until the snake was pinned under the front wheels. Then, with a well-aimed blow, Tom decapitated it with a long-handled shovel. Matters were not improved when a few nights later I was awoken from sleeping by little tentative scratchings of my hair and scalp. Light burbling snores from Tom indicated it wasn't the gentle husbandly rumplings of my hair and I froze. When I realised, however, that the action did not seem to be those of a snake either, I put up my hand to investigate and surprised a tiny mouse. It raced off squeaking indignantly at being interrupted in making a cosy nest in my hair. After that, my pains got worse and sleep became impossible with wondering how many more of the reptiles were hidden in the rafters, or under the bed, or curled up in the blankets, or about to slither through my hair.

And then! "Anybody home?" burbled a plaintive voice from somewhere out in the March rain. We rushed out of the shed to see the dripping form of a fair-haired, well-built young man dismounting from a decrepit old horse. I stoked the fire and put the billy on. "Hi," said the young man, "I'm Bill Dean. I've been over at Nourlangie caretaking and doing a bit of croc shooting while Allan Stewart's down south on one of his publicity tours, and I've run out of tobacco. I borrowed one of Yorky Billy's horses – the only one that hadn't gone walkabout – and I hoped you might have a spare tin?" Tom produced a tin of Ready Rub and papers and soon Bill was puffing away contentedly over a

The Muir aviation plane.

cup of hot tea. "Ouch," I said, as a twinge got me low down on the right side. "Crikey, you don't look too good," said Bill Dean, sympathetically, "What's the trouble?" "I think it might be an appendix or something," I said, doubling up. "Well, it's a lucky thing I came in with a horse then. Do you think you can ride to Muirella Park? Frank's got an airstrip there and radio contact and we'll have you out on a medical plane in no time." Frank Muir, a tall, white-haired, blue-eyed, distinguished looking man in his seventies, owned and ran Muirella Park as a safari camp. He had a beautiful setting under the shadow of the high Nourlangie Rock. His cabins for guests of antbed floors and sand palm walls had a rustic natural appearance in keeping with the surroundings.

The rain clouds had lifted slightly next morning as Tom saw us off on the trek to Muirella Park. A billy can and enamel mugs dangled from the horse's saddle bags which were filled with plastic-wrapped tea and sugar, tins of corned beef, dry biscuits and tobacco and matches. "Better walk as far as you can and just ride through the swamps," advised Bill, "This poor old nag is about time-expired." There were long stretches of water waist high, sometimes deeper in the buffalo wallows. Bill led the horse through the water-lilied swamps, occasionally disappearing under the water, but hanging on to the horse's reins and trying to keep the horse upright when it slithered on the muddy bottom. I hung on to the horse's neck and hoped for the best.

On the high ground, we stopped several times to boil the billy. The pain in my side came and went but did not make walking impossible. Towards evening, after crossing the last short, swift-flowing creek we approached Frank's camp. "Hello there, anyone home?" sang out Bill, in time-honoured fashion. Frank emerged from his kitchen hut. "G'day, Bill, and, why, bless my soul, it's Judy, too. What brings you here?" exclaimed Frank, "and not a thing ready to eat in the place, darn it. What are you like on making scones, Judy?" "I doubt if Judy's up to scone-making," said Bill, "she's probably in for appendicitis." "To tell you the truth," I said, "I feel much better, and I'll be glad to make some scones. We've got some tins of corned beef for you, too." Frank licked his lips. "Ha, haven't tasted such luxuries for months. Thanks. We'll get on to the Flying Doc first thing in the morning and he'll have you out in no time."

After the Flying Doctor had been advised of my case over the two-way radio, a plane which had business in the area, was duly diverted to Frank's airstrip next day. An ambulance was waiting at Darwin Airport to rush me to the Hospital and I was straightaway taken into the doctor's surgery. "Where's the pain now?" asked the doctor, pummelling and prodding me. "I can't seem to feel it," I said. It was true. I was completely pain free. There was nothing whatever the matter with me, physically that is. All I'd done was worry myself into acute symptoms. I felt an absolute fraud and went round to the Flying Doctor's Headquarters to offer to pay for the flight which is normally paid for by the Department of Health, and to apologise. The Chief Medical Officer was very understanding. "You were sick," he said, kindly. "Though fortunately not in the way you thought. You are one of those people cursed, or blessed, with a vivid imagination. You felt your pain all right but it was caused by your mind, not your body. Now go off and buy a new lipstick, go to a few parties, talk to lots of people and then go home. And if you can get a two-way radio out there, I don't think you'll have any further trouble. You'll be in contact with us all then, and if anything happens, well, we can always get a helicopter in to bring you to Darwin. It was the complete isolation that did it."

I bought a lipstick, a dress, had a hairdo and went to stay with friends. They took me out visiting every night for a week and at the end of that time I couldn't wait to get back to the Jim Jim. I returned in Arnhem Air Charter's little green twin-boom plane. We flew low over the shed at the Jim Jim and I dropped Tom a message in a tobacco tin to come over to Nourlangie and pick me up. Allan Stewart was back from Sydney and drove up to his airstrip to greet me when we landed. Tom walked in over the boggy track early next afternoon. He hadn't expected to see me for several weeks because he had thought, as I did, that I'd be laid up in hospital for a while.

In a much fitter condition than when I'd made the journey to Muirella Park, but without the benefit of a horse this time, Tom and I walked back the 20 odd miles to the Jim Jim. Halfway there a herd of buffalo, guarded by an old bull, contested our right to the track. After some desultory stompings, the herd wheeled about and made off into the scrub with the exception of their leader. "Better climb a tree," said Tom, shifting the .303 rifle he carried to an easier position for quick firing. I am not much of a climber of

The first tent store with the piers being erected to the side.

In the distance are the pillars Tom has made from his own bricks. This whole area goes under water in the Wet Season and the store will go on these.

straight up and down trees, and quickly sped up a nearby tree that fortuitously inclined at an easy angle. The bull took a menacing step nearer. "I'm right behind you," said Tom, and climbed up after me. The bull pawed the ground. "Could you go a little higher?" asked Tom, politely, "I still seem to be in his way if he charges." "I'm awfully sorry," I said, equally politely "but I seem to have run out of tree." "Oh, brilliant," said Tom rather scathingly, and lifted his rifle. Momentarily he unbalanced himself and dropped the rifle, which fell with a clatter to the stony ground below. Snorting derisively at such odd human cavortings, the bull turned and trotted off amiably after the herd and we were able to clamber down. Tom picked up the rifle and we walked on with me keeping a constant eye open for tall, leaning buffalo proof trees.

Bill Dean, who had walked back from Muirella Park to join Tom while I was away, was waiting for us with a feed of freshly caught barramundi. Bill's favourite food was the barramundi guts which he threw intact into the coals and roasted until they bulged and nearly burst. We rather preferred the firm white flesh. Bill stayed with us well into the Dry, helping us to build a temporary sand palm store which was more suitable than the tent we'd had the previous season. He also kept us in buffalo meat. One evening, after a larder filling expedition, he brought us in a tiny buffalo calf. Bill had been walking through the scrub when he'd been attacked by an irate buffalo cow. To save himself he had had to shoot her. The poor little orphan was obviously unhappy and could not be persuaded to drink milk. We tethered it to the central pole in our tent, where it twisted itself round and round and bleated pathetically. We did not know what to do for the best. During the night, we were aware of trampling sounds and squeaky buffalo snortings. Looking outside our tent, we shone our torch and saw about thirty pairs of green buffalo eyes looking back. We were half surrounded by a herd of buffalo cows who had heard the cries of the calf and come to investigate. We untethered the baby calf and it trotted outside, and immediately a buffalo cow, followed by its own calf, walked across and sniffed it. We watched developments through a slit in the tent wall. The large cow nuzzled the calf for a moment and then led it back to the herd, adopting it as her own. Quietly and happily they all trotted off into the moonlight. Our little orphan was being looked after.

By April, the Jim Jim Creek had subsided enough for us to wade over and then to bring over the necessary equipment to start the 1965 season. It wasn't long before we had our first customers in a slow stream. This picked up to 40 cars a week as the season progressed. By 30th June, 1965, we completed the necessary form put out by the Commonwealth Bureau of Census and Statistics and this gave us an idea of our takings. The figures, of course, were in pounds, shillings and pence at that time, but converted to dollars, we found we had taken a grand total of some $3,318 for the year since we opened, made up of groceries $774, refreshments $650, tobacco products $504, and petrol $1,390.

While I presided over the store for our second season, Tom's pile of bricks grew until he had an adequate supply to build up the piers for the main structure. Supplies of timber were brought in and then with the aid of strong and willing helpers from among the visitors, the wooden skeleton of the building began to take shape on top of the piers.

The store still needing the outer sand palm finish.

There was some urgency over building the proper store because to increase trade we needed a liquor licence and, before we could be granted one, we had to have a building approved by the Licensing Courts. Funds were stretched to the utmost to buy building material, but we weren't unduly worried as we understood from our bank that when the proper store was completed, we'd be able to borrow on it.

Tom worked without respite heaving great beams around, and strong customers lent willing hands to put the roof joists in position. Phil Harries, a young man we had got to know through correspondence, came out from England to help us. In the days when we were waiting for our lease to come through, I had put an advertisement in the English "Times," asking if anyone would like to give us a hand in exchange for a life in the sun. We received 78 replies, ranging from retired naval commanders to teenage girls dreaming of sun-tanned, lifesaving Australians. At the time the ad was inserted, we had nothing to offer anyone, and it was a case of keeping in touch until we did. Phil left us in no doubt as to his desire to come out and lend a hand and, at the earliest opportunity, we arranged his migrant passage. We had not seen

Tom and Judy on the front of their finished store.

The finished store.

any photos of him and I was not prepared when I met him at Darwin Airport, to see a good-looking curly-haired young man with the flaring aesthetic nostrils of a Rupert Brooke. He looked as though he would be more at home in an artistic world, and when I heard him speak in rich, well-modulated tones, I felt sure his vocation should be on the stage. But he was all for Adventure in the Outback, and he stood up for some months to the rough living conditions with a stout heart. He was later to find his niche in the world of real estate.

By September, 1965, Tom was nailing down the corrugated iron on the roof and decorating the front with sand palm. At last the building was finished, the licence granted and we sold our first beer. We had a grand opening party, well attended by locals from the other safari camps and buffalo shooting camps. There were many sore heads next day, not only from a surfeit of rum, but also from a light tap on the head I gave, using a large long-handled torch, which worked wonders in restoring order with an, at times, overly obstreperous crowd.

One of our customers at the store that year was a young archaeologist called Carmel Schrire, who was engaged on research excavations in the Oenpelli region for her PhD dissertation. The first time we met her was when she arrived as a passenger in a tourist's car and sought assistance from Tom in getting her Land Rover back on its wheels. She had inverted it whilst taking a notorious corner at the Barramundi Creek Crossing too enthusiastically. Occasionally she called at our store for supplies and seemed to relish telling a good story against herself. One of her tales was of misjudging the position of the

A horseman visits our store.

East Alligator River and of her Land Rover plunging down the sandy embankment into the incoming tidal bore. The vehicle had to be winched across by block and tackle and a great deal of time spent thereafter trying to jumpstart the vehicle. She said it never seemed to be the same after its dunking in the salty river. Carmel included such light-hearted tales in her otherwise more serious book *Digging for Darkness*.

I was, of course, totally captivated by her chosen profession. For two pins I would have volunteered to work on her excavations in any lowly capacity if I could have been the slightest use, or, more to the point, if I didn't have a store to run. I'd always had a romantic hankering to do something in archaeology, but without tertiary qualifications I'd hardly stand a chance in gaining entry to such a profession. All I really knew about archaeology was along the classic lines of Schliemann's discovery of Troy or the Minoan finds of Sir Arthur Evans, or Harold Carter and the Tomb of King Tutankhamun. Listening to Carmel I began to understand that Australia also had a valuable and different kind of archaeology to offer. She told me the prehistory of Australia was just beginning to emerge. Little had previously been known about where the first Australians came from, what they looked like, how they reached Australia, what routes they took once they reached land or what their impact on this huge unpeopled land may have been. A handful of radiocarbon dates suggested that people had come to Australia about 10,000 years ago, but Carmel was curious to learn if this date could be pushed back. By excavating rock shelters in Western Arnhem Land she certainly succeeded. She was to win fame with her discovery of edge ground axes over 20,000 years old. Before her discovery, the technique of edge grinding was a technology which was believed not to have developed until many thousands of years later, when such axes became part of the toolkit of Neolithic people setting up their agricultural lifestyle. What was it to say of the lifestyle and culture of the early Aborigines who were not considered to be an agricultural people? Many years later I was to have the joy of actually handling the material she had uncovered.

Trading figures leapt up but the season was drawing to a close. Could we make enough money to meet bills before the Wet set in? It seemed unlikely. And the loan we had so confidently anticipated from the bank was not forthcoming. A new policy did not permit them to make loans to any bush area project. We were frantic. Tom was expecting money from the sale of property in the south but solicitors were taking their time in settling the matter. Very nasty letters from creditors came pouring in. I wrote to them explaining the situation and begging for time to pay. With one exception, they agreed to give us a chance. The exception, Shell Petroleum, with its Head Quarters in Adelaide, threatened to bankrupt us.

With the crazy notion that perhaps if I called on them personally, they would understand and give us a chance too, I hitched a ride south with some people going down on their annual leave. The H.Q. Building in Adelaide was enormous. It took me quite a while to find out who I should see. Eventually I was shown into a small waiting room and the tall, thin Chief Accountant came in dry-washing his well-manicured reddened hands. He was coldly disinterested. He made me feel his time was precious and that I was wasting it. "Well, it looks like bankruptcy for you, doesn't it?" he said finally, as he turned on his heel and stalked out of the room. I was stunned. If he had shown some feeling or sympathy to soften the blow, it wouldn't have been so bad. I called at the Head Office of our bank, but it merely confirmed that bush projects did not merit a loan. Whoever heard of Arnhem Land anyway. There was nothing further to be done in Adelaide. Perhaps I should have tried to get help from a Darwin businessman. He, at least, would have heard of Arnhem Land and could surely see the potential of a tourist venture there. I boarded the *Ghan* train to Alice Springs and then took a Pioneer bus to Darwin, feeling guilty that the money spent on the fare north should have gone towards paying off the debt that was going to bankrupt us. Back in Darwin I called on several big businessmen. It was a humiliating experience and quite unsuccessful. In the end, Ningle Haritos, a Darwin businessman whom I hadn't even asked, tided us over with the Shell accountant being temporarily appeased.

To aid the situation still further, at the close of the 1965 season I moved into Darwin to stay with friends and work for a few months at my old job with the Department of Works, under Beth Campbell. Tom was left to grub trees on his own at the motel site. By now we had a two-way radio and a daily "sked" (as they were called – short for "schedule") so we could keep in contact and I would know all was going well with him. I returned to the Jim Jim at the start of the 1966 season which we hoped would be a busy one for us.

Thus it was that when our third season commenced in 1966, we were still in business though without the presence of young Phil Harries who had gone to Darwin to seek pastures new. One of our first necessities was an airstrip to service the motel site. An Airport Inspector came out to select a suitable area and by August the Department of Works advised us that upon receipt of the sum of $1,500 to the relevant Department, work would be put in hand to carry out the clearing and grading of the airstrip. Our all-weather one-mile long airstrip was completed shortly thereafter and was to be capable of taking DC3 aircraft.

Many caravans started to make the journey over the rough tracks now and in June of that year, a wagon train of some 20 caravans and a service vehicle, organised by Keith Odgers Wagon Train Safaris, camped at the Jim Jim Crossing. They boosted sales considerably, particularly fuel, with which we had been supplied adequately by Shell in advance. It was the first of several wagon train safaris operated by different people, one of whom got himself into a spot of bother leading his long train of caravans around the Mudginberry airstrip which had to be circuited to reach the outlet track onwards to Oenpelli, their destination. Unfortunately the leader missed the turning out and found himself catching up with the tail. Several circuits were made round the airfield with one vehicle following another, so the story goes, all nose to tail, until someone from the homestead interposed a vehicle and led them out and pointed the way onward.

Though the immediate financial situation had eased somewhat, the battle was by no means over. The year 1967 saw us still trying for a loan to expand. We simply could not get ahead without more money. Every known source was tried for a loan but it was the same old story. No finance company would look at a bush venture, however promising. We wrote hopefully to the Tourist Board. They replied that while being completely sympathetic to our proposals, they regretted to advise that at that time there were no funds available through the Northern Territory Tourist Board, or indeed, as they said, through any other official authority, for the purposes of development of tourist projects. However, they continued, they were able to confirm that the matter had been under careful study over the last two years, and they were hopeful that in the not too distant future development finance would be available through semi-official or official sources.

We couldn't wait that long. More money was vital immediately if we were not to be yet another undercapitalised business down the drain, with the wise ones sorrowfully shaking their heads and saying, "Well, what can you expect when you only had a capital of one thousand pounds ($2,000) to start with."

And then, in late 1967, a solution of sorts offered itself. We were loath to take on partners, knowing how such relationships can sometimes turn sour but it seemed the only solution to ease the problem. A couple, Fred and Jariyah Astell, who often came out fishing with their two children, showed interest in a partnership. With hopeful hearts we decided to take them on as partners. Papers were drawn up and the deed was done. We were hardly in a position to bargain and had to take the terms offered. There was a little more money in the kitty but it was not a happy alliance. We were temperamentally unsuited and it was probably a relief to all of us when, later, a temporary period of ill-health of one of the partners more or less forced a break-up. The partners sold their half of the business back to us – or rather to a group of shareholders, with Tom and I holding 50% of the shares – and a proprietary company came into being. Our project was at last starting to look interesting to investors.

CHAPTER FIVE

In the Motel Game – Jim Jim Motel

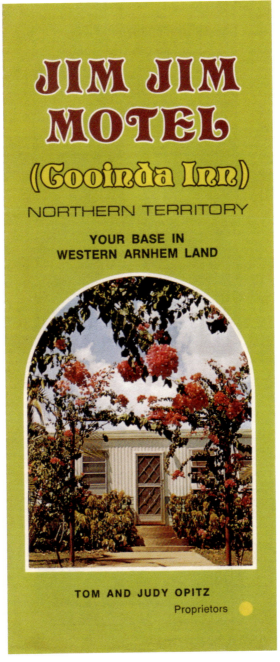

An early brochure cover for the motel.

The 1968 season saw the store site with its liquor availability a hive of activity, with up to 100 vehicles calling in at weekends. Although the name *Cooinda* had been chosen earlier to refer to both the store and the proposed motel, it seemed we should call one site by the Cooinda name and other by the Jim Jim name. But there always seemed to be confusion as to whether it was the Jim Jim or Cooinda Store, and later whether it was the Cooinda or the Jim Jim Motel. With official partners and a little more finance, our pleas for even further assistance were now being heeded and by mid-season, 1968, the E. S. and A. Bank granted us an overdraft of $6,000. Serious plans to build cabins and facilities over at the motel site were discussed but it was unlikely that any cabins could possibly be operational that year and, although brick making and site preparation were to continue, all other ideas were put on hold.

Storm ahead – the Wet Season approaches.

Road awash.

It was, nevertheless, a busy year in the store and Tom and I breathed a sigh of relief when November 1968 brought the rains and cut the track. We were, by now, not quite so isolated as we had been in our first Wet Season. We had an all-weather airstrip nearly 6,000 feet long, and a two-way radio. And our neighbours, Don McGregor and his tiny, raven-haired wife, Sandy, visited us nearly every week. If the track from his camp, Patonga, to ours was under water, he came the six odd miles down the flowing Jim Jim Creek by motorboat. Tall, brown-haired muscular Don had designed his house on the colonial style with rooms surrounding a large central hall. Polished bamboo, a crocodile skull lamp and an assortment of guns, rifles, and bullets decorated the walls. Bougainvillea, poincianas and mango trees were starting to flourish in his garden. Don catered mainly for the rich American hunter who preferred an exclusive hunt with personal attention, and he was already well-known in the higher hunting circles for the professional job he was doing.

By 1969, tourists were pouring into the Top End with Redline coaches alone bringing an average of 100 visitors into Darwin every week for a three day stopover, but no stopovers in the Western Arnhem Land area. In early June, 1969, Ansett Pioneer approached us with the idea of bringing a 4-day coach tour, called the "Arnhemlander" to stay at Cooinda. We had, of course, no accommodation to offer them – only the empty site we hadn't been able to raise the money to build on. Ansett Pioneer offered

pioneer's

ARNHEMLANDER

BUFFALO IN ARNHEM LAND

"Dreaming Waters", Nourlangie

THE ARNHEMLANDER

is an exciting journey into
the heart of Australia's Adven-
tureland. Here, in Arnhem Land,
you will find magnificent scenery,
abundant wild game, and see, in their
own country our aboriginal people — their
arts, their primitive skills, their tribal
dances. This is a fascinating part
of Australia, particularly for the
photographer, and one not
easily accessible by other
means — your ARNHEM-
LANDER holiday
will be a truly
unforgettable
experience.

NOURLANGIE is a camp originally
established for the buffalo hunter
which provides both permanent
flywired units and tented accommodation all with comfortable beds
and bedding.
Bearing in mind its remote location
in Arnhem Land, tourists will find
the facilities provided at Nourlangie are adequate and acceptable. These include hot showers,
septic toilet facilities and 240 volt
power.
Nourlangie is situated in a beautiful setting close to "Dreaming
Waters", a billabong of the Nourlangie Creek which runs into the
South Alligator River.

Part of a brochure for the Arnhemlander, 1967.

to finance us if we would take their passengers for a period. There was no time to build brick cabins, which had been our original intention, as they wanted to bring the first bus out in three months' time. WOWIC units were the answer. These units, ready made and furnished, put out by World Wide Camps Company, were able to be transported on semi-trailers to any site required. The proposition seemed to solve many problems of building brick cabins and after the usual discussion and drawing up of documents, arrangements were made for such demountables to be driven out to the motel site. Accommodation was to be for 30 passengers in five separate units, each unit containing three twin-bedded rooms with own shower and toilet. Another large unit would serve as

A truck gets dry-bogged on the track to Darwin. November 1965.

The WOWIC units arrive at Jim Jim Crossing.

a kitchen divided off from a dining-room recreation area. Payment for these facilities was to be recoverable from the anticipated guest stays.

A couple was engaged to manage the motel as Tom and I could not, at that stage, leave the store, and in due course the first bus arrived. But, alas, there were no WOWIC cabins for them to sleep in! Late rains on the track had bogged the semis with their extra heavy loads and they would be a few weeks late arriving. The "Arnhemlander" passengers were accommodated in tents spread around the store. Tall, grey-haired Gil Stone and his pretty, red-haired wife, Frances, looked after them. The kitchen facilities in the store weren't quite what Frances had expected or would have in the proper WOWIC kitchen, but she coped more than adequately. Gil found himself trotting up and down a ladder pushed out the back door, taking laden trays of food from the kitchen for the hungry passengers waiting to be fed at the tables set out underneath the store. The proper backdoor steps had been relegated to one of those "when we have enough money to spare" jobs.

Most of the passengers took the discomfort in good spirits. It was hard to remain long in the dumps with a coach captain like Doug Banks. Short, black-haired, brown-eyed bouncing Doug had been promoted from coach captain to Darwin manager of Ansett Pioneer, but was bringing the first few tours out to the Jim Jim himself. He coaxed the huge busses round the narrow tree-lined tracks whilst talking about the Aboriginal lore and the wildlife. For many it was a completely new experience. They had no idea that this northern part of Australia held such magic.

The cabins finally arrived and the passengers increased. It was a hectic

Even aircraft get bogged – at the Patonga airstrip near Cooinda.

Aerial view of Cooinda Motel with the WOWIC units, 1969.

season and we had some Very Important visitors that year, 1969. Colin Simpson, the well-known travel writer, came out on an "Arnhemlander" tour to take notes on the area for his book "The New Australia". Rolf Harris passed through on his TV Walkabout, and gave an impromptu singsong to the delighted guests at one of our buffalo and barramundi barbecues. Vincent Serventy, the writer and wildlife authority, also visited us, looking for material for his book on the area. Some V.I.P.'s and their entourages seemed to think we should provide them all with free accommodation and meals just for the pleasure of having their presence around the place. They said it would give us free publicity. So it may have done, but it wouldn't have been much use publicising a place that had gone out of business backwards paying staff to look after free-loaders. But possibly they didn't realise the razor's edge we were still operating on.

The end of 1969 brought more troubles. In late October Tom went swimming on the beach behind the store, with a party who had arrived in their own plane to stay at the motel. He dived in as he usually did. "Ho, ha, look at old Tom playing porpoises," said one of the party, then realised that Tom's flounderings on the top of the water were not in fun. Forgetting that the level of the billabong

The WOWIC demountable cabins. Cooinda Motel, 1973. Photo by Michael Jensen.

had dropped since he had last dived in, Tom had dived too deeply and struck his head on the sand. When they dragged him out, he was paralysed. The Flying Doctor was contacted by radio, and we flew in to Darwin in the guests' plane which they had immediately put at our disposal. An ambulance was waiting to take him to the Hospital. Extensive x-rays followed and it was clear he'd have to be flown south for surgery, as Darwin Hospital did not have the facilities to operate on such cases. I closed the store, found a couple, Grace and Allan Beckinsale, buffalo shooters with whom we had become friendly from their visits, to run the motel with its few off-season guests, and flew to Adelaide with Tom. He was one of the lucky ones. Some fine surgery in the Royal Adelaide Hospital pieced together his broken neck and, two months later, we flew home to the Jim Jim. He was later able to throw away his neck collar and back brace, and apart from a slight malfunction in one hand, appeared to be as good as new.

With Tom patched up again, we threw ourselves once more into the stresses and strains of running the business, always teetering on the edge of financial disaster but never quite falling into the pit. We had to spend out. We couldn't sit back and consolidate. We had to venture into erecting a full wayside inn at the motel site before somebody beat us to it. The large finds of uranium in the Jim Jim area would soon bring a bitumen road and a town site in its wake. We had never foreseen the country opening up to quite the extent it was obviously going to. Our dream of an eventual quiet life at the Jim Jim seemed to have vanished. Perhaps we had picked the right spot business-wise, but we were also caught up in a rat-race from which we could see no way to escape.

There were now four safari camps in the area, but none of us trod on each other's toes as we catered for different kinds of people. We, ourselves, were a strictly non-hunting operation. Allan Stewart at Nourlangie took mainly Australian hunting parties, though had his share of overseas visitors, while Frank Muir at Muirella Park ran an aerotel. With his many contacts in the flying world, Frank's camp was usually filled with aero club parties from all over Australia, or with members of RAAF 75 Squadron based at Darwin, who had "adopted" him. Frank had to sell out the following season, as the goring he had received from a wounded buffalo a few years back was affecting his health. He had been lucky to escape death from the enraged beast by wrenching at a vulnerable part of the bull's anatomy. He wasn't the only one to sell out. A few years later, both Allan Stewart and Don McGregor sold to the Wildlife Department, and Nourlangie and Patonga became Ranger Stations.

With our second Pioneer season, 1970, staff problems began. Gil and Frances Stone, who had left us at the end of the previous Dry, could not come back to us, and we were very fortunate in finding a young New Zealand girl, Anne Thurston, who turned out to be a most competent cook. She ruled the kitchen and dining area with great aplomb and was very popular with the guests with her cheery ways. She returned to work for us for several seasons, going home to New Zealand during the Wet.

We were not so well served by housemaids and had to restaff time and again. I was probably not a very good boss in that I didn't supervise as much as I should have done. I was far too lenient and trusted them to work without supervision while I tended to the store, or did weekly two-day trips to Darwin on business and to collect perishables.

The girls at the motel at first were left largely to their own devices and I hoped that their good sense would see to it that the jobs were done properly. This system didn't always work! Sometimes the cabins didn't get cleaned at all and we had complaints from irate guests. Then two disgruntled girls walked out after a week because I hadn't shown them how to clean the cabins. It hadn't occurred to me that anyone who applied for a job as a housemaid didn't know how to clean a room. It was certainly not a job that suited everyone. We needed girls who were not afraid of odd hours, who could work on their own initiative, and who could take the rough with the smooth. Fortunately there was never any shortage of girls eager to work a season in such surroundings where, on off duty times, they had opportunities to enjoy bushwalking, free helicopter or aircraft rides with visiting pilots, or tour around on the coaches if there was a spare seat.

The garden was starting to flourish under the loving care given it by Tom's brother, Ted, who had joined us. Ted was very popular with the guests with his profound knowledge of the bush and an inexhaustible supply of amusing stories. He left us to join the Forestry Department but became a frequent visitor when on leave. To his fund of yarns he added a repertoire of his own bush ballads.

A happy bar keeper.

Allan Stewart helping behind the motel bar, about 1971.

By 1971, the demountable which was to serve as the pub was *in situ* and being stocked up preparatory to a big opening night. A large ablution block and camping area was also set up near the motel, and campers' tents mushroomed up. Two large generators provided us with necessary power to run a large cold room to keep the beer at a happy temperature. This considerably sweetened the temper of those who had found the journey out to us to be hot, dusty and arduous. There were now two bush tracks to the Jim Jim: the original track from Pine Creek, and a shorter one through Humpty Doo and over the Mary River Bridge before passing Annaburro Station. This track cut off nearly 100 miles when travelling from Darwin. The owners of Annaburro Station, Terry and Kath Baldwin, were later to start up the Bark Hut Inn to service travellers on this route.

Tourists were visiting our store in ever increasing numbers, some of whom we

Front view of the new pub demountable, July 1972.

could well have done without. One hot, dry, morning, a green Volkswagen campmobile with N.S.W. number plates purred down the track from Darwin and pulled up at the Jim Jim Store. I got up from my desk in the back room, pushed my papers aside, and went out to check that the beer was cold. I flicked a duster over the store shelves again, and awaited developments. A dumpy little man heaved himself from the driver's seat and puffed his way up the steps into the store. "Where's all this wildlife they talk about?" he grumbled. "We haven't seen a single thing on the way out here. That's not what they told us at the Tourist Bureau. This is the Jim Jim, isn't it?" "Yes, this is the Jim Jim," I said, "and I'm sorry you haven't seen anything but it does sometimes happen that way. Wildlife is very elusive, you know. Can I get you something?" My hand hovered over the fridge door ready to whip out a nice, cold beer for him. The man mopped his florid, perspiring face with a pale, blue handkerchief. "No, ta," he said. "Just dropped in to see if you can tell us what to see around here and where to catch the fish."

He walked over to the doorway and called out to his wife who was still sitting in the vehicle. "Hey, bring us up a stubby, will you, luv, I'm dry." He flapped his handkerchief about and ran it round the back of his beefy neck. "Don't know how you stand this heat. Too much for me. And all that dust we've come through. Enough to choke a man to death. Why don't you improve your roads up here? Don't know what those corrugations have done to my springs." He broke off his grumbling to take the bottle of beer from his mousy little wife, who had quietly crept in and as quietly gone out again with never a smile or look in my direction. The man picked up the bottle opener from the counter and pulled the top off his stubby.

"Ah, that's better," he said, after a long mouthful," but it's our last cold one. What say you change some of our hotties from your coldies? Wouldn't like to see a couple of travellers die for want of a cold beer, eh?" He tilted the bottle again. "The wife and I call ourselves seasoned travellers now," he went on. "Retired, you know. Go away for six months every year. Always a different route, see different places. Can't think why. Everywhere is always hot and dusty and never like the tourist pamphlets tell us. They shouldn't be allowed to say the things they do. Still, it doesn't cost us a lot. The wife and I pride ourselves on the way we do it, not spending much." Absentmindedly, the man chinked some coins in his pocket. "Not that we have to be careful. Made quite a little packet out of our newsagent's business in Wollongong, but we're firm believers in that good old bush hospitality. Not a bad tradition that – if you arrive some place on meal time you're sure of a bite to eat. Though I can't say as how people are always too happy about it." The man glanced at a large gold watch on his wrist. "'Course it's a bit early for lunch yet but we're in no hurry. What's the good of a holiday if you've got to rush everywhere, I say."

At last he paused for breath. He looked around the store, evidently not finding it much to his taste, before he settled himself down on the row of full soft drink cartons that lined the walls. "And where are you going for your holidays this year?" he asked. Perhaps he thought it was time to include me in his conversation. I stifled a desire to scream with hollow laughter. Tom and I hadn't had a holiday for eight years. I was saved from the trouble of replying as the man went on: "I suppose you'd need a change every year to see a few people. Drive you mad out here all alone, wouldn't it? Can't be too many people want to come through here. Don't you get bored and lonely?" Hysterical feelings rose again. Lonely! When one saw people nearly every minute of every day and half way through the night, for seven or eight months at a stretch. Meeting people is fun but not when you have to talk to them or listen to them without respite. Bored? Yes, sometimes, when one had to answer the same questions over and over again. Yet one had to remember it was new information to each tourist and give him, so to speak, his money's worth.

The man rambled on: "I mean, what on earth do you do all day?" Do! I nearly choked. Did he think all I had to do was stand behind the counter. What about the bookwork that had fallen weeks behind, the letters to be answered, the orders to be made out for my next Darwin store trip, the wages to be calculated for the staff over at the motel. If I hadn't been wasting my time with his inane questions I could have been catching up on my work. But, of course, he didn't know that, and the customer must come first. "Oh," I said, as calmly as I could, "I'm usually kept quite busy serving people." He didn't seem to take the hint. In no way did he consider himself a customer. He pulled a packet of cigarettes out of his pocket and patted himself vaguely all over for matches. "Wouldn't have a match, would you?" he asked. "No, I don't want a whole box," he said hastily as I made to take one off the store shelf, "just one little match will do."

I handed him a half-used box from under the counter. "Do keep these," I said, " you might need another." "Ta," he said, pocketing them. How mean could the man get or was he just accepting that good old bush hospitality. He lit his cigarette, carefully broke the match in half and dropped the two ends on the floor. "Now, tell us," he said, "what's to see and where are the fish?" Suddenly I'd had enough of the man. I wasn't going to tell him a thing. "The fish aren't biting," I said, "and I don't think there's anything around here you'd be interested in seeing. Now if you'll excuse me I have some work to do out the back." "What about lunch?" he asked, plaintively. "I don't have time for lunch myself, and I'm certainly not cooking for anyone else. Try the motel, if you can spare the money," I snapped, and went through the three-quarter door that divided the front from the back store. "Hey, hang on a minute," he called out, "weren't you going to change some of my hot bottles of beer for your cold ones?"

I turned back, trembling with rage. "Not bloody likely," I shouted, and slammed the door. Unfortunately, being a swing door, it didn't rid me of my frustrations in a fine explosion of sound but merely caught me on the shins on the rebound. I could hear him clattering off down the stairs muttering about the rudeness of outback people and how could they expect to attract tourists if they didn't bother to make themselves pleasant. I heard him throw his bottle away and I dashed out to the top of the steps. "And don't mess up our lovely country with your beastly beer bottles," I screamed. Then I went back behind the counter and burst into tears. Clearly, a cup of tea, a Bex and a bit of a lie-down were indicated. I put the kettle on the Portagas stove and swallowed a powder. A lie-down was out of the question but I took my cup of tea out to the front porch and endeavoured to pull myself together, before the end-of-a-busy-season blues really took a hold. Oh, no! I heard another vehicle approaching.

A cream Land Rover with Victorian number plates came tearing down the hill and pulled up at the foot of the steps in a cloud of dust. I prepared to let the driver have a piece of my mind. A young couple tumbled out of their seats and leapt up the steps, two at a time, waving their arms about to disperse the dust they had generated. "Gosh, sorry about that, I really am," said a red-haired, freckle-faced young man of about 24, contritely. "Guess I was so thirsty and in such a hurry to reach your store, I was going a bit faster than I should." "Oh, don't worry about it, what's a bit of dust between friends," I said, and meant it, quite mollified by his pleasant manner. "We haven't been speeding all the way. Too much to see, wasn't there, darl?" The young man turned to the slim girl in a pink bikini by his side. "Never seen so much wildlife." The girl broke in. "Emus, wild horses, simply thousands of buffaloes, wallabies, a whole family of pigs, goannas, frilly-necked lizards, and ugh," she shuddered, "an enormous python we only just missed running over."

"Well, no good standing here getting drier," said the young man, turning to me. "I'd like a Coke please, and what for you, Jen, a lemonade?" The girl called Jen nodded her head vigorously, her long blonde hair caught back in a ponytail, bobbing up and down. "And one for you too, if you'd like one," added the young man. "No, thank you very much," I said, "as a matter of fact I was just going to have a cup of tea." The young couple took their drinks and sat down on the cartons by the wall. "Terrific little set-up you've got here. By the way, I'm Jack and this is Jennifer." "Howdy," I said to both of them, "I'm Judy and welcome to the Jim Jim." I sat down on the stool behind the counter and prepared to enjoy my tea and a chat.

"This your first time in the Territory?" I asked. Jennifer nodded. "Yes, and it certainly won't be the last." "But the heat," I said, thinking of my last visitors, "the dust, that awful corrugated track. Didn't it bother you?" "I don't think we really noticed, did we, Jen?" said Jack. "There've been so many exciting things taking our attention. It's all so new. We've never been out of Melbourne before." "This is a sort of honeymoon tour for us. We've just got married, you know," explained Jennifer, her fine-featured unmade-up little face glowing with happiness. "I like the way you've built on piers," said Jack. "Is that to make it cooler?" "No," I answered, "it's to keep the building out of the water. You may not think it, but that creek bed down there which hasn't a skerrick of water in it right now, flows a bit fastish come February/March time and water laps five feet or so up these piers."

"Good heavens, what do you do, stay inside?" asked Jennifer. "We close the store – no customers anyway, after the first big rains start to bring the rivers up," I said, "and we move over to our motel five miles away. We've got an airstrip there and guests can fly in during the Wet." "Wouldn't be much fun in the rain, would it?" asked Jack. "It doesn't rain non-stop, unless there's a cyclone brewing somewhere," I explained, "and personally I think the Wet is the prettiest time with the country green and lush and the billabongs brimming. But it's not the best time for fishermen. Most of the fish go out to sea to spawn as soon as the rivers run enough and they don't come back until the Wet's nearly over." "How are the fish biting now," asked Jack, eagerly. "It would be fun if we could catch a big one. Do you know any good spots where they might be?"

"I might at that," I said, pulling out a copy of one of my mudmaps from the stack under the counter (see page *vi* of this book). I pointed out Yellow Water and how to get to it a mile or so past the motel. "Try this point here," I said, and made a mark with my red pen. "They've been catching a few beauties there lately – 48 lbs is the record this year. But you can't beat those little 10 lb. fish for sweet eating." "Can we camp over there?" asked Jennifer, practically. "There are no facilities, if that's what you mean, and it gets a bit hot in the middle of the day as there isn't much shade. But lots of people do camp there because it's handy for the fishing. It's a good spot for waterbird life too. But if you want a shady camp, I suggest you go down to the waterhole about 300 yards behind the store. There's a sandy beach there which is fun to swim from." "What, no – er – crocodiles?" asked Jack, "though if there were I suppose they'd only be freshwater ones and wouldn't hurt you." "They are all salties round here," I said, "not that there are many left now. There is one old chap who lives on an island about halfway down the waterhole but he shouldn't worry you. He hasn't come up to the beach – or eaten any tourists – for ages." Jack laughed, then fell to studying the mud map again. "Hey, look, Jen, cave paintings. We must see them." He prodded his finger at some fanned out lines I had drawn on the map to indicate Obiri Rock near the East Alligator River. "I wish we knew more about them. We'll have to buy heaps of books when we get home."

"For a start," I said, groping under the counter again, "try reading this one." And I pulled out *Quest under Capricorn* by David Attenborough. "It was written a few years back and may be out of print. It's all about this country and the rocks at Obiri. I'll lend it to you if you like, if you're camping here. I'll lend you these too," I said, and produced Allan Stewart's *The Green Eyes are Buffaloes*, and *Top End Safari* by Vic McCrystal. "We do appreciate this," said Jack. "It's really kind of you. Do you know we wouldn't have had nearly such a good time or seen so much on this trip north if people like you hadn't been so kind to us. You wouldn't believe how nice people have been all the way up the track." I could most certainly believe it. They were the kind of people you wanted to do things for. Not like the previous couple who brought out the worst in one.

"Another drink and then we'd better get a tin of sardines in case we don't catch that fish for lunch," laughed Jack. Jennifer ran her eye along the shelves. "And you'd better hurry up, Jen. Looks like the shop is going to be invaded." Down the track from Darwin came not one but two coaches. Centralian? Sampsons? Greyhound? Rambler? Whichever coachline it was, there'd be nearly eighty people clamouring for sweets and cold drinks. I felt a moment of panic. Tom was over at the motel supervising some last minute details for the opening of our new pub the following week. I'd have to cope alone. "Want any help?" offered Jennifer, "I work in a milk bar in the evenings in Melbourne." "Thanks, I could use some," I said, beckoning her round behind the counter, "beer 0.40c, soft drinks 0.20c, everything else marked and there's the till."

The first of the eighty, led by a gangly youth in glasses with his camera case flapping round his sunburnt neck, tore up the steps determined that if there was only one cold drink left, he was going to get it. For twenty minutes bedlam reigned before the two coach parties drifted away and drove on down to the waterhole for a swim and a barbecue on the beach. Jennifer joined Jack on the other side of the counter and I pushed a Coke and a lemonade at them "That was a mighty effort, thank you, Jen," I said. "Quite a busy life you lead," laughed Jennifer, "I don't know that I could keep up with the pace myself. Whatever made you start all this. It must have been quite an adventure." I nodded. "You're English, aren't you?" Jennifer went on. "Do you like it in Australia? How long have you been here? Don't you ever get homesick? Have you seen much of Australia? What did you do before you started this?"

"Whoa, whoa," I laughed, "that's an awful lot of questions." "Take no notice of my wife," said Jack, giving her a hug, "she's nothing but a sticky beak." "But I like people," protested Jennifer, "and I'm always interested in why they do things and how they feel. I know there's a lot of personal questions there, but I'd be genuinely interested in the answers." "You're just like me, Jennifer," I said, "and I suspect many other women. I always want to know what people do, and how they met their husbands and wives, and where they were born and all that. But if I were to start answering all your questions, I'd probably get carried away and yarn on and on and you'd never get to see those caves." "Well, why don't you write a book about it," said Jennifer, thoughtfully. "Perhaps there'd be others like me who'd be interested in reading it." "You may be right," I mused. "I might just have a go one Wet Season when we're not quite so busy. Even if no-one but you, Jennifer, reads it, at least it will have been fun writing it."

The end of September 1971 saw the pub in full swing. Tom and I found ourselves busier than ever, dividing our time between the motel and pub. I certainly had no time

Postcard we produced in 1971-72 showing Tom and me serving behind the bar. One of the guests shown was our bank manager, Norman Thompson. He is fourth from left, wearing a white shirt, seen behind the chap with the orange shirt. Others are from the Haritos family. Norman later asked us for six of these postcards when I brought in the balance sheet for our company.

to write a book. The days of 10 cars a week to the Jim Jim when we opened in 1964, had increased to about 400 tourist cars a week in the peak season. This was augmented by Government vehicles, as well as mining transports, semi-trailers and road trains travelling to the mining interests or pastoral companies in the area. A cold beer in an outback pub was an attractive thought to nearly all the travellers. But all work and no play was having a serious effect on both Tom and myself. We were both mentally and physically exhausted, although Tom seemed better able to handle it than I. It is not possible to manage a place, particularly a place like ours in the bush with its peculiar difficulties, do a lot of the labour involved as well, and still be a relaxed host and hostess to visitors. Even the quiet Wet Season, which previously had been a time of respite from people so that we could recharge out batteries, was a thing of the past. Guests dropped in by air, not enough to warrant keeping on staff but quite enough to take up our own attention and nervous energy. Our guests by air also included those who used our facilities as their base for hunting uranium in the region from their specially equipped aircraft.

Ansett Pioneer, who could not, of course, bring out their passengers by road in the Wet Season, mooted the idea of operating light aircraft to bring out guests but this was not followed through. They also suggested bringing out passengers on a track being cut to the South Alligator River where a bridge was about to be built. Passengers would then be transported by boat up the river, across the flooded plains and finally through Yellow Water and into the Home Billabong. These tours did not eventuate at the time but we had a number of visiting fishermen who left their vehicles at the road river junction and made the journey in their own boats. It was a fantastic run but one on which it was very easy to get lost, until a Ranger marked out the route with small yellow painted drums hung in trees and coloured ribbons fluttering in the breeze at strategic points. One sweep across the featureless flooded plain needed the direction "turn right at the last blue ribbon and head for the tallest palm tree," a mere speck in the distance.

Business went so well during the 1972 season that Tom had the idea of setting up another motel near the soon-to-be completed South Alligator River Bridge. Coach passengers could then make use of both motels on their tours. In September of that year we were granted a Miner's Right so that we could stake claim for a site in the area and we spent some days measuring out and pegging what we considered a suitable site. I wasn't sure how I was going to cope with all that additional worry and by the end of the year I was at screaming pitch. The sight of another customer was starting to produce a nervous tension headache which didn't help customer relations. The result was hardly fair on the visitor and it certainly didn't make for a happy married life. What was the answer? We couldn't just down tools and go on strike and neither was it likely that anyone would be too keen to come in and manage the place without fantastic wages, long leave, air fares and all those fringe benefits which Government employees in Darwin enjoyed. Our small company was in no position to offer such benefits. The only alternative was to stifle the screams and carry on. But for how long could the screams be stifled? I wondered how I was going to get through another hectic season.

I had to have something to visualise which would make all that we were doing worthwhile. "I must have something to look forward to," I almost screamed at Tom, "or I shall wind up a raving ninny." I suddenly thought of the little white house with the red, front door which we hadn't thought about for nine years. Our dream of living in harmony with wildlife had somehow got lost along the way. Perhaps if I kept a vision of that house continually in my mind, I could get through another season – and then another if need be.

"That's it," I cried. "Our house. Let's choose where we'd like to build it and then I can start to furnish it – all in the mind, of course." Tom looked at me rather sideways but we trekked off into the bush outside the compound at the first possible moment. He led me to the site he had evidently had in mind for some time. I agreed with him that this was most definitely the spot. A natural clearing in the bush, surrounded by graceful white gums, and with a view of the never-never glades across the billabong, was just inviting us to put our house there. It was far enough from the motel to be secluded from any tourist activity but near enough not to be excluded entirely from contact with our fellow man. For some reason we called it the Place of the Whispering Shadows.

We started to dream-plan our house. It was going to offer us the best of all possible worlds by combining modern comforts with the natural wildness and ambience of the bush. I wanted a sewing and music room. Tom wanted a large shed where he could keep his special gardening gear for our own garden. "White roses trailing round the verandah, please," I said to Tom. "And perhaps some zinnias and marigolds for a splash of colour out the front?" "I've got plenty of my own ideas," said Tom," You just wait and see what it's going to look like. But there's a lot more water to flow down the creek before we can retire and throw off all our responsibilities from the motel." I sighed and thought about it for another glorious moment. Then I pushed all such thoughts to the back of my mind, knowing I could call them up at will, if necessary, in times of stress. The Dry Season was looming and there was still the spring cleaning to be done.

Tom and I greeting the Connair mail plane at our Jim Jim / Cooinda airstrip. I'm holding the mailbag and paperwork.

The year 1973 opened with a flourish and the company seemed to be catching up with itself finance-wise, but all was not plain sailing. At the start of the season we had decided to put a couple in to run the store at the crossing so that I could concentrate on the motel side of things. After going through a series of

Cooinda Motel, 1973. The pub demountable is at the left, the kitchen and dining section is left of centre, and the accommodation units are at the right. The track at the top of the photo leads to Home Billabong.

couples who discovered they didn't care for bush life and the rather spartan amenities and left in a hurry, we finally found an ideal pair – or so we thought. They didn't mind roughing it, appeared to be reliable, willing to stay open any hour and, according to reports which filtered back to us, cheerful and helpful with the customers. In spite of this admirable devotion to duty, however, the takings didn't seem consistent with the trade evidently taking place. Yet checks never revealed any discrepancies between takings and stock. And no wonder! Only a negligible amount of our stock was being sold and the clever couple, who no doubt were chortling all the way to the bank at our naivete in not realising the possibilities for such duplicity, were bringing in their own stock and selling it through our store. When they were dismissed we decided to close the store and concentrate solely on the motel.

We were also in contact with the relevant Department with regard to the availability of a site on the new road that was now called the Arnhem Highway. We had plans for a Wayside Inn type of business on the area we had already walked over on our Miner's Right the previous year. But it transpired that any lease the Department decided would be granted, had to be put up for auction. When, in October, 1973, we heard on the grapevine that a lease had been granted privately without going up for auction, we wrote with some indignation to Doug Anthony, the leader of the Australian Country

Tom of the Jim Jim receives a letter. This letter reached us despite our brief address! August 1972.

Party. He and his charming wife, Margo, had been among our visitors and knew of all our hopes and aspirations. Mr. Anthony was kind enough to contact the Secretary of the Department of the Northern Territory who advised him that the Department was very much aware of Tom's stake in the area. It transpired that no such direct grant had been made to anyone and an auction would be taking place in due course and we would have our chance. As we were still struggling for adequate cash flow our chances were, of course, slim. In the event, it was probably just as well we didn't get a lease granted to us as we were having quite enough problems running one motel, let alone two. Quite a large piece of land was eventually sold at auction for $30,000 to Roper Bar Trading Pty Ltd, and after a series of changes of hands was to become one of the leading resorts in the area.

Radio communication was by now something of a problem as speedy bookings were impossible. We applied for the provision of a radio telephone but were advised that although our need for telephone communication was fully recognised, such a facility could not be provided at that time.

To cap it all that year, we suffered nearly complete disaster in the shape of fire. Returning from Darwin after one stores trip, I stopped as usual at Moon Billabong on the Wildman River to admire the waterlilies and stretch my legs. A vehicle coming from the Jim Jim direction pulled up with the same idea. We passed the time of day and the driver told me he was heading for Darwin with a load of barra he'd caught at the East Alligator. "Did you call at the motel?" I asked. "No, we saw too much dirty, black smoke from the main track and didn't go in the four miles to the motel. What are you burning up there, old tyres or something?" My heart plummeted. I leapt into my vehicle without a word of farewell and drove like one possessed to the Jim Jim. I knew what it

N.T. NEWS, 3 JULY 1973

Braved flames to save vehicle

A truck driver who braved a raging petrol fire to save his prime mover said yesterday: "All I could think of trying to do was save my truck."

Bob Rasport (pictured) of Parap, was telling how he released the $10,000 prime mover from the trailer which had caught fire after an explosion.

The trailer carrying 500 gallons of petrol, burst into flames as he was discharging the load at the Jim Jim motel, 150 miles east of Darwin late Friday.

The flames spread to overhead fuel tanks and gutted a nearby shed housing three electricity generators for the motel.

EXPLODED

Mr Rasport, who was not injured, said, "It just exploded behind my back."

"When I turned around there were seven foot high flames in the air."

"I was very lucky because I had another tank on and I had just loaded that underground."

"If I hadn't the whole of Jim Jim would have blown up."

$20,000

He said that the generators and trailer would have been worth about $20,000.

He said the loss of the generators meant there was no water or electricity but that a generator had been loaned from Pine Creek.

NODE NORTH. N.T. NEWS 5/7/73

IT SEEMS that one way of keeping tourists happy is to have a good blaze. While helpers at the recent fire at Jim Jim were trying to stop flames spreading by hosing bulging petrol drums without thought for their own safety, one young lady was seen clapping her hands and dancing with excitement, exclaiming "oh isn't it thrilling!" She didn't seem to realise she could have been blown sky-high any second.

PUBLIC NOTICES

BUSSINESS as usual, after the fire at the Jim Jim motel, thanks to the magnificent efforts of those present at the time and subsequent help given by police department, Ron Thomas, Paul Porter, Wayne Cubis, Noranda, Pechiney Exploration, and many others.

was. A petrol fire. A semi-trailer had been due at the Jim Jim that day with a load of fuel for us, and heaven knew what ruins I would find when I got back.

It was dark when I reached the motel. No lights twinkled at me as I turned the last corner, though here and there a red glow sparked on the ground, but the bar and buildings were still standing. Tom came out and greeted me sombrely as I drew up. He took me over to where the engine shed should have been and I saw a charred ruin. The whole shed had burnt down, melting the generator, and destroying all the equipment stored inside. By the Grace of God it had not spread further, thanks to the courageous efforts of some young men who had been in the bar. Apparently the petrol had been unloaded and the semi driver had driven around to the tanks behind the motel to unload the diesel. During this operation the petrol pack, which was used to pump the diesel from the tank on the semi into our tanks, had backfired and burst into flames, setting the semi alight. With great coolness, the driver unhooked his prime mover and drove it clear, while yelling FIRE at the top of his lungs. Those in the bar heard the cry and rushed to his aid. The trailer was burning fiercely and the fire had spread to the engine shed. Neither could be saved. Flames shot thirty feet into the air to the delight of one tourist who stood at a respectful distance, jumping up and down with excitement and exclaiming "Ooh, isn't it fun, just look at those flames."

With no power we were virtually out of business. We couldn't pump water for our guests nor provide them with electric light, nor keep the beer cold or keep our well stocked-up deep freezers going. But Aussies are renowned at showing a helping hand and next day, Paul Porter, who ran the garage at Pine Creek, towed out a spare generator he had and we were in business again before the beer had gone hot or the frozen food spoiled. It all meant additional expense and worry. My health deteriorated to the point where I found myself in Darwin Hospital with high blood pressure and kidney problems and a temperature that would not come down.

Luckily we had some loyal and especially wonderful motel staff that year. With my fraying health, they suggested everything could now be left in their capable hands for the rest of the season and agreed they would all come back next year if I wanted to take myself off for a long, rejuvenating holiday. Tom decided to pack me off on the Women's Weekly World Tour Cruise for five months. We blessed the Go Now, Pay Later plan.

On a sunny afternoon in February, 1974, I boarded the P & O ship *Himalaya* in Sydney Harbour. Tom had flown down earlier with me from Darwin to see me off. I wished he could have come too, but we could not both be away from the Jim Jim for the length of the cruise. We had taken my gear to the wharf the day before, so that unusual packages, including a magnificent pair of albino buffalo horns, and a selection of bark paintings and Aboriginal artefacts as gifts for my family, could be stowed away in the hold. It had been quite a rigmarole getting official permission to take the artefacts out of the country, and my handbag was full of documents in triplicate from various Government Departments.

We got to the ship twenty minutes before sailing time, having dallied over our last lunch together for five months. The wharf was seething with people, and streamers were flying from ship to shore. We pressed through the throng of people on board and struggled down to find my cabin on "B" deck. The four-berth cabin, with its own facilities, was packed so tightly with farewelling visitors, that I couldn't even see my bunk space. Tom and I sat on the edge of the bath and sipped neat brandy from my emergency flask until the "all ashore that's going ashore" call came over the loud speakers. We rejoined the throng on deck and were borne along towards the gangplanks where I almost got swept down as well. Tom didn't wait for the final breaking of the streamers. As he disappeared into the crowd, I walked around to the empty side of the ship away from the wharf, repeating to myself over and over what a wonderful trip it was going to be. But at the same time I was wondering how I was going to be able to bear to be away from Tom for so long.

With hooters blaring and the band playing some jolly tune, the *Himalaya* cast off and headed gently out to sea. We should have gone to Brisbane to refuel but as Queensland was badly flooded we went to Port Kembla instead. No passengers were allowed ashore, apart from several farewelling visitors who had missed hearing the last call and found themselves at sea. A few cruise passengers who had been swept down the gangway in Sydney and had hastily made their way to Port Kembla, were picked up in exchange. Perhaps it was as well we weren't allowed ashore as I was so overcome with homesickness that I would have flown straight home to Tom and the Jim Jim. One of my cabin mates, Delia, was homesick too, and we gazed our last at Australia, telling each other our histories and howling quietly into our hankies.

Then the hankies were put out of sight, only coming out, I suspect with Delia as with me, when letter writing home was in progress. Putting on a brave front, we proceeded to get to know the other passengers and enjoy shipboard life. The scheduled stopover at Rabaul, a township in Papua New Guinea, was cancelled due to an oil strike and the necessity to go slow and conserve on fuel. We called briefly at Guam which I associated with gallant American marine landings, but all signs of war had long since gone. Here I began my collection of souvenirs from foreign parts with a hideous wooden face mask, not realising I would see the same type of mask on sale in most other ports of call.

Our next port of call was Kobe in Japan, followed by Yokohama, where I absorbed as much as I could of Japan on the organised tours offered, and enthused over Mount Fujiyama's majestic beauty. Clear white and stark against a blue sky, we saw her at her best. It was hardly cherry blossom time in the shrines and gardens we visited, but we could see how beautiful they would look in the Spring. The Japanese people were smiling, polite and anxious for us all to enjoy ourselves in their country.

Our stay at Honolulu was shortened due to the time factor and we missed the promised barbecue at Waikiki Beach. Instead we visited Pearl Harbour and the pineapple plantations and took a tour round the volcanic mountain scenery and golden beaches. Pulling away from shore in the early evening, we watched a rainbow appear and then fade over Diamond Head. A week later we called at San Francisco. No visit would be complete without seeing Fisherman's Wharf, the corkscrewing Lombard Street, riding on BART (Bay Area Rapid Transport), the fantastic computer controlled underground tube system, and going up and down the steep hills in cable cars. I added a tour to the

Muir Woods with its gigantic sequoia trees, but missed out on visiting China Town as again time was against us.

Los Angeles meant a tour of Disneyland, a completely captivating place for young and old, and a tour round Hollywood, stopping to marvel at the tiny foot and handprints of some of the famous film stars at Grauman's Chinese Theatre. The coach took us round the Beverley Hills area but it was an evening tour and we couldn't see the elegant houses the stars lived in. Acapulco was not one of my favourite ports of call, though it is apparently THE place for jet setters. The dive from the high cliff – a must for tourists – was naturally breathtaking to watch. The bazaars were fascinating and I was tempted by the silver type jewellery and onyx ware. I couldn't resist a blue and white onyx chessboard with carved onyx men. It weighed a considerable amount but I managed to stagger back to the ship with it. I later found I could not concentrate enough to play with such ornate pieces and preferred the more usual black and white set with standardised men.

And then the Panama Canal! What an operation! The opening and closing of the huge lock gates which controlled the rise and fall of our ship as it delicately manoeuvred its way through so as not to hit the lock walls, kept us all glued to the rails. Each side of the canal displayed the beauty of the jungle with its trees of brilliant coloured flowers. At the tropical island of Barbados, I bought a steel pan. This musical instrument looks like the top of a 44-gallon drum, which, after being beaten into the right shape, emits certain ringing notes when struck with a rubber tipped drum stick. Not only was the steel pan heavy, it was exceedingly awkward to carry. Madiera, the last port of call, was a neat, tidy and clean little island where the people seemed industrious and happy. I took a tour way, way up into the mountains above the mist before descending to walk around Funchal, the capital of Madiera, sampling their sweet wine and buying yet another awkward souvenir – a triple-tiered wickerwork sewing basket. I hoped there would be enough porters around on disembarkation to help me carry all my souvenirs.

On a foggy morning in March the *Himalaya* slid up the English Channel. Most of the passengers were on deck from 4.00 am onwards, eagerly awaiting their first sight of England. They didn't see much as they paraded about in thick coats, hands deep in pockets, coughing and sniffling in the cold, moist air and peering through the greyness. I strolled on deck with a studied nonchalance after breakfast in a very empty dining-room. I tried not to listen to the plaintive cry of the gulls as they followed the ship – surely one of the most heart-tugging sounds to an Englishman. "You must be excited at seeing the land of your birth again," said my cabin mate, Delia. "No, not really," I said, "beastly cold place, England. I'll be glad to get back to sunny Australia." "But you're out of the Aussie sun right now, so why are you wearing your dark glasses?" asked Delia. "You're not about to start bawling again, are you?" "Oh, no," I said, in a voice that by a supreme effort of will was quite steady, "it's just that glasses keep this infernal cold mist out of my eyes. It's making them water."

Yet, in truth, I had suddenly felt the whole of my earlier life flashing before my eyes and I was beginning to wonder who I really was. Pommie or Aussie? How deep were my English origins?

Part Two – Pommie Beginnings

CHAPTER SIX

Birthtime for Bonzo – London

My mother, Irene Molesworth (1897-1949), about 1914.

London, England, 16th June, 1924. I was unceremoniously eased into this world to the accompaniment of cries of "Oooh, she looks just like a Bonzo dog" – or so I was much later informed by those who had been present. In the early 1920s, Bonzo, a cartoon character created by George Studdy in 1922, reigned supreme in England with his antics. The distinguishing features of this pudgy pup were a laughing, crinkly face, big blue eyes, a golf-ball nose, elephant ears and large feet and I was evidently seen to be a carbon copy! Bonzo the dog had the happy knack of making the world laugh with him, so it was to be hoped that perhaps my similar appearance augured an ability to be of amusement to the world in some way. I was christened June Rose but the name of Bonzo stuck and, in my home circle of friends and relatives at any rate, I am still known by the nickname.

My father, Charles Rowley (1896-1934), about 1930.

My parents were Charles Donovan Rowley and Irene Evelyn Beatrice, née Molesworth. When, as children, some aspect of our family history was mentioned, it was always referred to as being either on the Rowley or the Moley side. The motto for the Rowley side of the family is *"Ventis secundis"* or "Favouring winds," from which it may be deduced that the family were connected with the Royal Navy, especially in the glorious days of sail. A series of Rowley admirals began with Rear Admiral Sir William Rowley (1690-1768). He was in the van (the leading ships) at the Battle of Toulon in February 1744 and later became Admiral of the Fleet.

Achievements in the Royal Navy continued with Admiral Sir Joshua Rowley (1730-1790) who took part in some of the many sea battles of the time, including the Battle of Quiberon Bay on 20th November, 1759, under Admiral Sir Edward Hawke's fleet. His deeds were remembered in the Second World War when a Captain Class frigate, *H.M.S. Rowley*, was named after him. Admiral Sir Charles Rowley (1770-1845) and his son, Captain Richard Freeman Rowley (1806-1854) also performed their own "Hornblower" style feats for their country.

Sir Charles was to experience the changeover from sail to steam and it appears had some difficulty in coming to grips with the new technology. The story noted in *The Oxford Illustrated History of the Royal Navy* shows this when, in 1834, apparently he read an examination paper for gunnery lieutenant, and found he could not understand the words "impact" and "initial velocity". The story continues that:

> He asked another member of the Admiralty Board, Sir John Beresford, who said, "I'll be hanged if I know, but I suppose it is some of Tom Hasting's scientific bosh; but I tell you what I think we had better do – we'll just go at once to Lord de Grey and get the *Excellent* paid off." However, Lord de Grey (the First Lord at the time) told him he could not sanction it, "for you have no idea how damned scientific that House of Commons has become."

One can sympathise with Sir Charles and wonder how he would have coped with the computerisation technology of today.

Other Rowley kinsmen similarly made names for themselves at sea. In particular, Sir Josias, nephew of Sir Joshua, was involved in the Battle of Mauritius in 1810, which indirectly put paid to Napoleon's dreams of invading Australia. His exploits in this battle were the basis for the Jack Aubrey adventures told by Patrick O'Brien in his book *The Mauritius Command*. Sir Josias also has some renown on the Australian scene when, in 1818, the hydrographer, Phillip Parker King, named the Rowley Shoals off the northwest coast of Australia after him.

The motto appearing on the Molesworth coat of arms, *Vincit Amor Patriae*, which is translated variously as "To love my country" or "The love of my country exceeds everything" was one of the guiding stars for my behaviour throughout my early life. For me, even today, although such love does not exceed everything, it still burns brightly and with gratitude in memory of England's earlier greatness and glories.

My mother, a "Moley," the elder daughter of George Bagot Molesworth, and Nina Alida, née Faulkner, was born in 1897, in the hill station of Chakrata, India. This was a time of the ascendancy of the British Raj, and my grandfather was serving in the Duke of Cornwall's Light Infantry. He was well acquainted with the turbulent events on the North West Frontier. After his death in 1947, I was given a cloth survey map he must have used in the area, and a *kukri* (a curved-blade Gurkha knife). Both of these had taken pride of place on a side table in their much later English home in Chorley Wood, Hertfordshire, and I had always admired them on my many happy visits there. Unfortunately, I am not aware of the precise history of how the *kukri* came into my grandfather's possession but I know he instilled in me at a very early age the distinction of the Gurkha soldier, and to this day I continue to speak of Gurkhas in almost reverential tones.

My grandfather took the title of 9th Viscount in 1906, on the death of his father, Samuel, the 8th Viscount. The 1st Viscount, Robert Molesworth, had set the ball rolling for family distinction in the time of George I, being advanced to the peerage in 1716 for his services in various offices of trust in Ireland. The title passed to his son, John, who became the 2nd Viscount, and then to his brother Richard, the 3rd Viscount. Richard had won fame in 1706 for saving the life of the Duke of Marlborough at the Battle of Ramillies, by mounting him on his horse when they were in danger of being run down by the French cavalry.

For those interested in the name of this line of Molesworths on the Australian scene, I have unearthed intriguing slices of family history through that wonder of modern technology, the Google search engine. John Joseph William Molesworth Oxley, explorer of vast tracts of Australia, had some connection with the 4th Viscount, while Molesworth Jeffrey, nephew of the 7th Viscount, caused the village of Molesworth in Tasmania to be so named after his uncle. In fact, I believe there are quite a number of Molesworth connections in Australia and New Zealand, just waiting to be brought to light.

On the return from India to England of my Molesworth grandparents in the early 1900s, two more children were born, a girl, Cicely, and a son, Charles, who was destined never to become the next Viscount. England was shaping up to a time of vast changes with the ghastly spectre of the First World War soon to confront them. In the first years of this war to end all wars, my mother lost both her brother and the young soldier she hoped to marry. My father, the man she married shortly before the War ended, was a chemical engineer, a graduate from the University of Chicago. After its earlier naval exploits, my branch of the Rowley family had taken up residence in

1920s early childhood – in bathtub. I'm on the left, then Billie, Gem, and another child.

the U.S.A. in the mid-nineteenth century. My father, however, had returned to live in England to take up his roots again and was fortunate, indeed, in escaping the slaughter in the trenches because his expertise on munitions meant his presence was required on the home front.

No doubt with memories of what might have been, after the first love of her life had been so cruelly taken from her, this marriage was to lack a certain joy. My mother became prone to moods of dark despair. As a VAD (Voluntary Aid Detachment) nursing the wounded and tending the dying during the War, and knowing the wreckage wrought on those young bodies, how often she must have pictured the last moments of her loved one. My eldest sister, Gem, born 1918, and Nina, known as Billie, born 1922, were to bear the brunt of my mother's rages when the tentacles of sadness closed in on her, her sadness increased by the death of a son, Charles, born 1920 and dying two years later.

By the mid-1920's, the pieces of shattered lives all over the country were gradually being brought together, although children born of that era were destined to carry a certain weight of remembrance of the war. Even though I was born some six years after the 1918 Armistice, I was still to be burdened with an empathetic understanding of what so many people had suffered. Both through my mother's grief and through my grandmother, whose loss of an only son had caused her, like so many other bereaved mothers, to take up spiritualism and attend seances, I was a witness to the grief of the period.

In the garden of the Chorley Wood residence, where I so often visited my grandparents as a child, a small wooden hut had been built called "The Sanctuary". It housed toys, books and other items which had belonged to my Uncle Charlie. My grandmother would often retire there to contemplate and "talk" to her son. I was

With my sister Billie. I'm on the left.

allowed to sit quietly in the hut at times and, young though I was, could feel the sadness of her thoughts whether she was there or not. But could I really understand her grief or my mother's grief if I had not actually experienced what they had endured? I could empathise in part but I could always spring back from that bitter well of consuming darkness which seemed, at times, to engulf both my grandmother and my mother.

But life goes on, the wounds would heal up to a point. The Great War was done. The future must now burgeon with the peaceful, confiding thrusts of humanity. The idea that the world was heading for another holocaust was never a consideration. And I was about to embark on my own growing up. If I were fortunate, I would be likely to experience only the normal share of unhappiness through childhood and into adulthood. Now, years later and growing "down," as one might say, rather than growing up, I look back at the various griefs that fell to my lot, some of which turned out to be not so minor. I find they have been outweighed by the ultimate incredible joy of life, and the feeling and belief for the richness lurking in the human condition – even if it is not always apparent.

CHAPTER SEVEN

The Formative Years in England

1920s – Early childhood.

Memories of my early life well up into my consciousness from time to time but at this distance seem almost like someone else's experiences. I suppose it can be said that I enjoyed a typical upper class upbringing of the period, such as would be the lot of those families who were of sufficient, albeit slender, means. Servants, in the shape of a couple who acted as cook and handyman/chauffeur, living in or out, graced the scene in many of the houses we lived in. For some reason, we moved house every two or so years. A house in Wadhurst and Frant in Sussex and three different houses in Tunbridge Wells in Kent feature in our places of residence in the ten years up to 1935. Early prints of the Rowley admirals always seemed to be placed to run up the staircases of these houses so that, as we ascended at bedtime, we could be reproved by their stern countenances for any misdemeanours committed during the day. An ever increasing number of cats were our main companions. Looking back, I often wonder how they were successfully transported when each move took place. It must have been a logistical nightmare.

We had a devoted Nanny who tended to most of our needs and, in supplying unremitting love, she acted as a kind of bulwark against my mother's blue moments. A succession of governesses also ruled our lives, some weak, some

With my father. Hastings area, 1930s.

strong, giving us a grounding in the attitudes expected of our class, such as enlightening us on the history of England and the British Empire, geography, basic maths, Latin and that most hated of subjects, English grammar. With one governess, splitting infinitives meant standing in the corner with a dunce's cap. Elder sisters, Gem, and Billie, later went on to a proper school in Tunbridge Wells, doing well scholastically. I also attended the same school for one day at the tender age of six, but quickly dissolved in such a welter of tears at the idea of being away from home and Nanny, that it was decided to keep on a governess for me.

My little sister, Julia, in later years at a beach in Norfolk.

My brother, John, was born in 1931, followed by my sister, Julia, born 1934, who was never to know her father. Sadly he died of encephalitis about a fortnight after her birth. To me, though I loved him dearly, he had always been rather a shadowy figure. A brilliant man in his field, he was away on business, mainly in Germany, for most of my young life. I really remember him only as a kind and handsome grey-haired man with a bristly moustache who always brought sweets and presents on his return from the Continent.

On his death, our big house in Tunbridge Wells was sold, the servants and the latest governess dismissed. My sister, Billie, and I were packed off to board at St. Michael's School, an Anglo-Catholic Convent at Leigh-on-Sea, Essex. Mother, Gem, who was by now a young lady and had stage aspirations, John and Julia and our faithful Nanny moved into a small flat in Battersea in south London. The cats were found alternate homes. After two years of homesickness and constant beseechings on my part to come home, it was time for a change to a day school for both Billie and me in London. But first the hurdle of entry exams into St. Paul's Girls School in Hammersmith had to be passed. Billie sailed through her exams but I failed quite dismally and wound up at the rather select Glendower School in South Kensington, which did not have quite such a rigid system of entry.

I look back with fondness to my time at Glendower, where such abilities as I had were praised and my shortcomings glossed over. Maths of all kinds continued to floor me. A blankness would descend if I were required to find out how much it would cost to paper a room so big if the paper measured such and such and cost 1/11d per yard. "You are a silly cuckoo, aren't you?" my maths teacher would pronounce when I simply could not fathom some problem, but there was always an encouraging pat on the shoulder to take the sting out of her words. However, on the up side, my history and composition marks soared, Latin and French just made the grade and other subjects passed muster. It was in more recreational subjects like tennis and especially acting that I really enjoyed myself. Indeed, acting in school plays was a great joy for me after I realised I could act out a part on stage, even if I could not project myself with any degree of confidence in real life.

Two years later, life was again disrupted by the looming threat of World War II. We were all staying in a rambling old house in Narborough, Norfolk, which we had taken for the summer holidays at the suggestion of a family friend, Frank Ash, who owned the Hall in the same village. I loved the village, and especially the beautiful old Hall. Frank, a tall man with a slight stoop, twinkling blue eyes hiding behind pince-nez, and a neat little moustache, was an ex-Captain of the 4th Hussars. He had been a friend of my father and had been a frequent visitor when I was a small child. I had always been intrigued by his stories of the Great War, particularly the attack by the first tanks at Cambrai in 1917, when he made the whole show seem to be almost a picnic. "There was this Jerry

Narborough Hall, Norfolk, owned by Frank Ash, who was later to marry my mother.

under this tank, y'see," he would tell me, "flat as a pancake filled with jam, and his legs stickin' up in the air." I didn't realise that this rather quaint frivolity of description was a kind of pose. It kept his own sanity free from the soul-destroying memories he had to bear of his time at the Front as a Cavalryman, and the appalling agonies he witnessed inflicted not only on human lives but also on the horses. At the time I couldn't understand his reluctance to keep any horses in the ample stable space available at the Hall. It was only years later, on his deathbed, that I believed I understood. Those who were with him at the end told me that his mind wandered back to his cavalry days, and that he spoke incoherently of "his" horses and what they had suffered.

When war was finally declared on 3rd September, 1939, the only immediate signs of war we saw in Norfolk were tents mushrooming up on empty ground usually covered in rabbit warrens, and khaki figures drilling enthusiastically. Our holiday house was commandeered by the War Office for a party of A.T.S. (Auxiliary Territorial Service) girls and my mother was detailed to look after them until her health broke down. Mother, Gem and Billie then found accommodation at the Vicarage in the village, while Nanny, John and Julia went to live in Chorley Wood with the grandparents. As Glendower, my school in London, had closed for the duration, I was sent to stay with friends in Winchester and attended a day school there. There were numerous military camps in the vicinity and the family hosted many tennis parties for the young Army officers. June, 1940, saw a marked decline of the visitors and I got my first real taste of the results of war. Most of the young lieutenants who visited in their glamorous uniforms, and upon whom I looked with schoolgirl awe, fell horrifically on the sands of Dunkirk. It seemed to affect my stability and my schoolwork, never brilliant at the best of times. Since it was becoming clear I would never pass an exam of consequence, it was eventually decided that to keep me any longer at school would be to throw good money away. I was just sixteen. I was sent in disgrace to join John and Julia in Hertfordshire where they were already settled in with the grandparents and the ever-faithful Nanny.

Presumably, had the war not intervened, my schooling would have proceeded until I was 17, but not necessarily fitting me for any useful purpose in life. My education so

Me, about seventeen years old.

Always a Godmother but never the mother. Holding my niece with Gem, my older sister, at the right.

far had been neither one thing nor the other. It was not leading me into any profession or even a menial job. Class distinction was still very much in vogue at that time, and there were barriers as to what the different classes could or could not do. Young ladies were not expected to join the labour force as it would take jobs away from the working classes who needed them to survive, or so we were told. It was the lot of young ladies to join the debutante trail and hope to snare a rich husband. Could I make the grade? I doubted it! The fact that there was now a war on and the debutante trail obviously temporarily on hold did not seem to enter the equation. All that was apparent to me was that because of a very sheltered upbringing and an inherent shyness, I had not learnt any of the necessary refinements of how one should act socially in one's own class. Clearly, this made it very unlikely that I would attract a suitable beau.

Even so, my mother in Norfolk, now married to Frank Ash, intimated she had visions of me being a social butterfly and, for a start, I was to come up to join her and live in the Hall with my new stepfather. The idea of being a social butterfly so frightened me that I begged to stay on in Chorley Wood and this respite was granted me for another two years. I knew my talents simply did not run in the direction she wanted. Even the most trifling points of etiquette bothered me. "Does one shake hands with one's gloves on?" I asked my grandmother, one day. "My dear child, you shouldn't have to ask me. A lady knows these things automatically," she said, and declined to tell me. The easiest thing to do now seemed to be to avoid meeting people "who mattered," so that I wouldn't do the wrong thing and disgrace the family name. She did, however, give me a piece of advice on how one should expect to be treated by any gentlemen acquaintances when attending a ball. "You must not let an admirer hold your hand or kiss you," she said, "you must rap him over the knuckles with your fan if he tries to do so." Evidently I had to wait until I was married before such actions were permissible.

But attending balls didn't seem to be an option at that time as a form of amusement and neither did there seem to be any purpose to where I was heading with my life. I found myself at an absolute loose end, with an active mind and nowhere to go with it. Although I may not have been a brilliant pupil at school, I now begged to be allowed to attend a Commercial College in the nearby town of Rickmansworth, to learn shorthand and typing. I desperately needed something to occupy my mind.

An interest in sailing (but never taking part!) and yachtsmen. A friend, Oliver Wells, after the war.

The idea was frowned on by my grandmother who felt that, by attending such a College, I wouldn't be meeting the "right people".

Somehow I got my way and suddenly found I was starting to come out of my introverted shell. It was true the girls at the College were hardly blue blood, but they were great fun. Every afternoon, after classes – and sometimes cutting classes – the girls and I would go to the nearby gravel pits which had been filled with water and were a popular swimming spot. Non-commissioned soldiers, sailors and airmen on leave found it a pleasant place to relax in. I liked them but I was having great difficulty in relating to them on any agreeable social level. There still seemed to be unconscious reservations on my part about joining in the fun and I earned the nickname "Duchess". One day, a young private picked up a book I had just changed at the Library for my grandfather. The soldier opened it at the borrower's tag and read the name out loud, but mispronounced it. "Who on earth is Vizzcount Molesworth?" he asked. I snatched the book back. "That's my grandfather, and you don't say 'izz,' you pronounce it 'i', as in I, myself" "Cor, listen to 'er. Proper little duchess, ain't she. No wonder she gets so hoity-toity at times," said the soldier. Hoity-toity was the last thing I wanted to be but I didn't know how to unbend and go against all that had been taught me about upper class behaviour. But any chance for change was denied me when my grandmother learned of the outings to the gravel pits. She gave me a stern lecture and forbade me to go there again.

I withdrew into a shell of morose unhappiness, until I discovered the comforting world of reading. I found a book on my grandmother's shelves called *The Wild Goose Chase* by Rex Warner. I read it and could not understand a word of it but whimsically I picked on the Wild Goose as my guiding symbol and knew that where the wild geese flew, there my happiness would lie. My own misery, of course, was of very little importance in an England fighting for its life. By day, the blue skies wrote the white trailing messages of dogfights, with blazing machines plummeting from the seething heights. By night, the sky glowed redly over London 25 miles away, as the bombs rained down on her and she burned. We knew in a very small way what it was like to be bombed. Nearly every night the moaning sirens preceded the sound of the desynchronised engines of the German bombers passing over us on their way to London. Occasionally they did not

My dog, Dubhe. Because he was a Pointer, I named him after the "pointer" star, Dubhe, which points to the north pole.

wait to get there but let drop their bombs in our area. Miraculously no-one was killed although several houses received direct hits. Rations were low; meat, jam and cheese portions were negligible. Two ounces of butter a week did not go far with growing children. The threat of invasion was very close and pitchforks were kept in handy places with the Home Guard practising their drill regularly. Few other weapons were available for them to protect us in the villages.

I wanted to join one of the Women's Services and do my bit but was too young. I was getting restless for change and my mother now sent for me to come and live in Norfolk. This greatly relieved my grandmother's mind as she was beginning to find me too much of a handful. I loved the village of Narborough and was glad to go home to my mother and stepfather. My mother met me at the village railway station. In my new-found confidence, I had bought a jaunty hat for the occasion – a navy boater of straw with a veil. With my new lipstick and powder which the shopgirl had assured me were just right for my colouring and which I had, perhaps inexpertly, just put on in the train, I felt a very proud and excited seventeen-year-old. I hoped my mother, whom I loved so much and hadn't seen for nearly two years, would be proud of me too. "Who do you think you are?" she greeted me in a rage, "You look like a tart. Go and wash that filthy stuff off your face before your stepfather sees you." It was not a very auspicious homecoming. I so badly wanted to please my mother but everything I did seemed to be wrong.

Settled in at the Hall and thinking to make use of what I had learnt at my short spell at the Commercial College, I asked if I could go to work. My mother found me a suitable job as a private secretary to a neighbouring squire farmer in the village of Cockley Cley, some 12 miles away from Narborough. I was to stay with the vicar and his family in the village and cycle the short distance to the farmhouse every day. My bicycle and I were duly delivered by my stepfather in his Bentley, and I was on my own. A week later, I sheepishly cycled back home. I was reasonably adequate on the shorthand curls and squiggles, but more was required of me. As my employer opened his mail, it would be "tell them this or that," and "reply to this invitation, you know what to say." Unfortunately I had no idea how to reply to invitations in the correct third person manner nor how to word a business letter. Again I found that my education and upbringing had misfired, resulting in nothing but an upper class veneer of respectability. It had made me totally useless. My inability to observe social niceties was only exceeded by an inability to offer any of the business skills an employer might expect. My next job proved it.

I had dared to find myself a position in King's Lynn, in Ladyman's Grocery Store, at 10/- a week. Part of my duties was to be a messenger girl from one department to another in the large building. I was instructed to run everywhere, but ingrained training surfaced and, feeling it beneath my dignity, I refused to run. After a fortnight I was called into the manager's office. He was irate. "I'm afraid you're no use to me," he said, scathingly. "I can't have you wasting my time and money by walking about like a duchess when there's work to be done." And he promptly fired me.

Fortunately, my older sister, Billie, came to the rescue. She was leaving her job at the local Gas Company for a job with more responsibility and suggested I might like to take her place, and share the same digs she had in King's Lynn, just going home at weekends. She had a quiet word with her boss, and more than a few quiet words with me. Thanks to her, I got the job which consisted mainly of filling envelopes with accounts to be sent out to customers, and stamping the envelopes. From diary notes I made at the time I see the other girls in the office made up a little poem about me called

"Our June" which goes:

> Within these walls we have a girl named June
> Who always makes us laugh from morn till noon.
> Her thoughts are way up in the blue,
> Wishing to be there too.
> You know she's going in the WAAFs
> To be with all the peaked-capped RAFs.
> She's crazy on the way they fly,
> I'm sure we'll lose her by and by.
> She feeds a cat to our disgust
> By putting horse meat in the cups.
> And though the warnings she has had
> The crockery stinks just as bad.
> Fuzz Face has told her once or twice
> About not being very nice.
> June takes no heed and worries not
> She'd just as leave tell him to pot.

My diary explains Fuzz Face was one of the senior clerks in the office and "a bit of a bind". Although I don't remember doing so, the diary also says that when I wasn't feeding stray cats I was hanging out of the window gazing skyward, or surreptitiously sliding out to the bookshop next door to peruse the odd Aircraft Recognition book, or "How to Fly in Three Easy Lessons". It was a wonder I was able to hold on to this job until I was old enough to join up.

CHAPTER EIGHT

WAAFling On – Wartime Service with Mosquito Pathfinders

British Second World War poster.
Imperial War Museum PC0143 Cat. No. IWM PST 3096

The idea of joining the WAAFs,[1] one of the branches of the Auxiliary Women's Services, had been a long recurring one. As I approached my eighteenth birthday I was able to give it deeper thought. Having decided I wanted to be a Driver, Motor Transport, I pestered my mother to sign the papers permitting me to do so. At last she said, "Well, if you must go into the Services, I'd rather you made it the Wrens[2]. WAAFS and ATS[3] are so common. It's a pity you'll have to go through the ranks but you'll soon get a commission." "I'm sure I'm not bright enough," I wailed. "Rubbish," said my mother, "you don't have to be bright to get a commission. People only have to hear you speak to know you're officer material." Whilst it was true I had developed a deep, drawling voice with a plum in it, I rather doubted my ability to command.

It was finally agreed that I could go into the WAAFs as a Motor Transport driver if I would go for a commission as soon as I could. I particularly wanted to go into the WAAFs as aeroplanes and flying sounded tremendous fun and I thought I might get a chance to actually fly. I gave in my notice at the Gas Company and told my boss why I'd chosen the WAAFs. He sniffed. "Hm, actually airmen, I suppose." And he may well have been right! After all, fighter pilots were always in the news and cutting very glamorous figures.

On my eighteenth birthday, I reported to the RAF Recruiting Centre in Norwich where I was pummelled and prodded and pronounced fit. Whilst waiting for the suitability test, I idly turned the pages of that day's *Daily Mirror*. "Paddy Finucane dead," I read, and could think of nothing but the death of one of my flying heroes, as I filled in more forms and answered questions. "Hrumph," grunted the Interviewing Officer, "didn't do so well in the maths test, did you? And you don't seem to have much mechanical bent. Don't know about M.T. (Motor Transport). And I see you haven't taken any exams and have no qualifying diplomas. What about being a batwoman? Would that appeal to you?" I cringed. A batwoman! A girl who looks after commissioned officers. And I was supposed to become an officer and have a batwoman look after me! "Oh, do give me a chance at M.T.," I pleaded, and the Interviewing Officer took pity on me. I could become a driver. And a driver I was to remain until the end of the War. In this I was a sad disappointment to my mother, as I never became more than a Leading Aircraftwoman. A Corporal's Course taken at one point had soon weeded me out as being quite unsuitable for any form of leadership. Even bellowing out drill commands on the right foot proved beyond me. My first effort at being in training charge of a squad left the girls bunched up against a wall as they waited for the "Halt" order from me, while I hesitated to give the command at the appropriate moment.

After my initial acceptance as a driver, the morning's batch of new recruits was sent to Bridgnorth in Shropshire. Part of the journey was by train and part by truck, my first taste of being squashed like a sardine in the back of a swaying vehicle. We were shown to our quarters, a huge barrack block with double tiered bunks, each room housing about 40 girls. Barely had we been allotted our bunks than a Tannoy (loudspeaker)

1   WAAF is the Women's Auxiliary Air Force.
2   Wrens is the Women's Royal Naval Service.
3   ATS was the Auxiliary Territorial Service, which was the women's branch of the British Army during the Second World War.

boomed out for us to line up at the Cookhouse for cocoa and buns.

Next day we were kitted out. Nothing fitted and had to be sent off to the tailor for a quick alteration. Eventually, all of us, at first rather overcome with self-consciousness in our new garb, met up at the NAAFI[4] and started to get better acquainted. Our time was free for the rest of the day and we toured the town in our new uniforms feeling very proud of ourselves. By evening I was beginning to feel very homesick and judging by the sniffles to be heard all over the barracks that night, so were a lot of other girls. But no time for tears! At 5.00 a.m. next morning, we were rounded up to clean the Ablutions Blocks and perform all sorts of menial tasks.

Three weeks of square bashing followed with sergeants and corporals shouting at us to pick up our feet, keep in line, swing those arms. Blisters appeared on heels unused to route marches in ill-fitting shoes, and girls fainted from standing long hours at attention waiting for the Officer of the Day to inspect us. A somewhat smarter body of girls than had entered the camp had to make a final appearance on the Parade Ground to the satisfaction of the Commanding Officer, before the recruits were broken up into their respective trades and sent to various parts of England for training. Drivers under training were sent to Morecambe in Lancashire, and billeted in the guest hotels which fronted the sea.

Most of the landladies, who were more used to catering for peacetime visitors, disliked having us forced on them, but could do nothing about it. My landlady certainly had no cause to like me. One evening she left me in her kitchen to look after the cabbage while she went calling. By the time she returned, the cabbage had boiled dry and the saucepan was a sorry mess. "Why didn't you put more water in it?" she cried, aghast. "I didn't know you had to," I replied. She threw up her hands in despair. "Lor, luv us, lass," she said. "How's tha goin' t'raise a family if tha doan't know how t'boil cabbage?"

But if I wasn't much use at boiling cabbages, I was proving quite adept at driving cars. Every day we went out, four girls to a vehicle with an instructor, careering over the lovely Lancashire countryside, deep into the Lake district. We had little time to appreciate the scenery, endeavouring as we were to take in the niceties of gear changing with double declutching, and stopping and starting heavy lorries on the steepest hills. A different vehicle was allotted to us each day. We never knew if it would be luxurious staff car, an outsize Albion ambulance with the accelerator in the middle where the clutch is more usually placed, or a 15 cwt. or 30 cwt. truck. Of the four girls in my group, one had absolutely no road sense and we were all terrified when it was her turn to take the wheel. She was eventually taken out alone by the Chief Instructor to see if solo coaching could do the trick. It couldn't. She landed them both upside down in a ditch and soon after found herself out of the service as unsuitable.

We were given instruction in the Otto cycle and what makes engines tick, how to grease the chassis, change a wheel and the vital importance of the Daily Inspection. I loved the driving but wasn't too keen on the discipline and regimentation. When the results of the final tests were announced, I found I had only just scraped through, one

---

4   Navy, Army, Air Force Institutes.

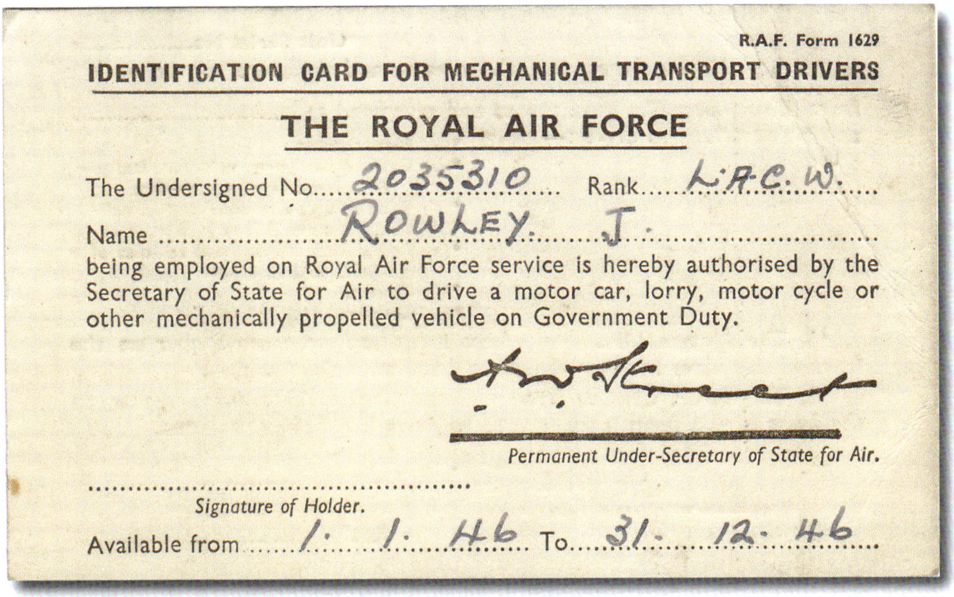

R.A.F. Form 1629

IDENTIFICATION CARD FOR MECHANICAL TRANSPORT DRIVERS

THE ROYAL AIR FORCE

The Undersigned No. *2035310* Rank *L.A.C.W.*

Name *ROWLEY J.*

being employed on Royal Air Force service is hereby authorised by the Secretary of State for Air to drive a motor car, lorry, motor cycle or other mechanically propelled vehicle on Government Duty.

Permanent Under-Secretary of State for Air.

....
Signature of Holder.

Available from *1. 1. 46* To *31. 12. 46*

mark above the lowest, and two marks above the minimum allowed. But at least I'd made it.

Training completed, by happy chance I was posted as a Driver Motor Transport to RAF Marham, in Norfolk, a bomber station only two miles from home at Narborough. The main hangars on the aerodrome housed some Blenheims which went out nightly on bombing sorties, and landed back in the small hours with a wrenching squeal of brakes. A small portion of the aerodrome was occupied by Tow Target Flight 1483. It consisted mainly of Lysanders, Martinets, Defiants and later a Hurricane, which towed the drogues for air-gunners-under-training to hit from one of the Flight's Wellingtons. The Flight was not actively engaged in war. The Lizzie pilots who towed the drogues and the Wimpey pilots who manoeuvred the plane for the gunners, had either done a tour of ops and were resting or were waiting to be posted to operational units. I note in my diary that "most of them went back on ops and bought it." I was provided with a small Standard van and assigned to 1483 Flight. My duties were to fetch and carry the pilots from their Mess to Flight H. Q., pick up the drogues when they were shot down by the pilots all over the countryside, and generally be at the beck and call of anyone in the Flight requiring transport. Unlike my first job at Ladyman's the Grocers, where I wouldn't run around the corridors, now I was more than happy to perform my duties at the double, and discovered that being the only girl among so many men was decidedly fun. Nevertheless, it appeared from the poem they wrote about me, all in good fun, that I still had certain reservations. They wrote:

> Where dipperdocas reign supreme
> The duchess is our uncrowned queen.
> She murmurs sometimes "Don't be mean"
> And "Try to keep the party clean".

I begged several rides in a Lysander, and a Martinet, as well as a Wellington. The Wimpey made me rather nervous as the wings waved up and down. I was told this made them safer, but the wings had frequently been known to break off in mid air. Later this did happen and there were some empty chairs in the Flight Offices for a couple of days until a replacement crew was sent.

On many off duty times that winter of 1942, Bob, a Canadian waiting for his second posting, and I would cycle along the Norfolk lanes for an evening meal at home in the Hall. The stars were clean and bright on our return to camp, the air sharp with frost, and Bob would point out the Pole Star and the Northern Cross, and other stars. But he never could show me his favourite star, Beetlejuice, or Betelgeuse, in Orion's Belt, because at that time of the year it didn't rise until well after the hour of 23.59 when all good little WAAF's had to be in bed. "I'll show it to you one day," he said, but he never did. The night he told me he was being posted back on ops, he gave me my very first kiss. It was like a gentle benediction, the fragile, innocent touch of a butterfly's wing, a magic moment I was to treasure for months. He flew off next day to join a Stirling Squadron and was shot down over Bremen soon after.

After that, I cycled home alone, spending most of my off-duty hours there. We were all issued with passes for leaving camp which were supposed to be returned to the Admin Office on our return to camp. But the wily ones told me how to retain such a pass and not bother with checking in and out, so I was often able to spend the whole night at home. One night as I cycled home I was picked up by the civvy police for riding without lights. Luckily, as Admin did not check whether I should or should not have been out of camp that night, all was well.

When Mosquitoes of 105 and 109 Squadrons, 8 Group Pathfinder Force, took the place of the obsolete Blenheim bombers, the Tow Target Flight moved to another station to give them more space. I remained as driver for 109 Squadron aircrew. My job was to drive the pilot and navigator of each Mosquito from the briefing area to where their aircraft was dispersed around the perimeter of the airfield at op time. I soon got to know each aircraft and its number or identifying letter and which aircrew flew what so that I could immediately deliver them to the right kite. Then I would collect them and take them back to base on their return from a raid. I loved this work but it had a kind of bleakness about it when the aircrew didn't return.

Such a bleakness became even worse when I was temporarily taken off this job to become ambulance driver when the usual girl went on leave. It really introduced me to the face of death. One of the previous ambulance drivers had gallantly saved lives from a badly damaged Halifax which, unable to reach its own station, had landed and burst into flames. Some of the crew were trapped until the girl drove at full speed into the middle of the aircraft and created a hole through which they could escape. I had no such experience but the experiences I did have were devastating enough.

One night a crippled Mosquito returned from ops with one bomb still hung up. The plane exploded on touchdown with disastrous consequences. Another time, an airgunner crew member of a daylight Flying Fortress, which was fast losing height on two engines but trying to make base at a nearby airfield, baled out. A farmer rang our aerodrome to say the gunner was sitting in his field and would we please come and do something about it. Locating the field, I drove straight across the newly ploughed earth to reach the man. The farmer was irate and demanded compensation. But how could I have known that time didn't matter, and it would only have been necessary to drive round the edge of the field and let the orderlies take a stretcher to the figure apparently sitting so upright in the field. The gunner wasn't worried about haste. His chute had failed to open and he was quite dead. Of another plane which crashed soon after take-off with bombs still on board, there was no need for an ambulance at all. All that could be found was the tailplane and some teeth hanging from strips of flesh in a tree.

Curiously enough, perhaps by blocking out the horror, none of this deterred me from wanting to fly. When the Air Transport Auxiliary called for volunteers, I applied. Here was the chance I had been hoping for. Could I be a ferry pilot? I passed all the medicals and was otherwise approved but was too young to pass the age requirement of 21. By the time I was old enough, they had enough volunteers.

When tarmac runways were put down in place of the grass runways at RAF Marham, both squadrons had to move. 109 Squadron went to Little Staughton and 105 Squadron to Bourn, near Cambridge. I didn't know I was later to be posted to join 105 Squadron at Bourn and was deeply saddened when I took the crews to their aircraft and watched them depart for the last time from Marham. I tried to capture my thoughts in heartfelt, though rather simple, poetry.

On 105 and 109 Squadrons leaving RAF Marham

> Empty hangers, empty field
> Desolate and bare
> Empty heart above all things
> Filled with bleak despair.
> One by one they took off proudly,
> Banked about and cut the grass
> Flying low in farewell greeting
> Which too soon has come to pass.
> No more the smell of dope[5] to greet me,
> A for Apple, D for Dog,
> No more flying times to enter
> In the well-thumbed log.
> No more the proudest mess shall know them,
> Talking quietly, shooting lines,
> But you can always hear their voices
> In the soughing of the pines,
> Bringing music from their new domain
> As they take off in the night,
> Exhausts flame-lit, engines revving,
> Ever climbing, gaining height.

---

5   Dope is a waterproof varnish used on planes. Here, it was sea-grey camouflage varnish to protect the fabric of the Mosquitoes.

But here the ground is empty
Till new ones take their place,
Different ground crews waiting
Till they return to base.
Empty skies and empty heart,
The two go hand in hand,
For to me they were the very best,
The best in all the land.

For some months after my posting to RAF Bourn, I drove the groundcrew about. This consisted of driving them to each Mosquito dispersal point, where they attended to any maintenance or did a preparatory warming run up of the aircraft before a scheduled op. The groundcrew allowed me to sit in the aircraft cockpit as they ran them up and a most exciting moment came when, quite unofficially, I was allowed to run one up myself, though I don't think it was quite full boost and revs.

Later I drove the aircrews to their kites. Ops were mainly at night. After delivering the crews, we had to sit in our vans outside the Briefing Room offices and freeze until, after a couple of hours, we would hear the sound of their engines returning and would go and collect them. A new Commanding Officer saw to it that we had a nice, cosy rest room to wait in. This was very welcome, as raids into enemy territory were getting longer and frequently we would not hear the sound of engines until the Mossies came back in the rosy tints of dawn.

Alec became one of my boyfriends on the squadron. He had brown, wavy hair and deep blue eyes. He was a wonderful pilot, but all Pathfinder pilots had that little edge of distinction – or all of us drivers liked to think they did. I wanted to marry him but when the question actually arose, I fell into doubt. He didn't have the right English background and my mother wouldn't approve. I turned my attention in a half-hearted fashion to Mac, a rather glamorous Canadian who had just joined the squadron. Colonials were acceptable.

Looking back on these 1944 times with the aid of my diary, I am able to recall many of the crew I knew, and their experiences. If any RAF bods of that era happen to read this book, they too may be amused at some of my jottings, such as:

Ducky Drake brought K King, LR 496, in on a crosswind on 252.
Kite swung violently causing a complete collapse. Both crew OK.

The runway they should have landed on was being lengthened after a fatal take-off. Even after such lengthening, it was still a hated runway with a hangar at one end causing some uncomfortable moments.

And another memory:

Bill Baker and Rex Lewis returned from ops in G George, ML 986, on one engine. Came in too low, tried to go round again, but other engine cut. They ended up at various angles in the hedge. How the bods got out is a mystery but they got off with just a few injuries.

And another:

Saw kite coming in on a right hand circuit which could only mean

DATE	Type	No.	1ST PILOT	OR PASSENGER	(INCLUDING RESULTS AND REMARKS)

TOTALS BROUGHT FORWARD

Taken at Markam. H Harry IV 319 usually flown by Tommy Thomas and Alec Wade. A good kite - even if she was only a IV. Pictured with Harry Cole, Pete Gilmore + Mac, who were her ground crew.

A quaint picture of a poor little fish (Poor little me, how I pity myself!) Taken in Morecambe and 'boy don't I look the compleat sprog!

GRAND TOTAL [Cols. (1) to (10)]
................Hrs.................Mins.

TOTALS CARRIED FORWARD

A page from my 1940s World War Two diary written in a Royal Air Force Pilot's Flying Log Book. I have written: A quaint picture of a poor little fish. (Poor little me, how I pity myself!) Taken in Morecambe and 'boy, don't I look the compleat sprog'.

A page from my World War II diary. The middle photo was taken during one of the bombing raids on Germany, and my caption reads: A simply superb photo of the ruins of Cologne taken by Sid Wingham, flown by George Hogg. Height about 2,500 feet. It looks kinda mangled. *My caption beside the photo below reads:* Outside the billet *(our "digs" or accommodation)* before stepping out on VE *(Victory in Europe)* night, Bourn. Left to right, Moi *(me)* Margery White, Babs Sheppard, Pat Wilford and Joy Bennington. Cambridge was a dead loss so returned to dance and finished the evening with little Georgie.

YEAR		AIRCRAFT		PILOT, OR	2ND PILOT, PUPIL	DUTY
MONTH	DATE	Type	No.	1ST PILOT	OR PASSENGER	(INCLUDING RESULTS AND REMARKS
—	—	—	—	—	—	TOTALS BROUGHT FORWARD

GRAND TOTAL [Cols. (1) to (10)]

TOTALS CARRIED FORWARD

Another diary page: Sid Wingham reclining at ease after a duty flip, probably rather cheesed with life in spite of the smirk. *A "duty flip" was a test or training flight and my comment related to the fact that he was bored, wanting real action. The same photo of Sid Wingham (S. Tom Wingham) appears on page 183 of* Mosquito Thunder: No. 105 Squadron RAF at War 1942-5, *by Stuart R. Scott, 1999, Sutton Publishing, U.K. I was attached to No. 105 squadron and knew the people mentioned in this book.*

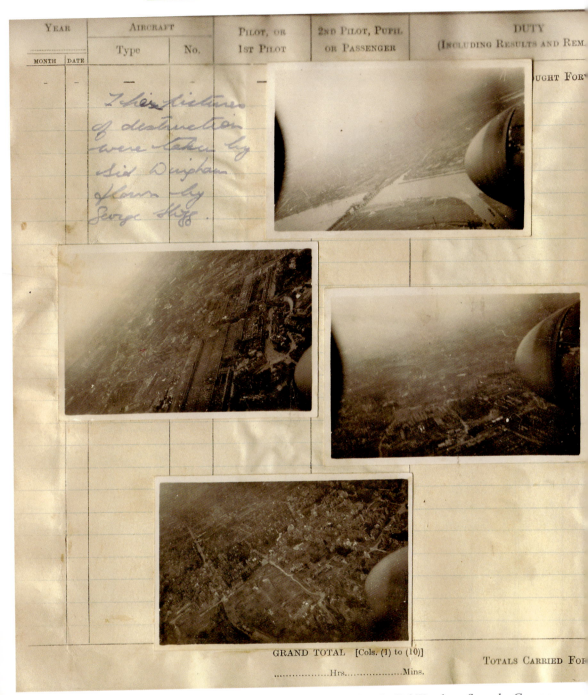

YEAR		AIRCRAFT		PILOT, OR	2ND PILOT, PUPIL	DUTY
MONTH	DATE	Type	No.	1ST PILOT	OR PASSENGER	(INCLUDING RESULTS AND REM.

These pictures of destruction were taken by Sid Wingham flown by George Hogg.

GRAND TOTAL [Cols. (1) to (10)]
..................Hrs..................Mins.

TOTALS CARRIED FOR

Another diary page: These pictures of destruction were taken by Sid Wingham flown by George Hogg.

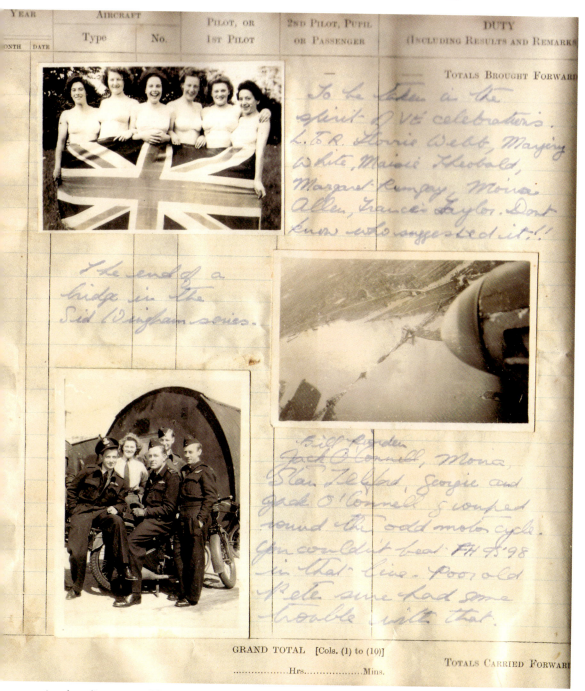

YEAR		AIRCRAFT		PILOT, OR	2ND PILOT, PUPIL	DUTY
MONTH	DATE	Type	No.	1ST PILOT	OR PASSENGER	(INCLUDING RESULTS AND REMARKS)

Another diary page. The top photo shows the girls stripped down to their bras, celebrating VE (Victory Europe) day. VE day was 8th May 1945. The second photo shows a bombed German bridge, the end of a bridge in the Sid Wingham series.

his port engine had gone bust. He tried a horribly shaky landing on 252.
A steep turn and he raced down the runway and looked as though
he would go on for ever but he heaved up his u/c and we went out to
inspect the bits. Tommy Horton and Jonah in ML 924 walked out
quite cheerily.

And:

Pat Enderby killed on WAAF site 4th May, 1944, in P Peter MM134.

I recall that clearly as Pat pranged into a barn at the entrance to the WAAF quarters. Those WAAFs who happened to be in the vicinity made a long chain from the Ablutions Block trying to put out the ensuing fire with buckets until the Fire Engine arrived, but Pat could not be saved.

And:

W/O Fox, flying with Eaton, killed after early return when he leapt
out of the kite and into the spinning propeller.

Photos and poems in the diary also bring back memories of those times. In particular, an "alphabetical" poem written at the time by Norm Hildyard recalls many of the foibles of the crews (some of whom were not to survive).

A is for Almond, whose landings are swell,
    He pranged with a load on and pranged bloody well.
B is for Baker who flies in the gloaming,
    His partner is Rex, so he calls for a homing.
C is for Comar, you know him as Johnnie,
    He has quite an eye for a WAAF who is bonnie.
D is for Danny, his surname is Moher,
    He's going back home when he's finished his tour.
E is for Enderby, Eaton and Co.,
    Each day to the top of the list they do go.
F is for Farrell, whose S.B.A.'s wizard.
    When I do the same, my heart's in my gizzard.
G is for Gallagher, known as the Vicar,
    At making out flight plans, nobody's quicker.
H is for Horton, who used to fly Blenheims,
    Back in the days when the Home Guard wore denims.
I is for Ivan, the terrible Acky,
    Who takes off as though the runways were tacky.
J is for Junior, short-arsed and stocky,
    The only fit rhyme is that he's cocky.
K is for Kirby, his Christian name's Neville,
    He wishes his pilot could fly straight and level.
L is for Litchfield who lays on the keys,
    And makes his own music with consummate ease.
M is for Millett, we all call him Les,

Geoff just ignores everything that he says.
N is for Norman, who's writing this song.
    If it gets widely read, he won't live very long.
O is for Oboe, the dream of the Boffins.
    It started one dark night and disturbed several coffins.
P is for Plunkett who flies with Bob Jordan.
    After his Lanc trip, he holds his ripcord on.
Q's for Mosquito, the QUEEN of the Air.
    To fly it correctly, you must have a flair.
R is for Runways, uphill and wavy,
    Bloody good training for joining the Navy.
S is for Slim, he who shapes all our ends.
    Above 20 thousand he always gets bends.
T is for Tidy, a rebel at heart.
    His hair is a work of tonsorial art.
U is for Umbrage, taken by Bish,
    If you talk about "C Flight" or cookie dazed fish.
V is for Victory, swift, certain and sure,
    Heralding copes by Mk I on the Ruhr.
W's for Walmsley who taught Yanks to fly.
    Unless he stands up, he can see only sky.
X is The first thing in dots that we get,
    If the wind hasn't changed very much from the Met.
Y is Young Bernard, also called Pop,
    Who does all the working in planning our Op.
Z's for the Zones, with which our friend Spike,
    Stacks all our aircraft by means of the mike.

I was in the habit of leaving my diary on one of the open shelves allotted to us in the Rest Room. One day, after some service visitors had called and waited in our room before meeting whoever they had come to see, I noted an addition to my diary. On the back page, the visitor had written:

    I don't know who you are – and yet
    Although it's true that we have never met,
    May I intrude and earn some humble name
    Amongst those people whom to you spell fame.

The note was signed: R. McKay Prentice, West Africa Frontier Force 1945. Yes, sir, your name is remembered too, and I hope you got through the war. If any of your family read this, I'll be so happy to say g'day to them in memory of those times.

With the Second Front looming, Dakotas painted with blue and white stripes, towing Horsa gliders similarly painted, flew over Bourn on their way to the bases in the South they would use on the Big Day. Pathfinder ops were stepped up to two and three raids a night, Walcheren and the dykes of the Dutch coast the objective, so that the

Germans could be flooded out of their gun emplacements. On D Day, the 6th of June, 1944, the Second Front started.

Barely a year later, it was seemingly all over. VE Day, the 8th May, 1945, and Victory in Europe set the church bells ringing in every village and town. But the war wasn't quite over. There was still Japan to settle and it was another couple of months before the horrors of Hiroshima and Nagasaki brought an unconditional surrender. VJ Day, the 8th August, 1945, and Victory in Japan was celebrated, finally denoting the cessation of all hostilities.

CHAPTER NINE

Civvy Street and Stage Life

Posing for an AA (Automobile Association) advertisement.

Just after my 22nd birthday, I went through a sort of reverse recruitment procedure and, demobilisation from the WAAF completed, found myself back in Civvy Street. Once again, I went to live with my grandmother in Chorley Wood. My stay with her was to prove even more disastrous than the earlier time. I just couldn't settle down. Perhaps I should join up again? It was a thought that was to plague me for many years. It was so much easier to have a secure job and be told what to do and how to do it than to have to find a niche for oneself in a world now being overrun with ex-servicemen and women seeking work. I quietened down a little after a Rehabilitation Centre found me a job as typist with BOAC (the forerunner of British Airways) in London. I commuted there daily from Chorley Wood by train and fell to talking with one of the passengers who took the same train there and back as I did. He was a young ex-major who had served in the army in India and Burma and was temporarily living with his parents just up the lane from my grandparents' house, while he studied at the London School of Economics. Tall, blond and good-looking, he was well-educated, had an excellent Army record, and was extremely intelligent. My grandmother thoroughly approved of the friendship.

What she didn't know was that he was a Communist. I hung on his every word and he had no difficulty in talking me into becoming a follower of the Red Flag as well. He pressed books on me about Dialectical Materialism and empirical polemics, or was it polemical empirics? He never realised I didn't understand a word of what he was saying because I fortuitously said "yes" and "no" in the right places when he talked about the books. He took me to Party Meetings and I found I was well received as Lady Molesworth's granddaughter – I was someone who had seen the light and they welcomed me. Mentally lazy, I believed everything that was told me and recounted these views as my own to my alarmed grandmother.

My mother was told of this and sharply requested my return to Norfolk. Brother John, sister Julia and Nanny were also due to leave Chorley Wood and live in Norfolk, so we would thus be a family again. I went, but the communism was still strong within me. At my order to the newsagent, the *Daily Worker* was delivered alongside the *Times* which my stepfather favoured as his breakfast reading matter. "Think of your stepfather. What will the villagers think?" cried my poor mother. But worse was to come. One day, over the machicolated roof of the mellowed pink, brick Hall, fluttered the Red Flag. It was a piece of red bunting I had found in the attic and hoisted up the flagpole, where it could be seen for miles across the low lying fields. That was going too far. My mother had hysterics and I obviously had to make the choice of going, so to speak, right into the communist camp, or living at the Hall. Not having the courage of convictions which were not really mine, I chose the Hall.

My mother breathed a sigh of relief and decided I must be presented at Court. Being way past the debutante age I was against the idea, and in any case the gracious old style presentation parties were a thing of the past. No longer did one dress up in gorgeous gowns with trains and ostrich feathers and make an entrance in the Presence to give one's Royal curtsey. Now it was a case of stand in line at a garden party for a handshake, wearing a simple afternoon dress. It was not a particularly exciting event. We waited for hours in a hired car in a queue stretching up and down the Mall several times, creeping forwards an inch at a time, until we eventually reached the regal doors of Buckingham Palace. Crowds of people lined the walls of the Presentation Rooms, two and three deep, and we waited where we were placed by liveried footmen. Then slowly the King and Queen passed down the line shaking a gloved hand here and there, with a longer pause for those actually being presented. The Queen's smile as she murmured suitable words was charming; the King looked shy and rather out of his element; the Princesses with beautiful, translucent complexions seemed to be quite enjoying it all. The presentation made no difference to my life whatsoever. There followed no jolly round of parties to launch me into society and life proceeded in its usual slow fashion at the Hall.

The question occurred to me that even if I were to be launched into society, did I know how to behave adequately? I believed I had the answer and knew what I wanted to do. Plans were put in train with my mother to send me to a finishing school in Switzerland – the kind one usually went to at 17 years of age. Much of my gaucheness had gone, but I badly lacked that veneer of sophistication to be at ease in the life I knew my mother still wanted for me. Surely a finishing school would do the trick. A fortnight before I was due to go I got cold feet. How could I go back to mixing with girls straight from school after four years in the Services. Apologetically I explained my feelings to my mother, afraid of her wrath after all the trouble she would have gone to in securing me a place. "Oh, that's all right," she said. "I never completed the arrangements as I had a feeling you'd change your mind."

So it was back to square one. There wasn't much to do at home and little to occupy my mind. I tried to sort my thoughts on where my useless life was leading. In restless mode I once again considered rejoining the WAAFs, as many of my friends were doing. Or should I embark on training? But for what? My mother couldn't understand I had hankerings for an independent life and suggested I could always work in a non-paying capacity in the garden. Growing flowers for the King's Lynn market were a large part of the Hall activities so I asked Ernest, our Head Gardener, if I could be of any use. The first job he found for me was to assist him and Albie, the gamekeeper who often lent a hand on his slack days, in tending some prize chrysanthemums being prepared for the market.

One day, Ernie, Albie and I were working in the chill of a fine October morning by the side of the high red brick wall which divided one part of the flower garden from the vegetable garden. On the other side of the wall, Dick, the gardener's boy, should have been hoeing the onion bed but, hearing no brisk working of metal on earth, Ernie demanded to know what went on. "Can't hoe no more, I want the rake," shouted young Dick. "Haven't you got legs?" asked Ernie, who had the rake on his side. "Oh, ar." grumbled Dick. " 'Alf a mo'," cried Albie, and singing out "Mark oooover" much as he would when a fine cock pheasant flew over the master's head on a shoot, he sent the rake sailing over the high wall. "Ar, ye've killed me," groaned Dick from the other side and then, more weakly, "I think I'm a-dying."

We raced round the wall to find young Dick collapsed against it, holding the rake upright, the prongs of which had neatly pierced the boy's scalp. "Ye've scalped me!" moaned Dick, piteously. "Cripes, so he has," said Ernie. "Tha's a rum'un and no mistake. Well, don't just sit there snivelling and carrying on so. Hold quiet and I'll heave it out for you." "No, no," yelled Dick, clutching the wobbling rake still teetering on top of his head, "Get the master. I got to see about me funeral." "You're not going to die, no such luck," said Ernie, cheerfully, turning to Albie to fetch the master, only to find him flat on his face among the onions in a dead faint. "Now there's two of 'em," muttered Ernie, as he turned back to Dick for a closer inspection. It was miraculously found that Dick had hardly been hurt at all. "Shame on you," cried Ernie. "All that squeal for a wee bit of a scratch. I've a mind to upend you in the dungheap." Instead, he separated rake from scalp and dunked the lad's head in a handy waterbutt, before sending him up to cook for first aid. Poor Albie was left to come round in his own time.

Occasionally I helped out in the apple orchards. These orchards were my stepfather's pride and joy, and in the late 1940s his Cox's Orange Pippins and Jonathans were widely known for their excellent quality. Her Majesty, the late Queen Mary, in residence at the time in Sandringham, apparently had a liking for apples and decided she would like to call and inspect the orchards. Due arrangements were made. John, Julia and I had been bidden to stay out of the way but decided we wanted to be in on a bit of the action. On the appointed day, we took up our positions in the battlements and waited for the arrival of the Royal Party. From our vantage point, we watched the tour around the orchards and then the Royal Party disappeared to take tea, cucumber sandwiches and cake in the gracious drawing room.

After a suitable interval, we ventured through the attic and down the backstairs so that we could watch the departure more closely from a downstairs window. Our faithful Nanny had evidently had the same idea and, emerging from the back kitchens, made her way towards the dining room which faced the front drive. Voices were heard coming from the drawing room as the door was opened preparatory to the Party leaving. But instead of receding, the voices got clearer. Brother, sister and I fell up the backstairs again out of sight before craning over the banisters to see what was going to happen. Nanny, incapable of darting anywhere with her very ample proportions, realised she wouldn't have time to reach the dining room nor return down the long corridor to the kitchens. With great presence of mind, she squeezed herself face first into the large vase cupboard under the backstairs, and pulled the door closed behind her. The Royal Party came round the corner. Her Majesty espied the closed door and asked what was behind it. Just a vase cupboard, she was told. I held my breath as Her Majesty, with a delightful curiosity, flung open the door. "What an extraordinary place to keep a servant," she commented, as she prodded Nanny's rear end with her famous umbrella and, closing the door again, led the way on to inspect the kitchens.

Climbing Mount Snowdon in Wales, 1950s.

In spite of such amusing moments, I was becoming more and more bored. I had to find some purpose in life. Didn't I have any ambition? It seemed not, as I aimlessly walked the banks of the stream that flowed, chuckling and peaceful, through the estate. It was very soothing. Then one day the wild geese flew over as I sat dangling my feet in the weeds at the water's edge. I felt a tremendous excitement. The wild geese! It was a long time since the thought of finding the geese had occurred to me. Perhaps they would tell me what to do. My heart was singing. I was singing. That was it! I danced back over the buttercup meadows to find my mother. "I think I'd like to learn singing," I cried, and my mother backed me in the idea. Together we went up to London and found a teacher by the name of Ernest Page listed in the telephone book. He bade me sing a scale or two. "Ah, glorious," he sighed, "never have I heard such a rich contralto in one so young. But it will mean years of work and your voice will not reach maturity until you're forty." "But I want to be a soprano," I protested, "I want to sing in musical comedy." "Ah," said my teacher, solemnly, "but it is not your choice. You must do as the voice dictates."

Once a week I travelled by train from Norfolk to London for singing lessons, returning home to practise in the attic so as not to disturb the rest of the household with repetitive scales. Deep and splendid would come out the notes below A above middle C and right down to my boots to low C. But, alas, around the note A itself there was nothing but breath and then, singing upwards a white soprano tone took over. The soprano tones did not please my teacher. I felt it was easier for me to be a soprano but "Sopranos are two a penny," he would say, "we're going to make a good contralto out of you." He forced the chest tones up and on good days I produced them with a resonance which astonished me. On bad days my voice simply broke around the wretched A note, leaving me in tears. I was consoled by being allowed to fling off a few arpeggios in the white tone, right up to the magical high F. But confidence was draining. I didn't want to give up singing but at the rate I was progressing, it certainly seemed that I would be forty before I could trust my voice not to break.

Restlessness took over, this time with an urge to get behind the wheel again. I ran into an old WAAF friend, resplendent in a neat, bottle-green uniform, who was driving for the Government Car Service. "Why don't you try it?" she asked, "and come and share my digs." After a very stiff driving test, I was fitted out in the smart, green uniform and was back on the road, learning the backways and shortcuts of London. My first job was to drive the King's Messengers around in a small van so that they could deliver Despatch Boxes to appropriate Government Departments. Later, I graduated to a shiny black car and chauffeured V.I.P.'s about. Singing lessons continued, but now took place in the evenings and practice sessions at Weekes Studios in Hanover Square.

"They are auditioning for the touring company of 'Annie Get Your Gun'," said my teacher, one evening. "Why don't you go along, just to get experience at auditioning?" The American star, Dolores Grey, as Annie, had taken London by storm. I'd seen her three times already and had dreamed of playing the part. The part was not a soprano one but neither did it really suit the way my voice was being trained. But, that was all quite irrelevant, as I was hardly likely to play the leading role of Annie. The audition was for chorus girls only and the idea of being a chorus girl felt quite exciting. But would my voice hold up?

"I can't possibly get the day off," I told my teacher. My feet had gone cold on me. How humiliating it would be if my voice broke. But it so happened that the next day I was parked almost outside

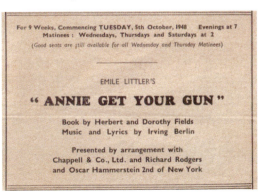

the Coliseum after driving some V.I.P.'s to a meeting nearby. I saw girls with music under their arms heading for the Stage Door and in a wave of bravery I joined them. As we waited in the wings, I in my plain, green uniform, the other girls decked out in their audition finery, the feeling of fright which had been threatening to take hold gradually fell away before the excitement rising within me. I fingered the scenery backstage and sniffed the air in ecstasy. Grease paint and hot lights! One day, perhaps, when my voice was sufficiently trained and I'd had some acting lessons, I could reach for the stars.

One by one, the girls were called on stage where they sang a few bars of music before a voice, echoing oddly in the nearly empty theatre, either said, "Thank you very much, next please," or "Come down to the stalls, dear, would you?" My turn came and I went on stage. I stood alone, the lights blazing up at me. "Where's your music?" hissed the pianist down in the pit. "I haven't brought any," I said, feebly. "Well, what are you going to sing then?" he asked. A fluttering in the stalls betrayed annoyance. "Could you play 'Abide with me' in the lowest key?" I asked. I hadn't even discussed with my teacher the best thing to sing, after I'd told him I wouldn't audition. Since my teacher was training me on churchy contralto lines, none of the songs I knew seemed quite right for auditioning for musical comedy. "Abide with Me" seemed a slightly better choice than 'There is no Death" or "The Lord's Prayer," solo songs made famous by the rich voice of Dame Clara Butt.

I bellowed out a few bars of the opening low notes of "Abide with Me" and then took fright as I neared the higher note which did not always ring out true. I stopped, fully expecting the voice in the stalls to say, "Thank you very much, dear." But the voice didn't. It said: "Very nice. Why did you stop, dear? Start again." I did so. The first few notes rang out richer than ever, and miracle of miracles, before I reached the dreaded higher note, I heard: "Come down to the stalls, dear." I flew through the Pass Door shivering with excitement. I was in! I WAS A CHORUS GIRL!

Rehearsals followed and the thrill of opening night in a north country town sparked an ambition for a career in show business. As part of the chorus, I was on in nearly every scene and in one scene even had to say "Frank Butler" in tones of adoration as he passed me by. We had lovely dresses. My favourite was a frothy creation like a white wedding gown, smothered in gardenias, which I wore near the finale. I was the Girl in White with flowers in her hair and who smelt of cologne; the type of girl Frank Butler wanted to marry in preference to Annie who went about in tattered old garments and stunk, by her own admission, like a polecat. It was my moment every night when Frank Butler, played by Neville Mapp, put out his arm for me to come to him across the stage during his song, and I was picked out in the spotlight as I advanced slowly towards him, my arm outstretched. There I stood, gazing up at him as he sang to me, before he beckoned the Girl in Pink to him and all three of us turned and slowly ascended the staircase. It was wonderful to be the centre of attraction – even if for less than a minute. It gave me a feeling of confidence I never seemed able to achieve offstage.

Soon after we opened we had an Understudy Call. All those who fancied understudying any of the principals went along. Just for fun, I decided to try for Annie without holding out much hope. It was certain most of the other girls would be after

At centre stage, on the stairs, the hero sings to each of the Girl in Pink (on the left) and the Girl in White (me, on the right).

the plum part. Luckily for me, only one other girl turned up, and as she was a quite unsuitable high soprano, I found myself as third understudy. In a touring show of the "Annie" calibre, a walker understudy was retained in London, ready at a moment's notice to take over the part if the principal of either the London or touring show fell ill. There was also a second understudy with a small part in the show, who took over if for some reason the walker could not get there in time. The third understudy merely appeared at understudy rehearsals in order to feed lines to all the other understudies. She was not really expected to play the part. Nevertheless I took the role seriously, learning even those lines which were not necessary for feeding. Every night after the show I would go through a scene in my digs, wielding an umbrella for a gun, and imagining myself actually on stage.

We travelled all over the north of England, staying two or three weeks at each place, until we reached Blackpool where we were to stay for the whole summer season. A few miles out of the city, an airfield advertised flying lessons. Recalling my Air Force days of being a passenger in an aeroplane, I had an urge to find out what it was like to be in sole control up there in "the long, delirious burning blue," as one poet, John McGee, had it. Unless we had a matinee or there were understudy calls, we were free until evening, so there was plenty of time to learn flying and I quickly picked up the theoretical rudiments of flight.

The day came when my flying instructor said I could go solo. Now to experience that burning blue! But the only thing I experienced as I took off alone in the little Auster for my first short solo circuit round the aerodrome, was a feeling that I'd forgotten some vital piece of cockpit drill for landing. The first solo went off without a hitch and next day I did another, away from the tarmacked aerodrome, out on the sands of Middleton, where circuits and bumps were often practised. The sand was sticky and I couldn't seem to get the Auster off the ground. The sea got nearer and nearer until finally in desperation I yanked the stick back and the aircraft staggered into the air. It could have been a fatal act as I must have been very near the stalling speed. When I eventually got the plane down, after a couple more than necessary circuits, my instructor on the ground was as white as I was. "Come on," he cried, "let's take her up again and whip her about a bit." Up we went once more, for a spin or two and a few jaunty manoeuvres under his experienced hands. "Another solo for you tomorrow," he said, "and you'll be as right as rain."

But the morrow brought news from home. My mother's health had been giving trouble for some time but no-one had told me what was wrong with her and I was not unduly worried. Now it was suggested that I go and see her in London where she had been placed in a hospital specialising in cancer ailments. I took the first available train and went to the hospital. Was this my mother? Gone the bright complexion, the glowing brown eyes. Gone the jet-black hair with its wisps of grey at the temples. Gone the trim figure. There lay in the bed a body, bloated out of all proportion, with yellow parchment skin, and white hair straggling over a sunken face I could not recognise. She barely knew me for the pain she was in, although the doctors were doing their best with drugs. It was the last time I ever saw her. My stepfather was there, and there was no point in my staying.

A week later the dreaded telegram came just before the afternoon performance. It would have mattered little if I had not played my small part in the chorus, but for some reason I kept repeating over and over to myself, "The show must go on," and I told no-one. Not even during the break between the matinee and evening performance. I would not think of it. It could not be. The reality caught up with me as I was taking off my make-up that night, and reaction set in. I was taken to one of the principal's digs, given sedation and put on a train next morning for a fortnight in Norfolk. At every turn I was confronted with remorse. How many times I had upset my mother, how many times I had been rude to her. How she had spoilt me and how I had taken it for granted. How often I must have hurt her with sometimes churlish and unthinking behaviour. Now there was no way of saying "I'm sorry."

When I returned to Blackpool a little later I found I could bury my mourning in that cover-up phrase "The show must go on" and was able to take my place onstage as before. The only difference was that I had completely lost my nerve for flying and did not resume my flying lessons. In any event, the opportunity to do so fell through when the Blackpool season came to an end and we moved to Liverpool where no handy flying lesson facilities existed. We were to play the Empire for three weeks.

We did our normal rehearsals in the new theatre and then came the opening night. I went through the Stage Door half-an-hour before curtain up as usual. The stage manager was waiting for me. "Hurry up," he said, "you're on." And he dragged me off to where the Wardrobe Mistress was waiting. "What do you mean?" I asked, nervously. "You've got to play Annie," explained the Stage manager, patiently. "Barbara (Shotter) has got laryngitis and can't sing a note, we can't get Peggy, our walking understudy, up from London because the fog is too thick down there for the plane to take off, and the second understudy is on sick leave as you know."

While the Wardrobe Mistress dressed me up in the various Annie costumes, sticking pins in here and there, the Stage Manager ran through the bits of business I would have to do that had never been rehearsed with me. "And only sing two choruses instead of the normal three," he said, "that'll save your voice a bit. It's got a long way to go tonight." Somehow I got my make-up on and dressed for the opening scene. The Stage Manager went out front and explained to the audience that the star was ill and the part would be played by an understudy, Rose Ash (my stage name). The house was packed for the opening night. The overture began and before I quite realised it, I was in the wings, making my entrance, gun in

As the third understudy, I played the role of Annie Oakley at regular rehearsals. On the opening night in Liverpool, both the star and second understudy were ill, so I played Annie.

hand. I stopped on stage, astonished. Those people out front were giving me one of the biggest hands I had heard for a long time. The leading lady normally got an ovation on her first appearance, but this seemed to be something special. Then I realised they were encouraging a newcomer. It was a moment to remember. I went through the part almost automatically. If I forgot my lines or some piece of action the rest of the cast pulled me through and carried me along. There was one awkward moment after singing "You can't get a man with a gun," when I forgot I had been told to sing only two choruses, and gaily started into the third verse without benefit of orchestra. By the time the orchestra had cottoned on to what was happening and had joined me, I had stopped. By the time I had started again to catch up with the orchestra, they had stopped. Had I had enough aplomb, it could have been quite amusing. As it was, it was rather a moment to forget.

I was ashamed of my whole performance. The applause for me at the end was little more than perfunctory, but it couldn't quite dim the joy of going back to No. 1 Dressing Room with a star over it, where a crowd of reporters awaited me. I was not panned. Perhaps reporters are kind on these occasions. The papers next day said I played the part with that

ANNIE GET YOUR GUN.

ACT I.

SCENE 1.

- - - - - - - - - while mother catches her breath.

       Bus. of bird on Dolly's hat.
       Suddenly we hear the sound of a rifle.
       The bird lands some place around stage

       ANNIE OAKLEY ENTERS.   She carries an
       old rifle; two birds are dangling
       over her shoulder. She strides
       towards the bird and picks it up.

- - - - - - - - - I'll thank you to give me that bird !

(Holding the bird above her head) What for ? It's mine.
I shot it !

- - - - - - - - - You shot it right off my hat !

(Surprised) I DID ! How'd she git up thar ?

- - - - - - - - - I SEWED it up there.

(Bewildered) What fer ? T'ain't no good.   Thar ain't no
meat in it.

Pages from my original script.

modicum of shyness which gave it an added appeal over the rumbustious way Annie Oakley was usually portrayed. What I fancied they meant was that it was an inhibited performance and I didn't have an ounce of talent for such a demanding and extrovert part. Even so, I received some fan mail and got stopped in the street several times over the next few days with the exciting words "Hello, weren't you Annie on opening night?"

I wished I could have played a second night to iron out some of my mistakes but the walking understudy was able to take over. Christmas came and went and the show moved from town to town. We were all getting a little stale. Then my flying instructor wired me that the Aero Club at Blackpool was giving a ball, and asked if I would like

<u>NUMBER: "THAT COMES NATURALLY"</u>

Annie   Folks are dumb -- where I come from
They ain't had any learnin'
Still they're happy as can be
Doin' what comes naturally.

Kids   Doin' what comes naturally.

Annie   Folks like us -- could never fuss
With schools and books and learnin'
Still we've gone from A to Z
Doin' what comes naturally.

Kids   Doin' what comes naturally.

Annie   You don't have to know how to read or write
When you're out with a feller in the pale moonlight
You don't have to look in a book to find
What he thinks of the moon and what is on his mind
That comes naturally.

Kids   That comes naturally.

Annie   My uncle out in Texas
Can't even write his name
He signs his cheques with X's
But they cash them just the same.
If you saw my paw and maw
You'd know they had no learnin'
Still they raised a family
Doin' what comes naturally.

Pages from my original script.

to be his partner. I decided to take French leave and go with him, little knowing it was to signal the end of my stage career. I asked the girls to cover up for me, taking my place in my small solo parts, as I had sometimes done for them. But they couldn't cover up for me when I was wanted to play "Annie" again, the very night I was away. That a third understudy is called upon to play the lead is very rare. Twice, well, that just doesn't happen. But it did. Even if my first performance was nothing to enthuse over, at least it could have meant the SHOW COULD GO ON, and because of my absence it very nearly didn't. Barbara Shotter had to play the part with a high temperature and barely able to stagger through. When I returned from Blackpool, I was on the carpet.

12 Daily Graphic, November 16, 1949

EX-CLERK STEPS IN AS GUN-GIRL— SAVES THE SHOW

AFTER half an hour's notice, a squire's 22-year-old step-daughter, with 12 months' stage experience, stepped into the leading role of "Annie Get Your Gun" at the Liverpool Empire last night.

Rose Ash was second understudy to Barbara Shotter, the show's "Annie," and was, until last night, a member of the chorus.

Born in Narborough, Norfolk, and step-daughter of the squire of Narborough Hall, Rose was a W.A.A.F. for four years during the war.

Joined Ministry

On her release she joined the Ministry of Supply as a clerk.

Barbara Shotter, on the advice of her doctor, stayed in her hotel room last night.

Her official understudy, Ann Kelly, was taken ill eight weeks ago and is in hospital.

No nervousness

Rose showed no signs of nervousness and got a tremendous reception from the audience.

She was almost collapsing when she reached her dressing room after spending more than an hour and a half on the stage in a two and three quarter-hour show.

Peggy Powell, who understudied Dolores Gray in the London Colliseum production of the show is expected in Liverpool to-morrow in time to take over as "Annie."

ROSE—*She got her chance.*

Under my stage name, Rose Ash. Daily Graphic, *November 16, 1949.*

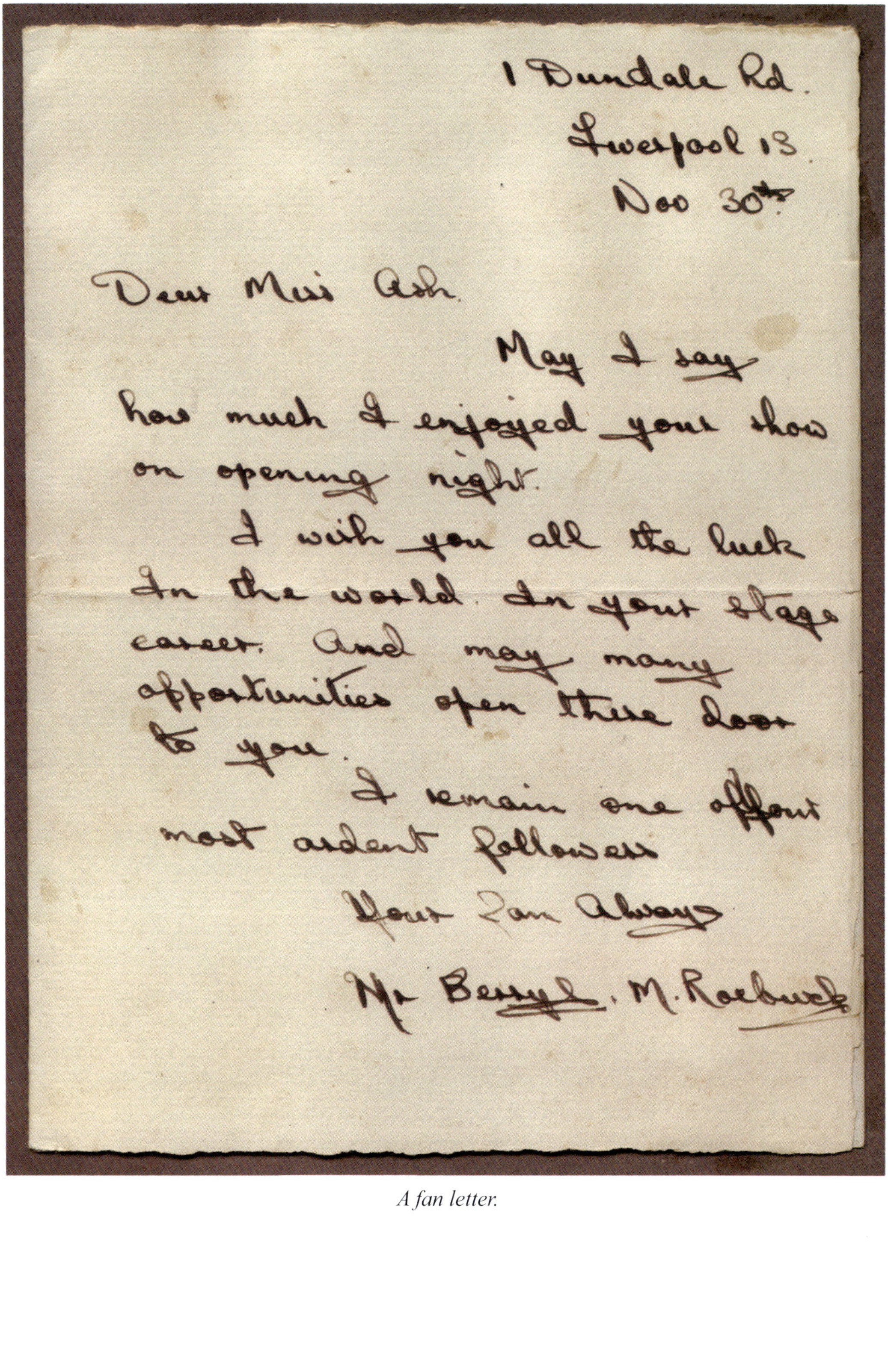

1 Dundale Rd.
Liverpool 13.
Dec 30th

Dear Miss Ash.

May I say
how much I enjoyed your show
on opening night.

I wish you all the luck
In the world. In your stage
career. And may many
opportunities open there door
to you.

I remain one of our
most ardent followers

Your fan always

Mr Berry, M. Roebuck

A fan letter.

One of many congratulatory telegrams received. Emile Littler, the theatrical impresario who produced the play, also sent me one.

I was suspended while Equity (the Stage Trade Union) decided what to do with me. If Equity sacked me, it meant I'd never be able to get another job on the stage. I wrote a letter to them making no excuses but telling them the whole silly truth, and suggesting I leave the cast. They accepted my explanation, apology and resignation from the show. Was that to be the end of my stage career?

I seemed to be at a loose end again! Perhaps this was the time to rejoin the WAAFS. Instead, I went back into the green uniform of the Government Car Service in London and found some rather dreary temporary digs to live in near the car depot.

Shortly thereafter, an advert appeared in The Times for a fifth girl to join others in a maisonette in Mayfair. This looked far more appealing and might offer some social life. I called at a vast house in Belgravia where prospective sharers were being interviewed. The door was opened by a pretty girl clad only in a bath towel. "Oops, sorry," she cried, clutching her wrapping modestly to her, "I thought you were Des." "No," I said, "I've come about the Mayfair house." "Oh, half a tick, I'll call Daph for you. She organises all that sort of thing. Hi, Daph, another customer," she yelled. She beckoned me into the entrance hall where I noticed another girl in a bath towel, crouching on the floor surrounded by a haze of cigarette smoke and drooling sweet nothings into a telephone. From somewhere upstairs came water splashings and the sound of a body rising from a bath. "Send her up, will you?" came back a disembodied voice.

I walked upstairs and, guided by wisps of steam coming from an open door, knocked and went into the bathroom. Daphne, blonde, shorthaired and pert, sat on

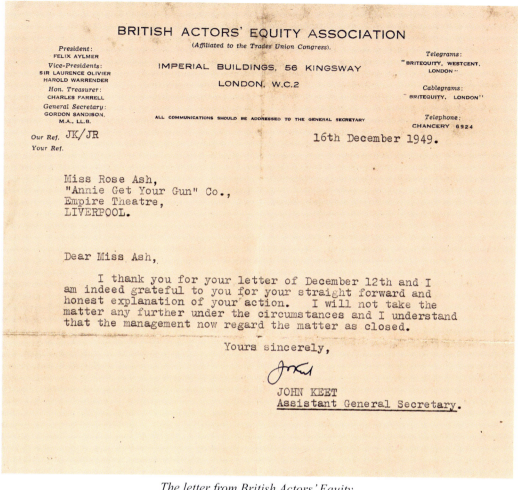

(Affiliated to the Trades Union Congress).

President:
FELIX AYLMER

Vice-Presidents:
SIR LAURENCE OLIVIER
HAROLD WARRENDER

Hon. Treasurer:
CHARLES FARRELL

General Secretary:
GORDON SANDISON,
M.A., LL.B.

IMPERIAL BUILDINGS, 56 KINGSWAY

LONDON, W.C.2

Telegrams:
"BRITEQUITY, WESTCENT,
LONDON"

Cablegrams:
"BRITEQUITY, LONDON"

ALL COMMUNICATIONS SHOULD BE ADDRESSED TO THE GENERAL SECRETARY

Telephone:
CHANCERY 6924

Our Ref. JK/JR
Your Ref.

16th December 1949.

Miss Rose Ash,
"Annie Get Your Gun" Co.,
Empire Theatre,
LIVERPOOL.

Dear Miss Ash,

I thank you for your letter of December 12th and I am indeed grateful to you for your straight forward and honest explanation of your action. I will not take the matter any further under the circumstances and I understand that the management now regard the matter as closed.

Yours sincerely,

JOHN KEET
Assistant General Secretary.

The letter from British Actors' Equity.

one end of the bath she had just vacated, with a towel thrown carelessly about her. On the other end of the bath sat what could be described in Mayfair parlance as a most divine young man. He was fully dressed but looked decidedly splashed. He held a long-handled bath-brush in his well manicured hands. "Sorry," I said, and backed hastily out of the room. Daphne screamed with laughter and the young man said in cultured accents "Come on in, the water's fine. It's bath time for girlies."

I sidled round the door again. "Actually," I said, "I've come about the room, but I think perhaps ...." I didn't know quite what to say. I didn't want to hurt Daphne's feelings by saying I wasn't a bathtowel type, but neither did I want her to think me a prude. I'd come a long way from the days when my grandmother told me a young man should not even be permitted to hold one's hand until married, let alone be kissed – service and stage life teach one a lot – but I still didn't quite feel able to participate with ease in mixed bath parties. "Look, buzz off for a tick, will you, hun," said Daphne, propelling the young man towards the door. "O.K." he said, lightly wielding his scrubbing brush, "I'll go and see who else wants a back scratch."

"Sorry about that," said Daphne in quite different tones, and proceeded to tell me in a businesslike manner about the room available, rent and so on. "And if you'll just hang on a mo, I'll get dressed and Dickie can take us over to see it." The knight of the bath drove us in his spruce red M.G. to Shepherd Street, where I met the girls with whom I was to share the house. They were all fully dressed. One was trying out a new dish in the kitchen with encouraging comments from a freckle-faced young man, two were discussing motor racing with their boyfriends over coffee and biscuits in the delightful little drawing-room, and the other, whose boyfriend was apparently at sea in the Merchant Navy, was quietly reading a book.

I moved in at once. At last I was in with a crowd of whom my mother would have thoroughly approved. They had all been to the right schools, they were all of the right class. Unfortunately they were not the right age group, being about five years younger than I was, but that didn't seem to matter. From time to time, girls moved out to get married and Daphne found replacements. Her hobby was finding flats and keeping them filled with girls. She had a happy knack of fitting the same type of girls in with each other, so that each flat had an entirely different personality background. The main interest of the group of girls with whom I now lived was following motor racing, which suited me down to the ground.

Daphne also threw frequent cocktail parties, inviting charming young men with whom she was acquainted through her family connections. There was never a lack of them about the place and dating was the order of the day for all of us. I may have missed out on the more formal debutante method of meeting the opposite sex, but I was certainly making up for it now. Proffered kisses from admirers did not meet with a rap over the knuckles with a fan as my grandmother had recommended, and whatever else was likely to ensue, simply ensued. So it was, that with a passing boyfriend of my own, on days off I would join the other girls going to some race track meeting or other with their boyfriend of the moment in his M.G., Jaguar or Austin Healey.

In the motor racing season, we visited Silverstone, Goodwood and Brands Hatch, to watch the greats like Stirling Moss, Mike Hawthorn and Fangio perform. We all belonged to some car sporting club or other, and although I did not have a car of my own, I joined the 500 cc Club whose members were allowed to take the tiny racing cars around Brands Hatch on practice runs. I tried a circuit or two on several occasions but my times were barely up to the qualifying mark for entering races.

When I wasn't at a race meeting with the crowd or alone with some boyfriend, I hired a self-drive car and went home to Norfolk for the weekends. "Are you going to drive for the rest of your life when you're not whooping it up with the guys?" the family started to ask. It was true I was in a nice, comfortable rut with the Government Car Service and an inability to even think of settling down with one of the many eligible young men about the place. Perhaps I should give stage life another go and see where that led. I approached Equity to see if they had any objection to my going back into another show after the "Annie" fiasco. They had no objection and wished me luck. I took a few refresher lessons with my old singing teacher, before auditioning for a touring show being put on the road by the same management with whom I had previously been.

I was warmed by being pleasantly greeted when I fronted up on stage. This time I had my music to give the pianist, and a suitable musical comedy number, Ivor Novello's "Fly home, little heart" to present. I started to sing. Oh, horror of horrors! My voice broke all over the place. "Try again, dear," they said, encouragingly. "Perhaps you're nervous. We'd like to have you back, you know." But I wasn't feeling unduly nervous and my voice had seemed quite stable during the refresher lessons. I tried again with the same result – and once more. I'd already had my fair share of time. Then, "Thank you for coming, dear," I heard from the stalls, "leave your address in case we want you."

That meant, of course, that they didn't. How could they want a broken down voice? I left the stage in tears and went straight to the studios to try my voice alone. Maybe I had been more nervous in front of an audience than I thought. A good deep note, crack, a breathy note, crack, a pale note, crack. I had no control over my singing voice whatsoever. "Well, that's that," I thought savagely, "that's the end of my singing days." And I went back to the flat in a state of utter despondency. I was greeted by one of the girls. "The firm where you always hire your cars have been chasing you," she said. I gave the firm a ring. "Are you interested in a driving job with us?" they asked. It promised to be more exciting than the present driving job which was confined to the London area. There were possibilities of driving all over England and even the Continent. I leapt at the chance and left the Government Car Service to become a J. Davy driver.

J. Davy Self Drive Car Hire had the reputation of being one of the best firms in the business. I drove all over England delivering cars, meeting people off boats and trains and aeroplanes. It was an enjoyable game picking out the right client from the pictures one had formed in one's mind from the correspondence in the client's file. Then the cars needed to be collected, usually from some different air or seaport where the overseas hirer had left them on departing the country. The plum jobs were deliveries to the Continent, and I became familiar with many of the major European cities. Clients would often want a Jaguar delivered to them in, say, Brussels, to be picked up later when their holiday was over, perhaps in Milan.

Sometimes in the English tourist season there would be multiple deliveries to one place and a batch of us would take cars to meet people at Liverpool or Southampton and would then return to base in a ferry car sent to pick us up. On one of these pick-ups we had a very lucky escape from disaster. Late one night, after a multiple delivery to the West Country, I was driving the ferry car, a Hereford, back to London. With five passengers aboard, I was making slow and steady time. "Can't you go any faster than this?" grumbled one of the young male drivers. "We won't get home till morning at this rate." I pulled up and handed over the wheel to him. No-one else wanted to drive, they just wanted to sleep and weren't particularly worried about speed. We started off again and the speedo needle crept steadily up and settled around the 70 m.p.h mark. "My," I thought, admiringly, "what nerve and skill to drive along these narrow, curving roads in the dark at that speed." Back seat driving is not a thing I indulged in, but when he approached a sharp right-hand corner on Salisbury Plain with which I was familiar, I

Delivering a brand new car while working for J. Davy Self Drive Car Hire.

ventured to say that I believed there was a wee bit of a corner ahead. "Don't you worry about that," he said, disdainfully, and kept his speed constant. I consoled myself with the thought that though it was a greater speed at which I would have approached the corner, perhaps other drivers had the knack of getting round bends at high speed which I didn't.

Then I realised that even Stirling Moss would have gathered the reins, so to speak, and, at this point, started a little judicious heeling and toeing. The driver obviously had no idea of what lay ahead. "Right-hand corner, you damn fool," I yelled, as a field with a high bank loomed into view, and a telegraph pole stared us in the face. It was by then too late to do any constructive driving, and the man panicked. His combination of violent braking and wheel turning caused the vehicle to career around the corner, going into a violent spin one way, followed by several gyrations in the opposite direction while it seemed to uncoil itself, before it came to rest in the middle of the narrow road with no damage whatsoever. A minor miracle had occurred. The others, very much awake now, wanted to know what had happened. The driver seemed to be suffering from shock. Shaking with rage and fear, I took the wheel back. "At the rate you were going, we would NEVER have got home," I told him angrily. "Now we'll go at MY rate. It may take a little longer but at least we'll have a better chance of getting there."

"If you want a cosy job with shorter hours, you've got one," said one of the girls one day when I'd returned to the digs exhausted. "I want to go abroad and can't until I've found someone to take my place." She was secretary/chauffeuse to a surgeon author and his wife. The girl took me along with her for an interview. Mr. Johnston-Abraham, short, white-haired with merry blue eyes and an Irish charm, had everyone eating out of his hand. His wife, suffering from a crippling bone disease, had obviously once been a very beautiful woman. Though frail and often wracked with pain, she had a dignity that held me rather in awe. I was very happy to be accepted as their "new girl".

Avidly I read the books my new employer had written under the non de plume of James Harpole. He had more or less retired from active surgery but retained a consulting room in Wimpole Street and also led a busy life as Chairman of Heinemann's Publishing Company. He was writing his autobiography *A Surgeon's Journey* and it was part of my duties to type out his manuscripts and read them aloud to his wife for her comments. Driving Mrs. Johnston-Abraham about London required special care, as any jolting, swerving or sudden stopping could cause great distress. She boosted my morale considerably when she said she felt so safe and comfortable with me driving. It meant great concentration all the time in the heavy London traffic – anticipate, anticipate, anticipate. It was a game one played, but the prize was a scratchless car and a relaxed passenger.

My employers were kind and thoughtful. When they found I was still hankering for a stage life but thought something had gone wrong with my voice, they took me to a colleague who specialised in throats. I felt sure I must be growing nodules on the voice box or something! The specialist probed my throat, asked questions, and took samples of scrapings from the throat lining. His diagnosis was that that there was nothing whatsoever wrong and there was no physical reason why I should not be able to sing. He suggested I go to a voice teacher he could recommend. The teacher listened to a few scales. "Lyric soprano," he pronounced. He was quite horrified when I told him I'd been training as a contralto. "You may have some rather nice low notes," he said "but that doesn't make you a contralto. You've been forcing the low notes too high, instead of blending the high quality into the low."

So there it was. I could either start all over again or just forget I ever wanted to be a singer. I couldn't make up my mind. I craved a little more excitement than I was finding in my present job and, much as I enjoyed and respected my employers, I kept an eye open for other possibilities. In the personal column of The Times I saw a position offered as secretary/chauffeuse to a Managing Director of a large company. I applied and attended for interview at his beautiful private house in Surrey. My duties would be to drive him daily from his home to his flat in Hampstead, from where he conducted business by telephone, and occasionally to his City offices. He had the latest model Bentley which an under-chauffeur cared for, so that I would not have to soil my hands with cleaning and greasing – something I had always had to do in my other driving jobs, with the exception, of course, of the car hire firm. I was to be supplied with my own small car to use for the trips to and from his country home, and was to have a clothes allowance so that I could dress in a manner befitting my position. My prospective employer showed me pictures of Amalfi in Italy, where I was to drive him every year for some annual conference. It seemed a job in a million. I wondered why he had picked me from the many applicants he had apparently had, after he offered the job, so I asked him outright. "You have a nice figure," he told me, "I think we'll get on well together." Rather naively I couldn't quite see what my figure had to do with my efficiency or driving ability, but was thrilled to have been chosen.

I took a train to his home the first day I reported for duty. The promised small car was to be bought for me later. The previous girl, who had been with him for many years, had been given her car to keep as a wedding present. My employer drove me himself to his Hampstead flat in the Bentley, explaining how to handle such a thoroughbred car. He thought I would pick up the finer points in Bentley handling quite quickly, but later dashed my confidence when he said I had much to learn when it came to my telephone technique. "State clearly what and whom you want," he said. "Don't say please and thankyou, it's entirely unnecessary." But I still found myself asking for so-and-so or some such, PLEASE, when I had to make various calls that first morning in his flat. I couldn't seem to help it, but he got quite angry about it.

At lunch time I had to set out the cold lunch his wife had packed in a hamper. All manner of delicacies were included and a bottle of champagne was apparently the normal daily drink to be shared with his secretary. I cleared away for the afternoon's work and found the snag to the job. My afternoon duties were not what I had imagined and certainly not to my taste. I walked out. That evening my stepfather had arranged to dine me at the Cavalry Club in Piccadilly to celebrate landing such a prestigious sounding job. He was keen to hear all about the latest Bentley – his own earlier model had been sold during the War. "You did quite rightly," he commented when I told him what had happened. "I think that shows you've got great guts." My own view was that through some squeamish streak of sexual distaste for the man, I was throwing away the chance of a life of easy money, pretty clothes and foreign travel.

I rang up the Johnston-Abraham's next day and told them the story. "Yes, I thought that might be the way of it, lassie," said the doctor, and then asked if I'd like to come back to them for a week or two as the girl who was taking my place hadn't proved very suitable. I returned to them but found the slow driving frustrating. I was quite relieved when the girl who had originally been with them before me, asked if they would like her back.

During the times I had spent waiting for V.I.P.s or clients on my driving jobs, I had revised my shorthand knowledge and I now joined the Brook Street Bureau as a temporary shorthand/typist. I was found a succession of pleasant office jobs with easy hours. A distant relative had recently died and left me some money. I bought a scarlet Triumph TR2 and at weekends zoomed over the flat, straight roads which led to Norfolk, to enjoy home

My stepfather, Frank Ash, on the left, with one of his relatives, Brian Ash, and my Triumph TR2 outside Narborough Hall. 1950s.

Jezebel, my scarlet Triumph TR2. My number plate included the letters "RGF" and I used to say this stood for "Rowley Goes Fast"!

life. Frequently I sat on 100 mph. I found fast driving was like a drug. It was impossible to drive fast safely and also think about what seemed an empty and purposeless future. When I wasn't driving, thoughts would come crowding into the mind, none of them leading anywhere. Perhaps a new life overseas would give me a fresh perspective on things. Surely I could move on and find my niche somewhere.

I knew I would never forget all that the Hall had come to mean to me over the years in its many different seasons and offerings of mists and mellowness, ghosts and graciousness, family and festivities. Wherever I went, memories of a fading way of life would surely never be erased. But that's just what they had to be. Memories.

Where should I try my luck next? My brother John now suggested I join him in Jamaica, relatives in New Zealand said come and stay with them, friends in Kenya announced they could find just the right job for me up country. But it was Australia, where I knew no-one, that for some reason – perhaps even the thought of bronzed Aussie life savers – pulled me more than any other place. So how was I going to get there? By ship? Fly? Or why not overland?

CHAPTER TEN

Bus Ride to India

Jaipur, India.

It was Julia who pointed out an advertisement in a Sunday paper, saying that seats were available on a bus travelling to Bombay in ten days' time. "Why don't you go overland as far as Bombay?" she jokingly asked, "and get a boat to Australia from there." Well, why not? Always ready for adventure, I called on Paddy Garrow-Fisher, a large, hearty Irishman, who was organising the tour. He knew the overland route backwards, having done it many times by motorbike. He was initiating a regular service by bus and had already made a successful run a few months earlier, in March, 1957, with a tolerant crowd of passengers who loved every minute of it. He was now preparing for his second trip.

"We'll be glad to have you aboard," said Paddy. "No doubt you'll be a bit mad like most of the others, so I don't suppose you'll mind if you're locked behind the Iron

Curtain, eaten by a pack of hungry wolves, boiled in oil by wild tribesmen, or become malaria ridden for the rest of your life." Unperturbed by what I hoped was just his sense of humour, I booked my seat, arranged visas, currency and inoculations, packed up clothes required, disposed of an accumulation of junk and bid numerous farewells in various parts of the country. Then I had to sell Jezebel, the scarlet Triumph, to get the money to pay for the bus ticket, leaving enough for the ship fare from Bombay to Australia, where I hoped to find work. Prosaically and yet how right, the bus was due to leave from London's Victoria Coach Station.

The passengers bound for India were easily distinguishable by the rolls of bedding and cardboard boxes which contained tins of food to sustain us over the desert stretches. Our bus was not quite the same as the others assembled in the station. It looked the same – it was, in fact, a 10 year old ex-Green Line Coach – but it had been painted a sandy colour and under the name *Indiaman*, a map of our route ran along each side. Inside the coach, half the rear seats had been removed to make room for luggage. An outsize plank lay along the aisle. "That's to get us out of boggy patches," explained Paddy, as we all tripped over it.

It was difficult for me to believe, as we nosed our way through the August holiday traffic out of London, that I was really going overland to India in this vehicle. Then I knew it was true when, after a brief stop for tea at Maidstone, the café's loudspeaker called, "All passengers for Bombay to return to their bus, please." We left Dover early next morning on the Lord Warden Ferry with the *Indiaman* firmly lashed down on the lower deck, as a rough crossing was expected. Peter, a tall, dark-haired

The white cliffs of Dover, England.

English boy, going to stay with relatives in Malaya, got a thorough soaking from the spray and had to retire below to the bus for a change of clothing. He joined us again, extremely green, muttering that having to contend with the roll of the bus and the rock of the boat together, was no joke.

By now we were all getting to know one another. There were sixteen passengers and Paddy, our Irish driver, with his Indian wife, Moti, whose early morning tea call was a sound we were soon to welcome. Paddy, in fact, was the brain behind this adventurous journey and it was his intention to make a regular service by road to India. This trip, in August, 1957, was his second scheduled trip. Curiosity was naturally rife among us concerning our reasons for making such an unusual journey. As Paddy said, there must be something a bit odd about us all!

Freddie, a white-haired, ruddy-faced Englishman of 67, was an ex-sailor tired of sea views who had joined the tour to get a dry land angle of the world. He was always offering tidbits of information on the most unlikely things. Norman, a Geordie sailor, hoped to work his passage across to Australia from Bombay. Eddy, a London policemen, after years of staunchly helping to uphold the law, was determined to taste freedom in the byways of travel, and Nigel, a very quiet boy who took on the absorbing hobby of collecting matchbox covers from the different countries, was also having his first slice of globe-trotting. Ron was a Canadian architect going the long way home after a successful spell in England. He found a fellow traveller in Robin, another Canadian with the same idea. John was a black-haired, stocky Australian of no particular profession but with a hankering to be a doctor. He was extremely intelligent and impatient with others not quite as bright as he was. He had found four months in England too long for his liking and, for some reason, was going home in somewhat bitter mood.

On the female side, Mildred, an English schoolteacher was getting unusual material for her teaching and had also been commissioned to send reports of her adventures back to her local paper. Her friend, Jemila, a teacher in the same school for a number of years, was returning to visit her home in Karachi. Sheila, whose father was one of the leading lights in the psychiatric world, had latterly left college in America, and held very advanced views on many subjects. She intended writing a book on Bombay. Betty and Joan were both Australian nurses going home. Renee, another girl from Down Under, whose plans to motorcycle home across the same route had fallen through, had decided a bus was the next best thing. Isabel, a delightful Englishwoman with a couple of grown-up children, and apparently well-versed in journeys such as this, was on her way to stay with friends in Karachi.

By the time we reached Paris in the early evening, we had sorted ourselves out into pairs. I teamed up with Isabel, and we found a room in a small hotel near the Rue Pigalle. As the hotel didn't serve food other than breakfast, we went in search of supper. Several left and right turns took us to the Rue Madeleine but there we got hopelessly lost. My French was excruciating and Isabel's non-existent, but nevertheless I bravely asked the way of a man who unhappily turned out to be Italian and thought I was German. When this had been sorted out he said he spoke a word of two of English and much Hebrew. With the aid of his wife, we had a long conversation in some obscure language before hands were clasped in farewell and we went off in the direction of the recommended eating house, with parting cries of "Bon appetit" ringing in our ears. Actually this was the last thing we wanted to be wished as our funds were low and food was expensive. But tightening our belts we entered the restaurant and let fly the francs on a small steak and beer.

Next day, Isabel and I trailed around Paris together in an endeavour to see as much as possible. After several times finding ourselves back at the station we had started from, we sorted out the system of the Metro underground and did the rounds of the Louvre, the Tuileries, and the Arc de Triomphe with its panoramic view of the city from the top. We marvelled at the Gothic nobility of the Notre-Dame and then turned our flagging steps along the Left Bank, gazing at books and pictures and people, while munching sticky buns, which was plainly quite the thing to do. We took a short river trip, gliding under bridge after bridge along the peaceful Seine. An American woman sat sulkily in the stern of the boat complaining bitterly that she had expected a guide to point out landmarks of interest. She would not refer to a most comprehensive little guide which was on sale: the good lady felt done down and was determined not to enjoy herself. For our part, we seemed to be enjoying ourselves too much. It seemed all wrong to dash about Paris in one day trying to see everything and lightly to dismiss the magnificence of the Louvre collection in half a breath yet, unwisely perhaps, we felt we had to see as much as we could.

In the evening, we found a cheaper restaurant than the previous night, nearer our hotel, where we were joined by a Swiss youth who had seen the *Indiaman* parked around the back. "You are, perhaps, on some mystic mission to the East?" he asked, with a fervent gleam in his eye. He was quite disappointed and disillusioned when we told him we were merely joyriding.

Lyons was our next scheduled night stop which we reached after an uneventful run across a scenically dull stretch of France. After Lyons, the endless straight roads and garish advertisement signs gave way to more hilly country and charming little villages, with streets narrow enough to make our passage a

Mont Cenis on the French - Italian border.

test of skill. Once I thought we had pinned a youth to the wall. "Ha, we missed him that time," said Isabel, drolly, who had a better view from her seat. "I think he stepped

Mont Cenis, with our bus, the Indiaman.

into a doorway at a happy moment." At Chambery, where the mountains overlook the village street, we all did our final shopping in France, disposing of our last few odd francs on this and that. Joan, in a flash of commendable foresight and wisdom, sought out a plasticware shop and bought a bucket and drinking bottle.

Past Modane, there were noticeable signs of a recent flooding of the River Arc. Waterlogged tree trunks lay around in ungainly attitudes by the side of the receded waters and odd bits of wood and rubbish were scattered everywhere. More important to us, however, we found the bridge had been washed away and we had to make a wide detour over a farm track at the base of Mont Cenis Pass to find another bridge. We were soon back on the proper road and climbing up and up, our big bus negotiating the bends with ease under Paddy's sure hands. Green fields tumbled down into the valley below and fir-treed slopes rose above us. A mile of two after passing an old Napoleonic fortress, we reached the bleak, windswept top of the Pass where the Douane is situated. In the short length of No Man's Land between the French and Italian Customs, we practised our "Si's" and "Grazie's" and pushed the "Oui's" and "Merci's" to the back of our minds. I was looking forward with relish to the next stage of the journey as we went through Customs and drove on to Italian soil.

Evening was drawing in as we drove down the other side of the Pass, though it was still light enough to notice the women working hard in the fields. We overtook one woman guiding a cart of hay down the hill while her lord and master had a ride in the back, trailing one leg leisurely on the ground. It seemed rather an ungallant thing to do, but we came to the conclusion he was not being lazy but was stopping the cart from running away.

The Cathedral at Milan, Italy.

Finding overnight accommodation in Turin was a problem, and Isabel and I ended up by sharing an enormous double bed which could easily have slept six at a time. Our deviation due to the flood had made us too late to see anything of the fine colonnaded city, and an early start in the morning gave us no chance to walk very far. As we drove out through the industrial area next morning, Freddie pointed out the Fiat Motor Works. "See that flat roof on that building over there," said Freddie, pointing, "that's where Fiat test out their racing cars." I wondered if any of the racing cars ever came hurtling through the air if the driver misjudged the edge on a corner, but considered there would surely be a nice, high parapet to stop such an event.

At Milan, we broke our journey for an hour or two and I made straight for the Cathedral with its hundreds of white marble pinnacles and statues and glorious stained glass windows. I didn't enter as I knew it well from previous visits when I was delivering cars as a driver for the J. Davy Self-Drive Car Hire firm. I just wanted to gaze at the noble building and gather my thoughts. Sitting outside in a small café nearby, I sipped an expresso coffee in meditative mood, feeling the summer sun tanning my face and wondering what lay in store for me. At the appointed rendezvous time we all converged on the *Indiaman* bearing huge bottles of chianti bought at varying prices from the tiny backstreet shops. Even the highest priced did not seem excessively so for a bottle of wine of such size. It looked as though we would be having a non-stop party for weeks.

Near Lake Garda, we stopped at a small village and stocked up with comestibles before finding a camping site on the shores of the Lake. I had never pitched a tent in my life but I soon got the hang of it. Hang is definitely the right word because instead of a properly taut tent such as most of the others had set up, mine hung in folds. We cooked our various eggs and beans on the primus stoves and prepared for a relaxing evening. "Anyone play chess?" asked John. Foolishly I said I played chess. While the evening shadows drifted over the water and misted the mountains, John and I sat on the low lake wall and played several games, fortifying ourselves against the chill night air with liberal draughts of chianti. I cannot have made a very exciting opponent for a skilled player such as he and after a while the games turned into lessons for me.

My first night under canvas was not a comfortable one. Most of us were doubling up in the just-big-enough-for-two tents provided by Paddy, but Isabel had brought her own camp bed and preferred to sleep under the stars so I was able to spread. I eased myself into my sagging tent and twisted about in an effort to get undressed and slide under the blankets without the whole thing collapsing on top me of. At last I closed my eyes with a weary sigh of sleep. About an hour later I awoke to find the air-mattress had gone down and I was lying on large, knobbly stones. And there I stayed, unable to find the mouthpiece to blow up the mattress again, and afraid to move lest my house folded up on me.

Paddy aroused us soon after sun-up. "Come on, me beauties, show a leg there," he cried, shaking each tent pole heartily. It was a fatal thing to do with my tent pole and it strengthened my determination to learn to put up a tent in proper fashion. A mild drizzle was falling as we set off for Verona and continued until we reached that romantic town. The sun came out as we strolled through the old market place with its gaily coloured umbrellas shielding the stalls piled high with fruit and vegetables, cheeses, meats, clothing and trinkets. A faint medieval air hung over the old narrow streets with their balconied houses which conjured up visions of Romeo and Juliet. Padua, with its wide streets and rather dark and sombre colonnaded shops and houses, did not have the magic of Verona, and our brief lunch stop allowed no time for more than a fleeting impression of the Basilica of San Antonio and the Arena Chapel with its beautiful Giotto murals.

A mile or two outside Venice, our scheduled night stop, we found an official camping site where, to our delight, hot water was provided in the ablutions hut. After pitching tents, we had a welcome shower before catching a local bus to the Railway Station where we transferred to a water-bus along the Grand Canal. This was my first visit to Venice, the city so much the flourishing pride of the Venetians in the Middle

Ages and where traces of past glory still linger in the houses facing on to the canals. I was completely captivated by it as each bend in the canal brought an enchanting picture of earlier days. If only we could have had longer than our allotted day to explore the residue of its history!

St Marks Cathedral and the Doge's Place, Venice.

Darkness was falling as we alighted at San Marco Square. Pigeons were having their last flutter of the evening over the pink and white chequered Doge's Palace, as we went in search of food. Feeling better after an outsize bowl of spaghetti, Isabel and I wandered along the dark, narrow passages, fearful of getting lost but impelled to find out what was round each corner. Countless people scurried by, obviously intent about their business or perhaps it was to get away from the slightly unwholesome odours which it must be admitted pervade some of the alleyways. Sleep was not easily wooed in camp that night as my air mattress went down again, this time landing me on a bed of little round pebbles. After I had blown it up three times, I ran out of wind and patience and decided discomfort was probably good for the character. The mosquitoes had not particularly troubled me but most of the others emerged from their tents looking decidedly spotty and it was a rather measly appearing crowd that set off for the centre of Venice once more, to pursue the delights of their choice. John meandered off alone with paintbrush and palette to capture some of the scenes with his art, the rest of us chose a partner for our wanderings.

"Let's take a boat trip to Murano," I suggested to Isabel, "and watch that beautiful glass being made." We bought tickets and boarded a boat but unfortunately found we were heading for Burano with its lace factory. Instead of the morning trip we had planned which would have given us time to explore Venice more thoroughly, the trip turned out to be a whole day tour, calling at San Franciso del Deserto with its Monastery founded by St. Francis of Assisi in 1220 A.D., and the island of Torcello, the birthplace of Marco Polo. When at last we arrived back in Venice, it was too late to do any sightseeing. Instead, we contented ourselves with walking round the well-lit passages which branch off the San Marco Square, gazing with wistful eyes at delicately moulded glassware and exquisitely set jewellery shown off in the shop windows. We bought none of this finery but spent our all too few lire on more mundane objects – tins of food and a frying pan for Isabel, who had left her cardboard box of emergency rations at the London bus station, and a sunhat, Malayan coolie style for me. I thought the hat might come in useful in warding off the sun in the desert, but a headscarf was more successful on the job, and the hat was destined to hang from a nail on the bus shelf and collect dust.

We walked on to the water bus, filling our eyes with the last sight of subtly floodlit Venice by night. A few minutes after leaving the landing stage, our boat caught up with a flotilla of gondolas winging swiftly along the Canal, poled silently by gondoliers. The leader boat carried instrumentalists and a singer, and snatches of the song floated to us when the engines of our motor launch were shut off as we edged to a landing place, and tantalisingly cut short as we started up again, until we outpaced the leisurely procession altogether. Alighting from the launch, we took our places in the queue for the last road bus back to the camping site. When it eventually came, the queue broke into a disorderly mob and it seemed to be a case of survival of the fittest. Isabel was encumbered with boxes of food but, armed as I was with her frying pan, I managed to lash out left and right giving as good as I got. With my free hand holding my hat high above my head so as not to squash the straw, I succeeded in retaining both our places in the queue. Since Isabel had formed the impression that I wouldn't say "boo" to a goose, her astonishment was considerable.

We left Venice with regret and headed for Trieste and the Yugoslavian border. We stopped for coffee at Trieste but I skipped the refreshment and had a quick walk down to the Harbour where I found the cruiser *H.M.S. Kenya* and other representatives of the British Navy gracing the scene. The town itself had clean, wide modern boulevards and there were many buildings of obvious antiquity tucked away in the narrow back streets and meaner looking quarters, but there was no time to peer closer. Climbing the winding hill out of Trieste, we had glimpses of the sun glinting on the blue waters of the Adriatic far below us before we lost sight of the sea and entered a stretch of cool, wooded country. A few miles on we reached the Yugoslavian border, where it seemed our days of whisking through Customs formalities were over. We had to fill in forms stating what moneys we held, and declaring all jewellery and effects – which, for all of us, was very little.

The country changed from rolling fir-covered rocky hills to lush green meadows and red-steepled churches nestling in the picturesque villages. Smiling peasants, mostly rosy-cheeked women, were gathering in the harvest and were quite thrilled when we all piled out of the *Indiaman* to take photos of them. As we approached Ljubljana, the lush country and the happy countenances disappeared and we drove through unkempt villages whose inhabitants looked as though a square meal would not be amiss. Ljubljana, with its austere grey buildings, redeemed by a castle perched on a hill overlooking the city, appeared to me to be rather an ugly town. I said as much to John. "You would," he said, scathingly, "but just because a town isn't chocolate box pretty at first sight doesn't mean it's ugly. This city has dignity and character and it's full of history." I resolved not to be so hasty in forming judgments on new places!

After several luckless tries, we all settled in a fairly cheap and comfortable hotel. It had only one hot water tap at the end of each passage and jugs and bowls in each room, so it took quite a time to clean up, after queuing with our jugs for an adequate supply of hot water. Changed and freshened up in a cool summer frock, I felt a little better than the blue-jeaned horror I had been a while ago. I drifted down to an enormous dinner served by attentive waiters, and marvelled at such homely things as white table cloths and choice cutlery, which a day or two of camping had made me appreciate. Later, I walked around the town with John, ending up in a small open-air café tucked away in a back street, from which we could see the floodlit castle. We drank coffee and discussed music and art: that is to say, John did the talking and I listened since his knowledge was far greater than mine.

Belgrade was our next port of call and, leaving Ljubljana, we were glad to see the country return again to its fresh, green prettiness. But there was a snag to it! The roads were composed of a white, dusty surface which crept through every crack and crevice in the bus and covered us all. The girls draped headscarves round their hair and over their mouths, yashmak style. The men at first suffered in silence, then they gave in and tied up their heads in handkerchiefs, berets, sunhats and even newspapers. We all got white-browed, dirty-faced and with our facial lines deeply etched. It took quite a lot of lick to make us look reasonably presentable to have a reviving coffee at Zagreb. Outside Zagreb, the road emerged on to an autobahn. Scenically this was dull and flat but at least it was clean. Sunflowers grew in profusion in the fields bordering the road. "That's what they make coffee from," volunteered our general informant, Freddie.

There were many restaurants at intervals along the autobahn, and we stopped for a large lunch. Later, cries for tea rent the air when we espied a modern pull-in. This turned out to be a lucky stop because, from chatting with a traveller, Paddy learnt that there was an Exhibition on in Belgrade which might make it difficult for us to find accommodation there. It was decided, therefore, that we should spend the night where we were. After an excellent yet inexpensive dinner, we were introduced by the locals to their famed brew of *slivavicz*, the hot and heady national drink. We were woken at 5.30 a.m. in mistake for 6.00 a.m. next morning which was no joke after an evening of slivavicz. But by managing to keep my head in an upright position I made good use of the extra half-hour by sweeping the dust from "my" space in the *Indiaman* and turning out some ruined sugar and cheese. As I did not like to throw it away in a country where there appeared to be great poverty, I offered it tentatively to the elderly women sweeping the yard. They fell on it with joy.

Our first stop in Belgrade was the Embassy to collect any mail, and a good few minutes were spent leaning against the trees that lined the side of the wide road, reading the latest from "home". "You've got the morning free," said Paddy, "so make the most of it." Isabel and I wandered off to find out if the Blue Danube was really that colour. Far from being blue, it was a dirty, muddy colour, though it undoubtedly changed to its more romantic hue outside the industrial area. Calling in at one of the many cafés for a coffee, we found a most odd system of payment. First you bought tickets for the amount you wished to spend on coffee and cakes and then took the tickets to the appropriate counters for the goods. As we were not familiar with the money or prices, we went round in circles, going from counter to counter, checking the price of cakes and falling over huge housewives cluttered with baskets and children, before getting what we wanted.

Although I had read that Belgrade was a city flourishing in the time of the Romans, and later an Oriental town under the Ottoman Turks, it was hard to associate it with either period of history with its overlay of many modern structures. In fact, Belgrade seems to have had a very stormy past, only in recent times emerging as the Communist capital of Yugoslavia. Communist or not, tourists were evidently well catered for, judging by the tourist-priced displays of traditional Balkan articles in some of the shops. As Isabel and I wandered back to the bus we window-shopped, casting our eyes over finely embroidered sheepskin jackets, beautifully handworked blouses, smoking hats, long pipes, leather shoes, filigree jewellery, carved tables and unusual musical instruments, but reluctantly bought nothing.

Some miles outside Belgrade, we stopped by a grassy bank and prepared to "do our stuff" with the primus stoves. It was a case of first get there, first eat. Hungry as we were, it was quite a rush to the front and, well to the fore, I soon mushed up a glutinous mess of eggs and chopped ham. A few of the others fancied their personal recipe stew but each one took such a long time to cook that those still waiting got impatient and chivvied on the proceedings. This resulted in half-cooked potatoes with bits of raw meat floating round in what was meant to be delicious gravy – but looked like dishwater – being eaten.

We should have stayed that night in the town of Nis but our long lunch break had delayed us too much. As dusk started to fall we had a conference and decided on camping after buying food for the evening meal at the next village. But we were too late and all the stores were closed. All we could get was quarts and quarts of goat's milk sold from the churn of an itinerant milkman. Finding a suitable field outside the village, we pitched our tents making haste to do so before the darkness enveloped us. The field was stubbly but the earth soft – indeed, one blow with the hammer and the tent peg disappeared in the direction of Australia. Our emergency food stores, intended for the desert stretches, had to be broken into and I ate a tin of my favourite baked beans, washed down with lashings of goat's milk and chianti.

About midnight, the rain started to fall. Heavier and heavier it splashed down, easing up only at dawn and ceasing as we were about to break camp. What a quagmire it left! Our tents were all but swimming. The groundsheets were soaked and it was quite a game folding up the equipment, next morning, without most of the sticky black field adhering to it. Our feet were caked inches deep in the thick gooey mud. A stream flowed between the ploughed field we had camped in and a sunflower field. As I plunged through the ten-foot high stalks of the sunflowers to find a spot for some private ablutions in the stream, I was seen by several angry peasants heading through the stalks from the other direction. Clearly, they thought I was about to harm their crop and with wild cries they pursued me, brandishing their pitchforks. I hastily turned about and skipped out of their way, running blindly through the forest of sunflowers back to the bus. I reached it, shoes in hand, having snatching them up from the oozy mud which had tried to claim them, and soaked to the skin and grazed where the tall, dripping wet sunflower stalks had lashed back at me as I ran. But at least I had managed to escape the indignity of being prodded along by the wrong end of a pitchfork. One good outcome from the storm was that it had settled the dust and we did not get our usual coating of it as we drove along the rough road.

We stopped at the small village of Aleksinac to get some provisions. Piling out of the bus, we made bee-lines for likely-looking shops which might sell eggs, butter, meat and bread. After about ten minutes we converged on the market-place where wizened peasants sat crouched over their wares which appeared to consist of nothing but melons in different colours, shapes and sizes. We compared notes on what success we had had with our shopping but it did not seem to amount to much. Butter was quite unobtainable and eggs apparently non-existent, although Robin furtively opened his jacket which he was clutching to himself, and proudly showed us six eggs he had somehow got from a black market source. The rest of us could produce nothing but loaves of coarse black bread. Striking out once more in a body, we found a meatshop which had just received its quota for the day. We bought some extremely unsavoury looking meat and hoped we weren't robbing the villagers of their ration. It had not been a very successful shopping expedition. Possibly if we had known a word of two of the language it might have been easier. Isabel's method of asking for eggs was to make oval shapes with her hands and cluck like an old hen! The faces of the shopkeepers at this pantomime was a picture.

The *Indiaman* looked quite out of place, parked in the dusty street with its bullock cart traffic. We were busily engaged in taking pictures of the incongruous sight when two solid-looking policemen loomed on the scene. The wily ones hid their cameras under coats and jackets but Robin and Peter were so engrossed in their photography that they did not notice anything amiss until the hand of the law fell heavily upon them and marched them off, protesting, to the Police Station. An hour or two later, they returned to the bus, trailing wet rolls of film. They had been kept in custody, all the time proclaiming their innocence – but in the wrong tongue – until the films had been developed and found to contain nothing of military importance. What possible secret could have been hidden away in that village is hard to guess.

At Nis, we bought provisions from what we were informed was the largest multiple store in Yugoslavia. The Food Department was extensive and we were able to buy all we needed at a fair price. We reached the Iron Curtain at dusk wondering if we were going to be greeted by the Customs men at the Bulgarian border with rifles at the ready. Instead, they proved most helpful and friendly, and though they certainly took their

Bullock cart traffic in Aleksinac, Yugoslavia.

time over the formalities, this may have been because they were curious and wanted to talk than for official reasons. Talk is perhaps not the right word since their English was very limited, but they gave us a strange but useful list of Bulgarian words to memorise and we all got along famously. We could see nothing of the country on the way to Sofia as it was very dark and raining hard. We were getting tired and hungry and our spirits were flagging, but Rene, who was always of good cheer, burst into song and soon the bus was ringing with harmony and laughing discord.

Sofia, the capital of Bulgaria, was an imposing city of large, square-cut, clean-lined buildings, many of them plastered with huge red stars. Slogans appeared on every available wall, usually accompanied by a picture of a Russian looking gentleman with close-cropped hair. No sooner had we entered the lighted area of the city, than we were surrounded by hordes of eager youths with black, curly hair and deep, sad, brown eyes with an expression that made me think of a maltreated spaniel. They cheered with gusto and flinging open the door of the *Indiaman*, tried to force themselves on board. Paddy quickly had the situation under control and picked out a boy, who seemed to have an admirable command of the English language, to be our guide through the town. The chosen boy shooed his comrades out of the way and, grasping what was required of him, led us to all the tourist hotels he knew. There was no room anywhere, which astonished us as we did not think tourism was encouraged behind the Iron Curtain. The boy finally guided us to a most expensive looking Ritz-class hotel in the main square where, after a hurried consultation with the manager, he got us in at tourist rates.

The rest of the youths had chased after us on their bicycles and now congregated round the bus wanting to help with our luggage, chat and exchange addresses for pen-friendships. It appeared they knew very little of what went on outside their own country and were anxious to find out, although with the strict censorship they said letters were subjected to, it was doubtful if we would be able to write them much about the Western way of life. Nevertheless, I gladly noted the address of a boy but was chagrined to find later that I had left the slip of paper in the hotel and my means of communication with one who might have proved to be an interesting and unusual correspondent was at an end. It was certainly poor public relations on our part after the wonderful welcome we had received, but we were just too tired to do much talking. A muddy bedraggled party, we staggered into the resplendent, chandelier-hung foyer, leaving a trail of dried mud in the deep-pile maroon carpet. Apart from the hovering liftboys who eyed us with distaste as we squeezed into the lifts trying to get out of sight as quickly as possible, the place was deserted. It turned out that the hotel was not yet officially opened. In some of the rooms the carpets still sported their price tags, and the blankets were fluffily new. I squeaked with joy at the sight of a private bathroom with its hot and cold taps, but the water was stone cold and the shiny chromium taps fell off as I touched them. No wonder tourist rates had been granted! But the beds were deliciously soft and we all had a good night's rest.

We went down to breakfast next morning thinking of bacon and eggs after the midnight feasts of bread and jam in our rooms. A troop of waiters bore down on us when we entered the dining-room, and showed us to our tables. Then four of them, with spotless napkins draped over their arms, hovered round each table, smoothing the starched, white tablecloths from time to time and re-arranging the salt cellars. Another waiter would then appear from somewhere and rearrange the salt cellars back to his way of thinking. For twenty minutes, they dashed smartly back and forth through the swing doors which led to the kitchen, bearing a plate here, and a cup there, before they were ready to take our orders. But again we were foiled as it appeared there was no choice in the menu. Placed before each of us was a couple of slices of grey bread, a knob of yellow grease and a tiny dish of most ersatz jam. The coffee, which we had hoped would put us on our feet again, was barely warm, looked like dishwater and tasted even worse.

With somewhat empty insides we threw our luggage into the *Indiaman* and headed through driving rain for Turkey. Turbulent torrents of water swirled deeply over the ditches in the villages, the peasants wading knee-deep through the brown foam, and geese huddled miserably together in whatever shelter they could find. It was not until we approached the Frontier in the early evening that the rain stopped. This Customs Post was well equipped with a most comfortable Rest Room. While Paddy was engaged with the formalities, Peter and Robin beat everyone to the chessboard provided and got in a quick game with all of us leaning over and shouting encouraging moves – which no doubt hastened the end of the game.

CHAPTER ELEVEN

Through Turkey

The Indianman and an overnight stop on a Turkish desert. We have our gear out to bed down for the night. The bus engine is covered with a blanket to prevent sand from entering with the sandstorms.

At the Turkish Frontier Post there was no Rest Room, only a rose garden and a lily pool to delight the eye while we waited for formalities to be completed. A storm was in progress over on the darkening Eastern horizon with thunder rolling constantly in muted fashion. Lightning stabbed the great, black cottonwool clouds with a magnesium brilliance and played around with a flickering magnificence. At any moment I expected to hear perhaps Holst's *Music from the Planets*, but only the rumbling thunder crashed forth. It was like no storm I had ever seen or heard in England in its magnificence and awe-inspiring beauty.

As we neared Edirne, a silhouetted skyline of mosque domes mushroomed up, accompanied by tall, graceful minarets pointing their fingers to the heavens. On reaching the town, however, these exciting new sights took second place and food was the uppermost thought. We invaded a building marked Lokantasi which looked hopefully like a restaurant. We were welcomed with open arms and initiated into the useful system of going behind the scenes to order food straight from the pot. This system certainly simplified the language difficulty in choosing food as we could just point at whatever took our fancy. Sometimes, however, we were to find the kitchens so uninviting that, after wading ankle deep through squashy cabbage leaves, stepping over sleeping goats, scattering hens and stirring up clouds of flies, we did not always feel much like partaking of the strong-smelling meat and vegetables which simmered in huge cauldrons over the open fires. This Lokantasi, however, was new and clean and we chose dish after strange dish of chops and chillies, yoghurt and stuffed tomatoes, aubergines (eggplant) and peppers, and kebabs in various guises.

Hunger appeased, Paddy held a consultation with us to decide whether to drive on through the night or find a suitable site for camping. As it was still inclined to rain Paddy decided to drive on. After driving for an hour or so, he suddenly pulled to the side of the road. "Me for forty winks," he said, and slumping over the wheel in his cabin, promptly went to sleep. Some of us nodded off in our seats, and others of us, in twos and threes, took short hikes up and down the road to stretch the legs. At the end of half-an-hour, Paddy appeared to need more sleeping time than forty winks, so we ventured a little further in our promenading. Isabel strayed off by herself in the now bright moonlight. She told us later that she had got lost and was challenged by a sentry outside a small Army Post. The sentry must have been somewhat perplexed to find an English lady wandering abroad at 2.00 a.m. on a road far from anywhere. She had great difficulty in persuading him in an alien tongue not to lock her up but to lead her back to the road where she was able to find the parked bus.

Suddenly Paddy stirred over the wheel and we made a dash for the bus. A roll call revealed Eddy missing. We waited a while longer, extremely impatient by now, but still he did not appear. We set off without him, hoping he had had the good sense to walk in the direction in which we were travelling. After some miles of peering into the darkness in vain, there was nothing for it but to go back to where we had parked. And there was Eddy calmly waiting for us to return, having unwisely gone for a walk in the opposite direction. Hauling him on board, Paddy drove off quickly before anyone else decided to disappear.

We slept fitfully as Paddy drove us through the night, waking to see the dawn breaking over the Sea of Marmora. The country had taken on a completely different aspect with low, rolling hills clothed in short, yellow grass. Smoke curled into the air from the campfires outside the many scattered tents of the local inhabitants, and boys darted about after their packs of geese, causing groups of handsome long-legged cranes to take flight if the boys approached too close. A couple of Englishmen, sitting by their car broken down at the side of the road, told us they were on their way back from Teheran when their car developed engine trouble. They were now waiting for the other member of their party to return from Istanbul with aid. There was nothing we could do, so, after handing over a quantity of fresh water, we carried on.

We entered the erstwhile capital of Turkey by the Edirne Gate – an ancient gateway in the remains of the crumbling outer wall of Istanbul, or Constantinople, as it then was. There appeared to be many walls, dating back, so I learnt, to 330 A.D. when Constantine the Great built the first inner wall to protect the city he had conquered. As the city grew with the years, so it became necessary to build another wall, and then another, and sections of these various battle-scarred and time-worn encircling walls still stand. Twisting our way through a maze of donkey traffic and trams, we reached the city

centre where we were lucky to find good accommodation in a hotel which provided plenty of warm, but not hot, water and comfortable rooms at reasonable cost. The Hilton Hotel, standing atop the city in glasshouse splendour, mostly patronised by wealthy tourists, was right out of our class. We had to put up with staying in a rather insalubrious quarter by the shunting yards of the noisy, main railway station.

Travelling through Turkey.

As usual, the first hour was spent in ridding ourselves of accumulated dust and dirt before we called at the Consulate for our mail. We read it sitting on a wall overlooking the Golden Horn, digesting the news as we gazed at the sun sparkling on the blue

waters of the Bosphorus far below. All around and receding into the hazy skyline were countless mosques and minarets. But although it looked beautiful from the top of the hill, when in the midst of it, squalor and dirt reigned with houses half demolished and others in the course of construction. Only the mosques seemed permanent. Even the Bosphorus did not look so inviting at close quarters with a surfeit of chicken feathers, dead cats, orange peel and other unwholesome garbage floating in the scum at the water's edge.

Istanbul.

After a good night's sleep, despite the noises erupting from the station, I set out on a tour of the city. I wandered through narrow back alleys and market places, up steep cobbled hills where donkeys vied with fast-ridden bicycles for right of way, and emerged quite by chance in the main and very fashionable shopping street thronging with well-heeled tourists. Wherever I went though the crowds, there always seemed to be huge armchairs, tables, and once an enormous refrigerator, walking about on human legs. When I overtook these oddities, they turned out to be human furniture removal vans with some poor man, or very often woman, bent double hauling these fantastic loads. I heard it said later that a man could carry half a ton on his back, provided someone went before him to sweep the path, as the smallest pebble would be driven right into his foot if he trod on it with such a load on his back.

Armed with the inevitable sticky buns, I left the tourist area and walked alongside the shores of the Bosphorus, through all the poorer quarters where life is still probably lived as it was hundreds of years ago. Dilapidated old wooden houses stood in tiers on the hillside. I was told these houses are only lived in for one generation and deserted when the head of the family dies, so that his spirit may return there and rest in peace. After hearing some of the women shrilling at their children I was not surprised that poor old Dad looked forward to a little peace and quiet on his demise, but it did seem rather a waste of a good house.

Darkness was falling as I retraced my steps and, footsore and weary, found a seat at the water's edge and contemplated what I saw.

Dilapidated old wooden houses stood in tiers on the hillside. Istanbul, Turkey.

> The stringy cat winnowing by,
> The stranger whistling on the seat.
> The sudden hoot of passing steamer
> And the lisping Bosphorus at my feet.
> Minarets in floodlit splendour,
> A bright moon in a cloudy sky.
> Stately hulking ships at anchor
> And the mournful water cry.

Hearing the water cry given by the many small boys trotting around with cups of fresh water for sale, reminded me that I was thirsty and hungry too, and I set off for the hotel. I was a little nervous at the thought of getting a knife in my back as I crept through the dark alleys but nothing untoward happened.

Renee came to my room saying she had met a couple of Americans staying at the hotel and they had asked her to bring another girl along to make up a party to "do" the town on the morrow. Foolishly I agreed to accept this blind date and regretted saying "Yes" as soon as I met our escorts next morning. However, it was too late to back out then and we drove off in their spacious car bound for a little restaurant that they knew, some miles up the coast. It transpired that our friends were American Naval Engineers, engaged in a secret project in the mountains on the other side of the Bay, and they knew quite a lot about the country around. From the delightful restaurant built out over the water, they pointed out where submarines were kept in secret, and stores of ammunition were stacked away in caves against a possible Russian invasion. But of course we could see nothing and it was forbidden territory to tourists.

Joe, the "leader" of the two, was a rough, tough character who intrigued me with his tales of tunny fishing off the East Coast of America. He had started fishing at the early age of 16 after first learning to throw a knife straight to protect himself from his ruffianly mates. His friend was a decidedly inferior character, whom I immediately nicknamed the "Octopus"! I spent most of the time on the way to the restaurant endeavouring to see as much as possible of the route while getting out of his clutches. The lads wanted to continue the party over drinks in their room but I had other ideas and left them, much to their disgust, taking Renee with me. She told me she had a revolver in her handbag – which she had – but it seemed silly to get as far involved as that!

Sheila had stayed in bed for the day with unspecified aches and pains and was feeling little better when the time came to leave next day. Her rounded cheeks had sunken and her long, brown hair, which hung halfway down her back, was lank and lifeless. She had to be carried to the bus where we propped her up with pillows and covered her with blankets on the front seat of the bus and hoped her condition would not worsen. Then it took a long time to get everyone on board as, at the last minute, someone or other found they had run out of jam or sugar or an essential commodity, and went dashing off to the stores. Neither was it an easy matter threading our way out through the narrow streets without knocking over barrowloads of fruit which kept appearing in our path, and we must have given heart attacks to dozens of skinny, limping sore-headed horses as we tried to inch by them. Their drivers thought nothing of cruelly cursing and swearing at the poor beasts as they cracked whips over their mangy rumps. A ferry took us across the Bosphorus, our last link with Europe, to the Asian side of Istanbul, where we proceeded to get lost with great thoroughness in the tortuous maze of streets. "I've been across on this wretched ferry dozens of times," said Paddy, "but it never seems to land at the same place twice and I never know where I am."

Eventually we got on track again, passing the hospital run so courageously by Florence Nightingale during the Crimean War. For some distance the road followed the Bay of Izmet, where several submarines were sporting themselves in the shining waters. Sandy wastes ran into the sea and sun-limned black spits of sand rose from out of it. Moss on the otherwise bare hills gave them the appearance of having caught measles. Rich alluvial deposits had settled at the foot of these hills and corn had evidently been growing there judging from the stubble. It was strange to see the primitive method still in use of blindfolded horses plodding in an endless, weary circle, in order to activate the water wheel which irrigated the crops. Soon vineyards edged the road and we feasted on the small, sweet, seedless grapes. Pastel-toned houses, mixed in with mudbrick hovels, added colour to an ever-changing already colourful scene.

After a night in a comfortable motel near Bolu, poor Sheila's condition had still not improved and Ron again nobly carried her to the bus, as she was running quite a temperature. A short run brought us to Ankara where Isabel and I volunteered for nursing duties, putting Sheila to bed in a hotel to await a doctor. Meanwhile, I invaded the kitchen and made an eggnog for her; the kitchen staff could not speak a word of English but they grasped the situation and obligingly let me rout around until I found all the ingredients I needed. The doctor diagnosed a mild attack of Asian flu, which was quite a relief to all of us, as well as Sheila, as we could not delay our journey for sick passengers and yet had no wish to leave her behind in a strange country. I spent the afternoon sitting in the hotel lounge, taking it in turns with Isabel to look in on the patient and give her the prescribed laudanum and belladonna pills on time.

Our ministrations and the medicine were clearly effective because by morning Sheila's temperature was right down and the crisis was over.

We should have been on our way but Paddy decided to give Sheila another twenty four hours to recover so I had time, after all, to see something of the town. Ankara, which dates back to 1,500 B.C., was rebuilt into the very modern city it is today, by Mustapha Kemal, who, in 1923, made it the capital of Turkey. My efforts to find some trace of the old Ankara were rudely interrupted by a terrifying noise and immediate uproar. The dam, high above the town, had broken. Water cascaded down the hill, gathering up lorries, houses, people, cattle and anything that happened to be in the path of the mad rush. One of the hotels where some of us were staying was flooded, though not demolished and it was sheer luck that none of us had been in the way of the water.

Our exit from the town next day we found blocked with mud and debris. Soldiers and other willing helpers were dragging drowned bodies from the now subsided waters and we could see twisted wrecks of vehicles tangled with each other. One man was trying to get his horse and cart across a fairly deep stretch of water, but the unfortunate animal skidded on the soft mud underfoot and dragged the cart over with it as it fell. Frenzied, the man beat it about its just-visible head while other men rushed to his aid. Whether the horse was rescued or drowned we never knew, as Paddy, anxious not to waste any more time drove off to find another exit road.

Flood damage in Ankara, Turkey, after the dam burst the night we arrived.

We had covered some miles of dry, dirt road when, for no apparent reason, a wide wet patch barred our path, bypassed only by a high-rutted track. A large lorry was already stuck axle deep in the thick mud and was being dug out. The fields on either side of the road offered no solution as the earth was soft and powdery, and the *Indiaman* had too low a ground clearance to take the diversionary ruts. There was nothing for it but to take shovel in hands and start digging a path through the squelchy mud. Shirt after shirt came off, the better for the boys to put their backs into it, with the girls cheering them on. But, with only four shovels available, little headway was made. Meanwhile, other lorries and local busses with their very high clearance – not to mention a couple of tough little Volkswagens – had safely negotiated the detour. Paddy decided the only thing to be done was ride the bus over the ruts by means of the plank we carried down the centre aisle and which we had so often sworn at as we stubbed our toes on the wretched thing. With all of us lending a hand, amid gruntings, groanings and cheerings the feat was accomplished and we were under way again. Brows were mopped and shirts donned with sighs of relief but these were soon quelled when Paddy said gleefully "Ha, that was nothing. Wait till you see what's coming!"

We drove on over country which was for the most part dull and flat with mountains a mere shadow in the distance. Every so often we passed a sprouting of mud huts which passed as a village. Children ran around barefoot in bright but dirty costume and enjoyed themselves riding on a flat board hitched to a horse. The horse trotted round and round over the grain to be threshed, sometimes breaking into a canter if egged on by the excited children. Far off three towering mountains gradually took shape. The light was beginning to fade as we got abreast of them and saw them in all their beauty, changing from dull grey to pink, to gold, to copper, before blackening into silhouettes.

A village in Turkey.

In the small town of Nigde, we found a travellers' hotel – it could hardly be called a tourists' hotel – where we got a clean bed for the reasonable sum of three shillings. Washing was an hilariously hectic procedure. In a tiny room, about six feet by six feet, we found a sink and three bowls, which, in our usual time-saving attitude of mind, meant four of us could wash at the same time. We were all in fits of laughter playing a sort of "boomps-a-daisy" as we scrubbed ourselves down in the freezing water. Before leaving Nigde we trudged around the market buying peppers, potatoes and goat's meat, for we were now in the country where eating houses were few and far between and we certainly didn't want to go without supper.

The dust on the road began to be excessively troublesome and past the joking stage. I wore a headscarf well down over my forehead, dark glasses and another kerchief across my nose tied like a *yashmak* – the face veil worn by Muslim women. I hoped this would serve to keep the dust from my face and lungs, even if it did make me look rather like an insect from outer space. The bare mountains were creeping nearer and nearer to our road and fascinated me with their different colours and texture. My favourites were the pink ones with a petrified flow look about them; they seemed to be playing *Grandmother's Step* and would move another yard or two towards you if you turned your back on them. Then there were the dirty putty-coloured mountains that resembled a child's efforts at pastry making, complete with pudgy finger marks in the dough. "And to think those mountains were once green and had trees growing all over them," remarked Freddie. "Then, why are they so bare now?" I asked. "Because," explained Freddie, patiently, "people cut down the trees for firewood and the soil just slipped away as there was nothing to hold it." In my ignorance I didn't know if he was pulling my leg or if the mountain slopes really had been thickly forested in the dim distant past.

Magpies were not so prolific here as they had been in Yugoslavia. Going through that country, I had changed the old jingle of one for sorrow, two for mirth, three for a wedding, four for a birth, to ten for sorrow, twenty for mirth and so on. Now it was only five for sorrow! Lovely blue birds flashed by and an occasional eagle winged its way in stately fashion high over the plain. Little rat-like gophers darted across the road in front of us, narrowly missing the wheel, and once the kind-hearted Moti insisted on stopping for two tortoises which she spotted wandering down the middle of the road. Putting them gently on one side, she left them with a stack of lettuce leaves to feast on.

When we got tired of bird watching or mountain gazing, we turned to books which we could read quite well in spite of the continual jolting. Various tales changed hands from a Whodunit, surprisingly brought by Mildred, to *Ulysses* by James Joyce, not so surprisingly brought by John. In truth it cannot be said that *Ulysses* went very far round; it was rather hard to digest on a bumpy track and in any case the fine volume would have been ruined. My cheap edition of Ogden Nash that went the rounds finally came back to me as a few barely recognisable pages.

Once rounding a fairly steep downgrade bend we saw a large, red lorry upside down in a deep gully at the edge of the road. It had clearly had brake failure and could not take the corner. We got out to investigate what was to become a commonplace sight. Indeed, it was unusual if we did not see one accident (or more) a day. We did not feel very cheerful when Paddy informed us that on the morrow we would be facing the worst mountain crossing of the journey. As soon as the first faint tinge of dawn tipped the horizon he was up and checking on the brakes and making sure that the engine was in good form. And

The inverted red lorry.

when we saw the bends we realised why he'd taken so much trouble. Hairpin bend followed hairpin bend in quick succession. Many times we had to stop and reverse in order to get the length of the bus around. "This is where the local laddies carry a mate to leap out and put large rocks under the back wheel, so that they don't slide over the edge during backing manoeuvres," said Paddy. Immediately he had several volunteers to perform the task. Paddy waved them away. "Not to worry – we've got good brakes," he laughed. "I hope," he added.

At noon we stopped at a small eating-house and got a veritable feast for about 1/6d. Armed with a large ladle and bowl, we helped ourselves from the weird concoctions simmering over a range of fires: bits of meat swimming in grease, stuffed limp-looking aubergines, sodden rice, boiled grass, and other delicacies swarming in flies were there for our choice. A group of youngsters gathered round when we had eaten and went into gales of mimicking laughter when the girls repaired their lipstick.

The second half of the mountains which we now had to tackle was even more hazardous than the first half. At one section there was no room to reverse to get round the hairpin bend as the apex was too great. A precipice fell away down one side and a huge rock overhung the other. Paddy took the corner with great elan, lurching on the gravel, while we held our breath and closed our eyes. When we reached level ground once more and were able to laugh at the experience, the passengers at the back of the bus told Paddy that it felt as though "their" wheel had gone right out into nothing. "I wouldn't be surprised," said Paddy. "I had the same feeling myself. It's very difficult to know on those corners how much of the bus is on the road and how much poised in space. I find the best way to take them is to turn the wheel, close the eyes and hold the breath." We were all very thankful when we once more reached level ground.

On the far side of Erzincan we found a good camping site on a patch of hard ground covered with prickly cactus which was to play havoc with our air mattresses. I did not feel too good – perhaps it was a touch of the Asian flu – and was in no mood for fighting the hard earth to knock the bending tent pegs in. Gallantly Robin and Ron put up theirs in a twinkling and helped me with mine. Meanwhile, Norman had gone off in search of firewood and came back with his arms full of dried brush which made an excellent flame, and Jemila brewed some Nescafé which she had miraculously produced from a hidden hoard. Dosing the coffee liberally with my precious brandy I crawled on to my soon-to-be airless mattress and wooed sleep with little success.

Bodies started crawling out of tents soon after dawn and I found myself with barely enough energy to haul down my tent. Sitting on this, I had more coffee well laced with brandy and got very cross with John who wanted a swig of the neat spirit to clean his teeth in! Tempers were frequently frayed from the lack of water for anything but drinking. Pepsicola was one thing to share with a friend for tooth cleaning, if one's teacup ration of washing water had given out, but I drew the line at using my favourite medicine for such a purpose. We delayed washing until we had covered some miles and the road converged on a deep flowing river. While the others practically stripped and disported themselves gleefully in the cool water, I staggered out of sight around the hillock and almost "lay me doon to dee," only descending when from the sounds below I gathered the party was ready to be on its way.

We entered the garrison town of Erzerum around mid-day, spotting rows of guns on trucks and camouflaged, tarpaulined shapes tucked away behind military buildings. This was evidently a most closely guarded and secret area of Turkey and we were kept waiting at a picket post for some time until an escort was available to take us to the town centre. He took our passports to check on and make sure we were not spies and kept them until we had had lunch and were once more assembled in the *Indiaman*. That is to say, most of us were assembled, but a count of heads showed Eddy and Frank short. It appeared they had gone off in search of a Post Office, disobeying our escort's request that we should remain together. It caused the poor man great anxiety – maybe he would have been shot if any of his herd escaped – and on their return he hustled us out of the town and put us on our road before we could perpetrate any other crime.

At some unknown point on the map, we pitched tents at sundown on an incredibly dusty site. One's very breathing disturbed the loose soil. I tossed and turned on the hard ground, dog tired and feeling like death, yet unable to sleep. Finally, in desperation, I left my dust-clouded tent and walked out into the night. The stars scintillated against a rich velvet backdrop and an icy wind whistled round my legs, carrying with it a plaintive and eerie song from the high mountains. Perhaps it was a shepherd boy on a lonely vigil, singing to his flock of goats. Sitting on a stony outcrop until dawn, I gazed out over the distant mountains shimmering in the early light, and drank in the solitary grandeur and desolation of the scene. I found myself thinking "I will lift up mine eyes unto the hills, from whence cometh my help," though I wasn't sure what help I needed or was available anyway. On my return to camp I ran into Eddy who had also been on the prowl. We both agreed that the cold, wild mountain air was magically invigorating. In fact, I felt so vastly improved that I had no hesitation in eating a cold, greasy chop and baked beans that John had left over from supper and could not face for his own breakfast.

Mount Ararat, Turkey.

We were almost within sight of that beautiful, majestic snow-capped mountain, Mount Ararat, where Noah's Ark is popularly supposed to have rested during the time of the biblical floods. Its summit is usually shrouded in a fleecy white cloud, but we were very fortunate to reach it at a moment when the peak was visible against a piercingly blue sky. Almost in the shadow of the great mountain lies the compound of what was then known as the Turkish/Persian Customs. The name Persia, of course, was later to be changed to Iran. "Don't step over that white line, whatever you do," warned Paddy, as we trooped out of the bus, "or you'll get interned for entering Persia without a passport." We watched our steps and kept well clear of it for the next three hours while waiting for clearance on the Turkish side. With traffic non-existent, I filled in the time admirably by laying myself out flat on the dried, prickly apology for grass at the roadside and having a nap. In this part of the world, it appeared that nobody thinks anything of seeing what looks like a dead body at the side of a road, taking a siesta. Cleared at last, we walked across the dreaded white line to the Persian Compound, where we were treated with courtesy and efficiency and speedily sent on our way.

CHAPTER TWELVE

Through Persia

Crossing the Persian Desert.

Over the border the road turned into a single line cart-track with axle-breaking corrugations which threw us up and down unmercifully. Pieces of luggage that had been stowed away in the rack above, came tumbling down and had to be anchored more securely. Even so, the cry of "Heads!" frequently echoed down the aisles of the *Indiaman* as some bag or other came adrift again and threatened a nasty headache to whoever was underneath. The mountains soon lost their smooth, rounded contours and sandstone quality and looked to my uninformed eye more like grey granite, with stickleback peaks. I wondered why they had changed their shape so markedly, but there was no geologist aboard to tell me.

While it was still daylight we stopped by the side of a swift flowing stream. The stream was neither very wide nor deep, which was just as well because Sheila, when making a grab at an article of underclothing which was whisked out of her hand as she was doing her laundry, overbalanced and fell in. Perhaps it was unkind of us but it afforded us some much-needed light relief! Most of us put up our tents by the stream but I thought I'd try sleeping in the bus for a change as I was getting tired of cold nights under canvas. I stretched my air-mattress across the width of the bus, in company with Renee, who was coughing up blood at this time for some obscure reason – probably an over-intake of dust – and was also feeling rather sorry for herself. Provided the mattress stayed up, this was a fairly comfortable method. If it did not, one found the handle of the suitcase used to support the mattress in the aisle between the seats, sticking in the small of one's back. One was also in a slightly twisted position because the seats were not in line with each other across the aisle: but at least it was warm!

An old beggar came to our camp as we were breakfasting and we piled bread on him until he couldn't have known what to do with it. Then a camel train passed with jingling bells and set us dashing about with food in one hand and cameras ready for action in the other, before we piled on board the *Indiaman* again for the next stage of our journey. The small village of Khoi was overrun with zealous police who stop all who enter and try to take away their passports – usually for a day or two. Paddy had had experience of this before and told us to say we all came under his passport as one big family, and to leave him to do the rest of the talking. This he did in his inimitable way to some effect, although the policeman obviously understood little of what was said. But Paddy made him quite happy by giving him a piece of paper with all our names on it.

Every few miles we passed a couple of Persian men, armed with long rakes, who were engaged in sweeping the grit back into the middle of the road to try and stop corrugations forming. It was a never ending task for them as the heavy lorries immediately sprayed it to the edges again as they passed, but it did help to keep the road comparatively even. From time to time the road ran close to the mountains. Whole villages were built into the cliff face and, in some places, houses had been completely demolished by heavy falls of rock. Camel trains were on the move by the score and, in the far distance, we spotted herds of wild camels galloping over the scrub. Vultures wheeled in vast numbers overhead and once we saw them making an excellent meal of a recently dead horse at the side of the road. We also noticed many sad, little heaps of whitened bones that told of drought or some other mishap in that forlorn, arid country.

In this flat terrain, it was becoming increasingly difficult to find cover when the cry "Bushes, please" was made to Paddy. We soon got quite adept at finding culverts, folds in the ground or even a two-foot high patch of the prickly camelthorn bush, to hide our modesty in times of need. It always caused me vast amusement as we fanned out in different directions searching for a suitable site!

We reached Tabriz at dusk and checked in at a reasonably appointed hotel. The washing arrangements were new to us but we found them repeated in similar class hotels throughout Persia. Although we had a basin in each of our rooms, it was fed from a small container behind the basin cabinet and, of course, was soon exhausted after the demands we made on it. Some of us chose a shower which could be had for payment of a rial or two, but the shower room consisted of a shower only with no hooks or bench. The floor naturally got flooded and it was an art holding one's clothes and towel out of reach of the spray with one hand and washing with the other! Perhaps one was supposed to have a servant waiting outside to assist.

The hotel certainly gave us a sumptuous meal of roast chicken but unwisely in my effort to make up for lack of food I rather overdid it and retired hurriedly to bed in agonies of indigestion. I almost repeated that mistake at breakfast when I tasted the delicious honey they served with several kinds of brown bread. Persian bread usually resembled rather dry Yorkshire pudding, and quickly staled. It came out of the oven in thin flaps sometimes three feet long, and about a dozen layers were then carried off over the shoulders of the bread-sellers.

The streets of Tabriz were wide, edged with water-running gullies called *jubes*, which carried away all refuse. Smart little patisseries and Western-style shops were interspersed with the open-fronted shops which sold the cheaper local wares. Most of the Persians wore sloppy European suits, although in the areas outside the town we noticed they seemed to favour blue and white striped pyjamas for day wear. The women were encased in a long, flowing black garment, or *chador*. This covered them to the eyes and, if necessary in the presence of strangers, a corner of the cloth would be held in the teeth to hide the entire rest of the face.

Leaving Tabriz behind us – well stocked up with albeit highly priced Nescafé and dried milk which had hitherto been unobtainable – we continued down the road, so bumpy now that it was impossible to read on the duller stretches. After one stop Paddy found he could not start the bus on the self-starter which, it appeared, had broken a cable, and he had to "get out and get under" to get us going again. Indeed, he had to go through this slow performance several times more after various stops were made for tea or pepsicola at the many little wayside *chaikhanas*. Presently the road ran adjacent to a brown, gurgling river, very different from the dried-up river beds we had been crossing. An ancient bridge had once spanned this river but it had long since lost its middle portion and a modern structure was now built alongside. A spring gushed from the mountains overhanging the road, and we drew up to replenish our waterbottles. A young blind beggar-girl seated by the spring gratefully accepted some food we put in her hands.

Suddenly the sky, which had been clouding over, burst into a monsoon shower. The poor beggar-girl was getting drenched with no cover so we led her on board the *Indiaman* to shelter until the storm had passed: she may well have thought she was being kidnapped by a strange-tongued people but she made no protest. Chips of rock, loosened by the heavy drops of rain, hurtled down from the mountain towering over us and landed with frightening clonks on the roof of the bus. Paddy got a shade alarmed, thinking a landslide might well be precipitated, but a quick getaway was out of the question with a dead starter motor. "Righto," yelled Paddy, "everyone out and shove for your lives." Without more ado, we all piled out of the *Indiaman* again in a rush and shoved, heaved and cajoled that great monster to a push start. Luckily a slight incline was with us, and we soon heard the motor pick up our efforts enough to carry us out of harm's way. But what a dripping bunch of beings we were as we charged back into the bus. For about fifteen crazy minutes we proceeded to fall over each other trying to find dry clothes and put them on in the confined space. At length, towelled down and dry again, we resumed our journey with an odd collection of wet blouses, skirts, shorts and shirts, hanging from every available hook in the bus. Well out of range of danger, Paddy stopped again without stopping the engine, and halted a passing lorry. The driver took over the blind beggar-girl, promising in broken English to drop her at the next village. We hoped that from there, someone would claim her.

The storm was certainly short, if not sweet, but a brilliant rainbow cheered us over the next few miles. The old town of Zanjan, a former Royal capital of Persia, welcomed us. A local official led us up a long driveway to a school, fronted by a bright, flower-surrounded pool. There we were offered the floor of the Assembly Room which was spread with thick Persian rugs. It was indicated that we should choose our bedspace where we liked, and we lined up our blankets in a row in the middle of the room. On waking at dawn, we found ourselves hemmed in by snoring Persian bodies who had bedded down after us, and were now curled up on blankets over every inch of space.

We continued travelling on the dusty road to Teheran, the now capital city of Persia. A mile or two outside the city, built in the shadow of the stately Elburz Mountains, we found ourselves on a well-surfaced dual carriageway. Factories sprouted on either side, the Pepsicola Factory taking pride of place. Pepsicola could almost be called the national beverage, and our feverish drinking of it must certainly have sent the sales rocketing.

Teheran's streets were wide and tree-lined with the usual gully at the road's edge. The buildings looked modern and spacious though there were still many of the overcrowded older houses standing in the poverty stricken back streets. We booked in to the Hotel Persepolis, quite a three-star affair. I straightaway flew to the room allotted to me and, dumping my filthy bits of luggage on the nice, clean carpet, grabbed first bath before such a move seemed to have occurred to anyone. It was heaven to lie back and soak in the boiling hot water, trying to rid myself of some of the ingrained dirt. I was rudely awakened by thumpings on the door reminding me that my time was up. Perhaps the drain got clogged by the dirt sponged off me, but for some reason the water would not run away properly through a grid in the floor to which the drainpipe led, and I had to paddle to the door. Fortunately the doorway had a slight sill or the carpet outside might have suffered. There was plenty of hot water available in our bedroom basins too, so we soon had our clothes washed and hung out on the verandahs to dry. I do not think we could have been very popular with hotel staff: we must have left quite a mess for them to clear up on our departure and we couldn't afford to tip extravagantly.

A long rest on the super-soft bed and a really good dinner served in the outside restaurant which was decorated with coloured lights amid potted palm trees, brought me back to a civilised state of mind again. From the upper balconies of the hotel we could see an enormous cinema screen which was giving a free show to all who watched. The sound was somewhat distorted, but that did not matter too much since it was all in Persian. Though we could not make much headway with the story, it seemed to be quite a romantic affair and gave us something else to think about than the rigours of travel. In the morning Isobel and I walked down to the Embassy to collect our mail. The heat beat off the pavements and we had to revive ourselves several times with Pepsis. The unbottled drinks on sale did not attract us as they consisted of either fruit or carrots pulped through a machine into glasses. The resultant oozy mixture was swarming with flies. The heat, and perhaps lack of vitamins and sleep over the past few days, had worn me out, so instead of accompanying Isobel who wanted to see the Peacock Throne that afternoon, I collapsed into bed and slept the all too short time away.

Paddy had bidden us be ready by 8.00 o'clock next morning, but by the time the bills had been paid and the baggage loaded in the *Indiaman*, it was nearer 9.00 a.m. Then, of course, came the usual shriek for last minute stamps. The Post Office was near the main square and, business finally completed, we were caught in a traffic maelstrom similar to Piccadilly Circus and Paddy had to make several revolutions round the square before he could exit on the road he wanted. The dual carriageway continued for some miles out of the city before general groans greeted the appearance of dirt track corrugations ahead. Hastily we donned headscarves and other anti-dust equipment.

The Golden Domed Mosque, Qum.

Not far from Teheran we entered Qum, one of the holy Moslem cities of Persia. Here, traditionally, any bad character is able to claim sanctuary. Infidels in the city are greatly frowned upon, especially women who dared to walk about with their faces uncovered, so it was impossible to stop in order to see at closer quarters the Golden Domed Mosque. However, our way was baulked by a donkey cart as we cruised slowly down the street, and we had no option but to stop for a few minutes while the traffic jam sorted itself. Leaning out of the windows of the bus, we managed to get in a quick shot with our cameras.

Our way led over mountains covered with copper-brown soil cracking in the sun. We all felt that we were cracking somewhat in the sun too! We arrived at the outskirts of Isfahan too tired, hot and hungry to appreciate the gradual change from arid waste to fruit orchards shaded by silver chenar trees. Mere trickles of water, that would be running streams in spring, surrounded each orchard. I looked at the dried earth banks and felt desperately in need of a cool spring day and a grassy slope lined with primroses on which to rest my weary bones. But such is the way of travellers! Had I been sitting on a primrose bank in an English April, tucked up in an overcoat and with a wet wind whistling round my ears, I should doubtless have yearned for the heat of this moment.

Settled in a small hotel, our rooms looking into a courtyard below, we could do no more than summon enough energy to wash, and then feast on fried chicken and rice and mast (sour milk). The fried chicken in its cooked state looked more like chopped-up cats' feet and tasted slightly burnt – possibly because it was cooked over open coals. We knew it really was chicken, though, because we had gone to the kitchen and chosen the pieces of meat we fancied, as was the custom. But even so, there was no guarantee that the goods on view were those delivered!

One of the mosques in Isfahan, Persia (Iran).

Early in the morning I set off with the other girls on foot, along the wide dual carriageway separated by a dusty strip, which led to the centre of the town. Modern but dilapidated American cars, ancient and likewise dilapidated donkeys led by pedlars, and carriages pulled by emaciated horses, crept or swept past us. Small shops lining each side of the road showed a fine window display of intricate silverwork, brass bowls and trays depicting scenes from Persian life in pin-hammer work, jewellery of all kinds, and plates and coffee sets enamelled in rich colours. It was possible to buy any of these articles for a reasonable sum for their worth, provided one haggled for a good half hour. As I am not a good haggler, and had no money anyway, I bought nothing.

We stopped to watch the figured trays being hammered out, the workers tapping away at extraordinary speed as they squatted on the earth floor of their workshops, which opened on to the street. I strayed into a mosque with an exquisite blue and yellow tiled dome, covered with inscriptions. Its many smaller rooms surrounding the courtyard were decayed and crumbling but there was an air of peace and quietness over all. Pondering long and gazing into the still waters of the lily pool, I conjured up visions of the romantic Persia of roses and nightingales and love, of which the poets Hafiz and Ferdouwsi spoke, forgetting for a moment that even then there was poverty and sudden death, just as now.

After a belated breakfast of milky coffee and some sticky sweet doughnuts at one of the less noisome cafés, we split up. One group went in search of the mosque with the shaking towers, so built that a slight push would set them trembling, and Isobel and I to find the Palace of Chehil Sitoun, or the Palace of Forty Columns. In actual fact, there are only twenty columns of thin spindly wood supporting a heavy porch; the other twenty are reflected in the long pool facing the Palace. Unfortunately

Courtyard inside a mosque in Isfahan.

we could not admire the reflection as a large, very dead dog right at the front of the pool was now the meeting place of countless flies. The open columned porchway led to audience chambers, the roof and walls of which were covered in mirror mosaic work which glinted in the strong sunlight. It was said that Shah Abbas, who had ordered the Palace to be built during his 16th century reign, had originally intended huge mirrors to line the walls of the Audience Chambers. But the mirrors had broken in the course of transportation and, rather than waste the pieces, the Shah, or his advisers, thought of a way to use the bits of glass in this novel manner.

Leaving Isfahan behind and passing through a succession of mud villages with the inevitable blue-domed mosques, we were mystified at seeing what looked like large mud turrets dotted over the landscape. We stopped and scrambled to the top of one crumbling structure by means of a dried mud staircase that had once wound itself round to the top but was now half missing. From our vantage point, we could see endless chains of these turrets and could not conceive to what possible use they had been put in days of old, as they hardly seemed strong enough for fortification purposes. We learnt later that these are the famous pigeon towers where these birds are encouraged to roost so that their droppings could be used in the cultivation of crops.

A large pigeon tower near Isfahan, Persia.

With many stops for Pepsicola to quench our ever-present thirst, we drove on to the small town of Yezd, where we bought the usual provisions. These now always included melons and dates. Indeed, melons were devoured in great quantities, one person generally buying one big one at a time and sharing it round the bus. The cutting of it was not an enviable job as the cutter tended to get smothered in sticky juice, which took a lot of removing with the little water available.

We had barely left our camping site next morning when Paddy found we had a broken main spring. There was nothing for it but to go back some 30 miles to Yezd, where he knew a "little man" in a garage who could repair it speedily. On the outskirts of the town Paddy turned into an obscure gateway and routed out the mechanic, clearly a past master at repairing broken springs from all the practice that came his way. How he must have blessed the rough roads that gave him such a lucrative living! Repairs were immediately put in hand and we were promised the mended *Indiaman* at sundown.

Armed with books, writing papers, and spongebag to cool the heated brow, we made for the centre of the town. There was little to see in Yezd beyond a few mangy camels and the usual small bazaar. The local trade was pottery and I bought a very pretty little green glazed bowl for the equivalent of four pence. Isabel bought a large jar so as to increase her water supply, but it turned out to be quite useless for the purpose as it leaked at a high rate, even when stuck up with Bostik. It was obviously necessary to test all water vessels for porosity before buying. We spent the morning in quiet discomfort writing letters in a café, to the bubbling accompaniment of many of the locals sucking away at their *hookahs*.

Robin found a Public Bathhouse and came back, pink and well-scrubbed, with a flowing tale of having been rubbed and pummelled by a male attendant till all the dirt was forced from his skin. With three of the girls I ventured into the steamy atmosphere of the Baths but it appeared that men did the massaging in the Women's Section also. We declined the cleansing massage but took a bath apiece in sole comfort. The individual bath arrangements consisted of two rooms with very hot floors. The first room was for undressing and in the second was a bowl and ledge on which you could lie in the steam and almost watch the dirt floating from your pores. It meant many fillings of the bowl before I considered myself clean again. As Joan seemed to be taking a very long time over her bath, we charged in to collect her corpse only to find that she had washed all her clothes as well and was waiting for them to dry!

Our skin tingling with its new cleanness, we returned to the bus where we were glad to see the repair operations nearly completed. One helpful little Persian lad was diligently trying to sweep out some of the dust which had accumulated rather badly and which we had long ago decided might as well stay where it was. But he had other ideas and heartily banged the seats in an effort to shake out some dirt. Alas, the only result was a thick, choking cloud of dust which would not settle anywhere except, of course, in our still open pores.

On the way at last, we passed our camping site of the night before but could not face the thought of bedding down there again. We carried on despite the darkness falling, till we came to a very small village boasting a fast moving stream. Out came the water bottles and we filled them and drank plentifully of the warm, slightly brackish water, undeterred by the thought of any impurities there might have been lurking in it. When we finally found a suitable resting place, I considered it was warm enough not to curl up inside the bus and indeed, not only did I sleep outside it, but like the others, could not even be bothered to put up my tent. Small groups of us were huddled fairly closely together because the ground with its prickly plants and stones had to be treated rather circumspectly and we took what gaps in these uncomfortablenesses that we could find. The night was perfect in its velvet brightness, the Milky Way looking more like a searchlight than the tenuous thread of light visible from England. Stargazing practically forced itself upon us. As we sipped our black tea, snugly embedded in sleeping bags, I was called upon to give a "lecture" on the stars to my little group, and gladly pointed out the new constellations I had learned from my well-thumbed "Handy Stargazer's Book".

Our road next day passed series after series of odd moonlike craters, stretching in lines from the mountains. We thought at once what excellent bush cover. "Sure, use them by all means," said Paddy, "if you want to find yourselves at the bottom of a deep well." The purpose of the wells, or *qanats* as they are called, is to bring the irrigating life-water down from the mountains to the villages, often for a distance of sixty miles. The wells reach a depth of 300 to 400 feet and are connected below ground by tunnels. The lip around the top of each shaft is formed to prevent soil blowing down and clogging the wells. This is vitally important because if the water supply dries up the village dies and the inhabitants have to move.

We approached Kerman around noon. It had taken us barely two days to reach here from Yezd, a journey that had taken Marco Polo seven days some 700 years ago. He mentions in his Travels that "there are only three places for shelter along the route but many groves of date palms and an abundance of wild game." He was certainly right about the dearth of *chaikhanas* but over the intervening years hungry travellers must have eaten all the dates and wild game for we saw no sign of either. As we were getting low in the necessary currency, our first stop in Kerman was to look for a bank in order to change some of our Traveller's Cheques. Whilst we were waiting for those engaged in this business, Norman, our Geordie sailor, foolishly washed his hair in one of the *jubes* (kerbside gullies) running with clear water. He was all but lynched on the spot for despoiling their water supply with his infidel person. We had been under the mistaken impression that the purpose of these gullies was to carry refuse away, but it appeared that at certain hours of the day fresh water was gushed through them for drinking purposes.

We strolled down the main covered bazaar, or *souk*, dodging bicycles and donkeys, hoping for some unusual souvenirs, but surprisingly the goods on sale were mostly inferior Birmingham ware. Lunch consisted of great mounds of saffron rice and thin, skewered slices of minced and pounded meat which had been cooked over the usual open coals. In the afternoon we were taken round a carpet factory and watched one of the famous Kerman carpets being made. As it was a holy day no work was in progress, but a special show was put on for our benefit. The factory was little more than a shack and the machinery merely two large wooden poles, one of which supported the weight of the framework of the carpet, with the lower pole having the carpet rolled on to it as it took shape. Two men worked in unison at great speed, one singing out the colours and stitches from a chart and the other complying with his orders. Very young boys also work on the carpets for an absurdly low wage, about 8d (eight pence) per day, and are in great demand for the finer knots which their small, deft fingers can accomplish.

Having seen how they were made, we were led to a magnificent chamber where the carpets were shown off to prospective buyers. We sat in a cool room overlooking a palmed indoor courtyard, and tea, poured into glasses placed in wrought silver containers, was brought to us. Cigarettes were pressed on us and small samples of the beautiful carpets handed round. All to no avail as far as sales were concerned, of course, as we obviously could not afford to buy one, as they must have known. Meanwhile, many people had gathered in the courtyard and soon the chanting of low voices filled the room. The hour of prayer had come and it was time for us to leave. This pleasurable delay meant we had to make up time, however, and we made good speed into the night. At about midnight, Paddy drew up and we flung ourselves from the *Indiaman* intending to bed down on tarpaulins with all haste. But the wind had other ideas for it suddenly sprang up into gale force and no sooner was a tarpaulin laid out than it blew itself in knots around everyone else's. Rene's favourite headscarf was whipped from her head and she pursued it helplessly into the night with much encouragement from the onlookers.

Large shapes of baked earth, near Bam, Persia.

It was a sleepless night for all of us and at the first signs of dawn paling the sky, we were up and away. Travelling on, we passed what I thought was a dead town, but it stretched for miles on either side of the track and it became obvious that no city of mud houses could have been so large. Paddy told us that the 60-foot high shapes of baked earth had once been a high mountain range, and wind and weather erosion had brought it to its present state. I was overawed at the sight and wondered how many thousands of years it had take to kill such a mighty mountain. Then there was nothing but scrubby desert, and soon even the scrub disappeared leaving flat, black gravel reaching into infinity. Nothing relieved the deadly monotony except a high tower at the start of this particular stretch, a beacon which had stood there for centuries as a guide to the camel caravans. It was not advisable to wander off the track here or, indeed, even to drive along it without an adequate supply of water. There had been one or two cases of foolhardy Europeans ignoring this warning and dying of thirst.

The black desert changed to sand dunes reminiscent of "Desert Song" scenery, and we came to a portion of the track, barely 500 yards in length, where loose sand had blown across in a drift. A Persian lorry was stuck in the middle of this, and another, in trying to bypass it, had sunk up to its axles through the false crust to the soft sand beneath. Several more lorries were drawn up at either end of the drift, and we tagged ourselves on at our end.

The heat, although it was only 8.00 a.m. was already fierce, and heavy digging out work was quite out of the question. There was nothing for it but to remain becalmed all day until the heat died away at sundown. Luckily, after Paddy's warnings, we had plenty of water on board, though it became warm and unpleasant as the day wore on. The Persian lorry drivers were most friendly and insisted on us drinking some of their cold water poured straight from a

Truck bogged in the Persian desert.

goatskin. There were rust drips in it from the radiator, under which the skin is hung, and a few goats' hairs and other unrecognisable oddments floated about in it, giving some of us a moment of doubt as to the wisdom of drinking. Nevertheless, we gratefully drank the refreshing water so kindly offered, hoping our weak stomachs wouldn't suffer too badly if the water was not as pure as it might be. Our Persian friends also spread out rugs for us under their very high chassised lorries, and offered to share their chicken mash lunch with us. This meant digging with our right hands into the communal bowl and shovelling the food into our mouths in turn. I felt a little doubtful about joining in this feast but didn't want to churlishly refuse such hospitality through any feeling of European squeamishness. I joined in with relish and ate heartily of the tasty meal.

Regardless of the heat, and to while away the time, I set out with Rene to examine a sand dune at close quarters. For fun, we childishly climbed to the top of a dune which had a nice, hard crust, intending to slide down the other side which fell away at quite an angle for about 20 feet. But to our horror, the sand on the downward side was too soft and for the first few feet we sank up to our knees, floundering through what felt like boiling water. Rene's shoe came off and it was a painful task finding it again, plunging our arms up to the elbows in the hot grains. We took good care to find another way back down around the edge of the dune. To further pass the time in a more sedentary manner, Nigel, Robin, Ron and I set up a bridge school under one of the lorries – quite the most novel setting for a game of bridge. Play was not really brilliant as the heat made us all a little hazy, and a strong, hot wind had arisen which tended to blow dummy all over the place, until we pinned him down with pebbles. When, finally, all the tricks we had taken had to be put in our pockets so that they would not decorate the desert, we gave up.

Around a quarter to four, the situation was surveyed and the boys went into battle armed with shovels to help dig out the lorry causing the first obstruction. After much digging, pushing, swearing and shoving, the lorry was freed and moved off to a rousing chorus of cheers. The boys who had helped in this achievement were revived on melon and had a brief respite while the other lorries in the queue got under way. There is, of course, an art in getting over ground such as this, and with all their practice, the Persians knew the best way to do it. Planks are placed in front of each back wheel and the vehicle run on to them. Further planks are then placed immediately in front of the first lot and when the back set are cleared, they are snatched up and placed in front again. And so on. If done with speed, the vehicle can be kept moving over the planks at a cracking pace but, if the rhythm goes and the lorry beats the plank changers, it comes to a halt in the sand and the process has to be started all over again.

We did not have four planks and the one we did have was far too long and heavy for the job, but the crew of the Persian lorry preceding us said that if we gave him a hand to get clear, he would in turn help us. It meant keeping the *Indiaman* within a short distance of the lorry ahead so that when he had freed himself the driver would be able to take us in tow. While the men went ahead to free the Persian vehicle, the girls, directed by Paddy from the driver's seat, pushed and heaved the *Indiaman* a few inches at a time in the right direction. We trod on each other's toes and fell in heaps when the bus jerked forward. To add to the general giggly excitement which was getting hold of us, there were plenty of scorpions about and when the cry of "Scorpion" rent the air, we all stopped work and leapt after it with, or without, shovels. The "Scorpion" cry was alternated with the cry ahead for "Shovels," which meant the lorry up front had rolled off the planks and had to be dug out again. Then the chase for shovels began at the place they were last used and thrown down. This didn't seem very satisfactory to me so, tired of being trampled underfoot in the pushing squad, I appointed myself Chief Shovel Carrier. It was no easy matter dashing about with four of them, ankle deep in soft sand. If I swung them ahead as I walked, I was in danger of chopping off my feet. If I dragged them behind me, I had a horror of churning up the scorpions. If I hoisted them on my shoulders, two a side, they just slipped off. In the end I managed a sort of relay race with them.

When the Persians were out of the worst of it, the boys brought the planks back to help us along. At last we were within towing distance and the *Indiaman* was secured firmly to the lorry, but we still had to aid matters with a combined plank-and-push routine. From somewhere out of the night other Persians had arrived, one of whom appointed himself as Cheer Leader, evidently thinking our spirits were flagging. He greatly encouraged the pushers with shouts of what sounded like "Gully, gully, hay" and on the last rousing "hay" we were all supposed to give one concerted heave as the towrope took up the slack. If we didn't do it to his satisfaction, he threw himself on the ground, buried his face in his hands and rolled about in a most alarming manner. The thought of creepy crawlies in the sand didn't seem to worry him. Then he would leap up and dash ahead to see how his countryman's lorry was faring, followed by the cry "Choop, choop," which meant planks were required to get the vehicle over a soft yard or two. I still do not know how we weren't all brained by the huge lengths of wood being flung around in the air. Hours later – or so it seemed – the *Indiaman* was out of trouble. We felt the whole effort called for a midnight feast and we went haywire on melon and boiled eggs, washed down with warm water.

The ground was not very inviting for sleeping out and I, for one, certainly had no wish to share my bed with a scorpion, so we decided to snatch a couple of winks in the *Indiaman*. Everyone seemed to drop asleep almost immediately but first I got pins and needles, then cramp curled me up and I slowly froze under my thin blanket. But even so, I hadn't the heart to wake up Sheila who was soundly snoring at my side, in order to limp out of the bus and prowl around the whispering desert. I watched the stars gradually turn round and the Plough disappear only to reappear again just before dawn. It was well after the light had caught and held the edges of the dunes that general stirrings began. We were soon all awake and anxious to get moving but our Persian friends, who had promised to lead us out of the desert at first light, seemed disinclined to wake up. The driver had tea brought to him by his mate as he lay on his bed under the lorry, and then lay back for fully half-an-hour to digest it. Then, slowing rolling off his *charpoy* he spent a further ten minutes either saying his prayers or washing his face in the sand – in my ignorance I couldn't quite determine which from his actions. Without haste, we ate a melon and boiled egg breakfast left over from supper and wandered about, but still the Persians showed no real signs of getting under way. So bidding them a most grateful farewell for all their help the previous night, we set off to find our own way out of the desert. This was not as formidable a task as had been feared and we soon reached Zahedin, the last town of any size before the Persian border.

Our first call at Zahedin was at the pumps in the main street to refill our water vessels. The water had an unpleasant salty taste but it was a case of take-it-or-go-without, so we took it! We were assisted, or perhaps I should say hindered, in our shopping expedition round the town by hordes of small boys who trailed along behind us, trying to lead us this way and that to the best buys. Their words of English consisted solely of, "How are you?" This was followed by a quick, coy, dash into a doorway, as though they had frightened themselves with their knowledge of another language. Any answer to this question as they dashed up to us once more, merely brought forth the reply "How are you?" again. There was one bright youth in the group, however, who spoke reasonably good English although we gathered he had never been out of Zahedin.

Leaving Zahedin behind, we travelled only a short distance further before reaching Mirjawa, the Persian border village. The Custom Offices were contained in a large compound and here we bedded down for the night. Again we didn't bother to put up our tents. We just spread out our tarpaulins under the walls before scrubbing ourselves clean under a pump which ran into a pool overhung by sweet-smelling white flowers. Other sanitary arrangements in the Compound consisted of the usual unwholesome holes in the ground inside a cubicle. Outside one of these little doorless huts there was a gaping cavern where part of the ground had subsided into what appeared to be a bottomless pit. It was sheer luck that no-one in our party had used this one during the night, and disappeared down the hole or perhaps twisted an ankle, as we didn't discover this trap for the unwary until morning light.

CHAPTER THIRTEEN

Through Pakistan to India

Jhalrapatan effigies are made for the annual festival, Rajasthan, India.

We had to cover some miles of No Man's Land before we reached the Pakistani Customs Compound at Nok Kundi. The roads were even bumpier than before, if that were possible, but not so dusty. Driving on the left is the rule of the road in Pakistan, but Paddy could not remember if this applied in the No Man's Land portion also. However, he drove on the left side of the road and hoped something would approach us from the other direction while the road remained straight, which might give us some indication. Nothing did come towards us, however, and only one well-laden Hillman overtook us, whose driver was pursuing such a middle of the road course that we were no wiser.

The heat was getting intense and mirages appeared in the shimmering mountains in the distance making villages appear to rest on lakes of water. Tops of bright copper brown hills looked as though they were floating in the air and disappeared into nothingness as we got nearer to them. In the blazing heat of noon, we pulled up at the Nok Kundi Rest House and Customs, where we were kept waiting an hour in the sweltering bus until our passports had been checked.

Nok Kundi is set alongside the railway line which our road had followed since leaving the railhead at Zahedin. To the few inhabitants of Nok Kundi, the railway is a very important line as it is the sole means of getting food and water from Quetta, some 300 miles away. Trains only run once or twice a week so food must be carefully rationed. Apart from a few chickens, no animals could be kept and certainly no food would grow in the arid, sandy soil. Huge heaps of stones were lying near the railway line which, on close inspection, proved to be chunks of onyx which had been mined somewhere near. We were informed it was a highly prized stone, chunks of which were sent to Japan. I picked up a couple of small, choice thrown out pieces for my stone collection which had by now grown considerably. Admiration had mounted for the way in which, after a trip to the bushes, I generally managed to come back either with a pretty stone or a flower. Peter had paid me the nicest compliment by saying he believed I could find a flower however barren the desert looked.

The Pakistani couple who ran the Rest House set about preparing a meal for us by wringing the neck of a stringy looking fowl. On inspecting the quarters while waiting for the food to be cooked, I found a couple of *charpoys*. Selfishly keeping quiet about my find in case a dozen other sleepy bodies contested my right to one of them, I laid myself out to rest. And there I stayed in splendid isolation until the call for lunch came. One mangy bird to feed eighteen hungry people was rather optimistic, even if it is stretched into a curry. However, there was plateful after plateful of glutinous rice and this, moistened with a drop of skin and bone curry – especially weakened since it was thought our European stomachs could not take the real Indian curry – made up a very welcome lunch.

We continued on through the Sind Desert. Little stickleback mountains obtruded themselves from the scrub and made a lovely setting for the waning sun as it slid in fiery, orange glory behind the miniature peaks. Endless herds of black goats ran down the mountainside, the late sun glinting on their shiny coats. I drew Isabel's attention to the sight. "Doesn't it look like the long rippling black tresses of a fairy tale damsel?" I said. Isabel laughed. "Yes, it does rather, now you mention it." John snorted from way down the back of the bus and muttered "trust a woman to think of something silly like that. I can't see anything but a lot of stupid goats running about."

Some miles on we pulled on to a flat piece of ground and set up camp in the dark. During the night I heard curious muffled snufflings and stompings and fully expected to be attacked by a mob of wild animals, but daylight showed us to have parked hard by the Nushki Camel Corps Depot. Freddie walked over to the lines to have a few friendly words with the Camp Commander. It was extraordinary how he always managed to have long conversations with people regardless of whether they spoke the same language or not.

Lak Pass.

The road to Quetta wound up and round the dry, brown mountains of the Lak Pass. Although it was supposedly quite safe to travel through these passes, it needed little imagination to conjure up visions of Pathans brandishing *jezails* and surging down from the hills with frenzied war-cries, ripe for a plundering party. Quetta still retained its English street names and there were many signs of the British occupation in its military quarters. I thought of the *mem-sahibs*, including my grandmother, running the now peeling large white houses.

We booked in at a hotel which could only offer us two rooms and four beds between us. Our first thought – after the ritual clean-up – was a long, iced beer brought to us as we sat in wickerwork chairs under the shade of a large *deodar* tree. After an enormous, very English lunch of Windsor soup, roast beef and Yorkshire pudding, followed by apple pie and cream served by waiters attired like Bengal Lancers, some of the crowd went off to explore Quetta. I just couldn't summon the energy required and lazed away the afternoon sitting in the garden, listening to John playing the piano. The flowers had wilted long ago in the heat and the grass was dead and brown. Not a breath of air stirred the leaves of the trees and I had a longing for an English garden drenched in summer rain. Towards evening, I began to feel decidedly odd and collapsed myself on one of the beds. I was past caring about the rest of the girls fighting for the other beds or curling up on the hard floor.

Our departure in the morning was marred for me by the fact that we were leaving Isabel behind, as she was taking a train to Karachi to meet her friends. She had been a wonderful and amusing companion and I felt I might be going to need a little of her nursing skills during the next few days. We headed for the Bolan Pass, passing group after group of migrating tribes, with the whole of their possessions – wives, children, chickens, tents and saucepans – strapped to their camels' backs. In endless numbers they plodded along the dried-up riverbeds, the reds of their cloaks and blankets their only touch of colour.

The road tied itself in knots round the mountainside. Here and there black entrances to coal mines gaped in the rock face. Back on the plains once more, bullock carts plying between the many little villages made the road look overcrowded. But the bullocks were well-trained beasts and, on hearing a distant horn, obligingly pulled to the left while their driver slept on unheedingly. Perhaps that is one reason why Pakistan and India cannot change to a Drive on the Right rule of the road, as it would confuse the bullocks!

We had little to eat all day, not feeling too hungry in the burning heat, but most of us were famished by nightfall. We stopped at Rohti Junction and walked about half a mile through the village to the Station, where a meal of some sort is generally to be obtained at the Buffet. While the others tucked into something substantial, I managed to down a glassful of hot milk, in between shivering fits and watching people grow to an impossible size and then vanish into thin air. Eddy gallantly helped me back to the *Indiaman* on his strong policeman's arm. By the time we had covered a few more miles and reached a Dak Bungalow for the night, it was obvious I was in for a bout of dysentery.

Dak Bungalows, or Government Rest Houses, which are to be found all over India and Pakistan at intervals of several miles, were built by the British for their touring officials. All personal bedding equipment and food was carried by the bearers of each visiting officer, so that the bungalows, which are now mostly used by tourists, are usually sparsely furnished. The *chowkidar,* or watchman, was summoned, or perhaps I should say serenaded, to our side by Peter who, having learnt and savoured the new word, sung out "Chowkidar" in a fine, bass voice in the manner of the "Wunderbar" chorus from the musical *Kiss me, Kate*.

I was taking little interest in the proceedings and only too glad to be put to bed by Sheila. Joan dosed me with sulpha guanadine pills which she produced from her emergency store. In the middle of the night I had to make a very hasty call to what is known inelegantly in India as the "Thunder Box". With no light in the bungalow and my torch left in the bus by mistake, there was nothing for it but to try and remember in which direction the little room was and feel my way to it. Perched on the "throne" and remaining there for a most uncomfortable hour in the pitch blackness, I wondered how many cobras were lying at my feet, carefully positioning themselves to strike!

Sheila took my temperature at daylight and greatly alarmed everyone, including myself as I had thought I felt much better, by announcing that the thermometer read 105°. Joan and Betty, the trained nurses, rushed to my side armed with bowls of cold water and sponges and proceeded to cool me off, while Paddy looked on worriedly and wondered whether to carry on, leave me there, call an ambulance, the hearse, or what. I really felt quite proud of myself being able to struggle to a sitting position and protest, whilst clearly almost at death's door, that WE MUST CARRY ON. A second reading of the thermometer rather spoiled all this as it barely reached a couple of points over the normal! Probably Sheila had forgotten to shake the mercury down. Even so, I felt pretty wretched and was glad to lie down on a made up bed on the front seat of the bus. This front seat was now known as the Hospital Seat, as from time to time, one or the other of us, not feeling too happy with life, stretched out on it.

It was a pity that from my reclining position I could not see the lush, palm tree country we were now passing through. The next thing I knew I was being rudely awoken from a health-giving slumber by the bus lurching down into a muddy ditch. The escape hatch being on the ditch side, everyone had to clamber over me to get out to inspect the damage. Fortunately the angle was not too great and there was no danger of the bus rolling over, but we were badly stuck. The locals gathered round by the score,

The bus bogged in a ditch and locals helping, bringing brushwood. West Pakistan.

gesticulating and shouting among themselves as to how best to help us, and then set off to gather brushwood to put under the wheels to get a grip. Whilst thus engaged, one poor fellow got bitten on the leg by a snake. Eddy immediately applied a tourniquet and cut the fang marks and made the man rest quietly. Meantime, operations continued. No-one seemed to bother very much that one of their number had been bitten and took it quite as a matter of course.

It was soon apparent that their efforts at digging us out were unavailing. "Looks like we'll have to get a tractor from somewhere," announced Paddy, and sent off Eddy with a party of locals to see what help he could summon up in the next village. When a tractor eventually arrived, we were dragged out in no time at all. Taking our snake-bitten friend on board, who was by now very pale and quiet, we took him to his home in the village at his request, and there left him with all our thoughts and good wishes. Whether he survived without proper medical aid we never found out.

In the early evening we crossed over the barrages of two rivers, which were part of the Punjabi Canal Scheme. I leaned over from my front seat, almost falling out of the door, and watched the brown waters foaming creamily through the sluice gates. This, the Lloyd Barrage, is a magnificent piece of British engineering started in the early thirties. It was designed to hold back the waters of the five rivers meeting at this point, and filter them through as necessary to irrigate the dry plains in the area. There had been floods near there quite recently and, the barrages crossed, we slowly drove through a forest of palms along a flooded road. As the sun set, brilliant orange, it almost seemed as though we were afloat on some technicolour film adventure. We found some dry ground on which to camp in darkness made light by the myriads of fireflies which danced around us.

The road we followed next day was dry and dusty, sealed for about a car and a half's width, with soft, sandy shoulders. When two vehicles approached one another head on, it was a moot point as to who was going to get off the road into the sand. Any vehicle following behind the one forced off the road was, of course, completely dust-blinded. We came upon a local bus whose driver had just been blinded in such a fashion and had run off the side of the road into a tree. The vehicle was not badly damaged but a man who had been resting his arm on the window ledge, trying to keep it cool, had had it crushed against the tree. He was bleeding badly. He could not be freed and the bus could not be moved. The rest of the passengers were jabbering away at the tops of their voices not knowing what to do for the best. Eddy did what he could, which was very little, and we hastened to a railway signal box, where Paddy asked for an ambulance and a breakdown van to be sent to move the vehicle and save the man's life. But the signalman said he could not send any such message over his wires as they were reserved solely for railway business. With time running out for the poor man, we raced to the next railway station some miles up the line, where Paddy sent in a proper report requesting aid. But it was too late. We learnt afterwards that the man had died from loss of blood.

It was really going to be a day, it seemed, when we passed a dog which the car ahead had just knocked over and injured, being torn to pieces by vultures. Then, entering Gambar, we saw the remains of a head-on smash between the down-train Karachi Express and an oil train, which had occurred the day before. Many people had been killed and sad, canvas bundles were stacked in rows by the track awaiting removal. A tangled mass of wood and steel was still smoking. When we came to yet another head-on road smash, Paddy began to wonder whether it was going to be our turn next. We all felt greatly relieved when we were settled into the Sunny View Hotel at Lahore.

The India/Pakistan border.

This time there were enough beds and rooms for all of us. We even had our own bathroom, sitting-room and verandah. Little green geckos darted up and down the walls in a friendly fashion but never ventured across the floor so there was no fear of treading on them. A sleep in comfort that night did wonders for us. After a vast English breakfast, I set out townwards with Sheila and Rene. Along the road's edge, *dhobies* crouched in their numbers over the ditches, washing gaily-coloured *saris*. They pounded the saris on handy flat rocks before rinsing them in the scummy ditch water and spreading the yards of flimsy material out to dry on any odd bush or scrap of spare ground.

Despite the copious directions the hotel manager had given us, we very soon got lost in a maze of narrow streets, overflowing with garbage and humanity. Cross-legged figures sat at the front of shops that were little more than shelves set above ground level and underneath which the stores were presumably kept. In some shops the vendor still lay on his charpoy surrounded by his wares of furniture or cheap brass goods. Fruit and vegetable sellers, however, took more interest and tried to invite sales before their supplies withered in the heat. The smell everywhere was rather rank and we were glad eventually to find ourselves out in the main street, right opposite

Shalimar Gardens, Lahore, Pakistan.

a clean-looking restaurant. No sooner had we entered and ordered our Cokes than we were approached by an Indian of splendid military bearing. "I am at your service," he told us, bowing low. "I run this café now, but I was once a Catering Sergeant in your Indian Army. Please be my guests. It is an honour to have you."

The rest of Lahore proved to be something of a disappointment as the tourist season was over and the Red Fort closed. Even the famed Shalimar Gardens laid out by Shah Jehan to remind him of his beloved Kashmir, were hardly worth inspection. No fountains played in the terraced pools and the dried-up vegetation gave little idea of the large variety of fruit trees and shrubs that had been planted there.

The frontiers of Pakistan were met and left behind. The old question of which way up does the banana grow was solved for me at last, as they seemed to grow profusely both ways in the gardens of the Indian Customs post. We were now on Indian soil. Parking the *Indiaman* in a square in Amritsar, Paddy led us through endless, narrow streets to the grounds of the Golden Temple – the sacred building of the *Sikhs*. At one of the entrances we had to leave our shoes and walk barefoot over the uncomfortably hot stones to the Temple itself, which is built in the middle of a pool and reached by a short causeway. The Temple shone brilliantly gold, reflected in the calm waters of the Sacred Pool, where Sikhs are allowed to bathe and purify themselves in the holy water. Inside the Temple, not a scrap of wall was left without a scroll, figure or pattern painted on, and a fragrant aroma pervaded the air from the flowers scattered everywhere. A monotonous chant rumbled on as the Reader of the Hour intoned from the Holy Book. This Book is read continuously through the twenty-four hour period, each holy man relieving the other so that the reading is carried on without a break. Other priests in attendance were handing out the traditional sweetmeats or cakes to all who asked, and I was told that anyone homeless may sleep there free for a night or two.

I fell into a kind of trance watching the proceedings and came out of the Temple to find most of the others had already gone back for their shoes. They were now impatiently waiting for me by a gate right opposite the Temple, having walked round outside by a devious route. Promising to be no longer than a jiffy, I hopped back over the hot bricks and retrieved my shoes. Then, of course, I found I was not allowed to wear them through the holy grounds to the other gate! I tried to conceal them in my cardigan and still go barefoot, but was hauled back and told even that was forbidden. I tried to explain that I HAD to go back through the grounds to reach my friends who would not wait very long for me, and I HAD to have my shoes. But it was no use. I just got redder in the face with explaining and the Keeper of the Shoes got calmer and more adamant.

A tall, handsome Sikh, who had been looking on with amusement at this exchange, came up to me. "Pray do not disturb yourself so over such a minor matter" he said, in perfectly enunciated English. I turned to him hopefully. "But what am I going to do," I said. "I must reach my friends and I'll never be able to find my way round the outside in time." He waved a beautifully manicured hand in the direction of the lines of bicycle rickshaws drawn up at the gate. "But I have no Indian rupees," I said, helplessly. Without more ado, the Sikh hailed a rickshaw, spoke to the driver, smilingly paid him in advance and, in spite of my protestations, charmingly bowed me on my way.

The rickshaw boy, a man of about 60, seemed to realise the urgency of the occasion and pedalled like one bewitched through the crowded bazaars. Naturally, the inevitable happened and in next to no time, I was being catapulted over his head into the lap of another passenger being ridden posthaste in the opposite direction. My rickshaw boy ruefully disentangled the entwined handlebars before condescending to pick up the other fallen driver, while a gathering crowd looked on with appreciation. Seeing no blood spilled and knowing how much talk was bound to follow between the two men, I fled off on foot to try and find the gate. I was too late, of course. The gateway held no familiar white faces. As I looked around, bewildered, a man – if man he could be called being merely bones encased in skin – dragged himself towards me on his knees and elbows, looking horribly like a nightmare spider, croaking for alms. I had none to give and fled off again through another maze of streets to find the *Indiaman*. By happy chance I located the square where the bus was parked but no familiar faces were to be seen. There was nothing to be done but sit on a bench in some nearby gardens and wait. Connecting my pale face and the bus together, an Indian courteously approached me and asked a few pertinent questions. Before five minutes had passed I found myself surrounded by quite a large group of people eager to hear all about the trip, their total grasp of the English language making such a task easy.

Leaving our Dak Bungalow and setting course for Delhi next morning, I noticed from my map that the foothills of the Himalayas were a bare 40 miles distant, but they were just out of our range of vision. It was tantalising to be so close and yet see nothing of these magic mountains. New Delhi is a modern and neatly arranged city, having been designed as a Government Centre by Sir Edward Lutyens in 1930. After a highly civilised lunch in Qwality's Restaurant in the heart of this clean, new city, Paddy drove us out some miles to the old part of the city to see the 13th century Qutb Minar. Built to commemorate the Islamic victory over the Hindus in Delhi, this structure is a magnificent pillar of red granite, fashioned in narrowing layers rather like a wedding cake, with fancy brick drapery at each layer.

With several of the others, I climbed the nearly 400 unevenly spaced, winding steps to the top. It was a case of feeling one's way up as, apart from slits in the stonework at long intervals which let in a feeble glimmer of light just at that point, it was pitch black. One is forbidden to go up alone as so many suicides have chosen to jump dramatically from the highest platform, but it seemed to me to be too easy to fall off without intent with the wind swaying the tower and trying to pluck one from it. The rest of the grounds, dating back to 300 B.C., included a 1,500 year old solid iron pillar, about 20 feet high. "Modern" legend has it that if you stand with your back to it and can reach round with your arms so that your fingertips touch, your antecedents are somewhat questionable. Without knowing the reason, we were put through the test, as are all visitors, but only Peter's long arms made the unwanted grade. The Dak Bungalow in the grounds of the Qutb Minar was locked up, but when night fell we made up our beds in rows on the verandah. My diary reads – "Eddy snored, dogs fought, birds screeched, mosquitoes bit, rather a torn night." Which, still clearly remembering that night, was a definite understatement.

The 13th century Qutb Minar, Delhi.

Paddy dropped us back in the centre of New Delhi next day and I took a hair-raising motorcycle taxi ride to the largest mosque in India – the Jamma Masjid. Its lofty domed white ceilings of the praying rooms abutting onto the huge, main courtyard, gave almost the same air of uplifting spaciousness as our more Western decorated cathedral spires reaching to the sky. Apart from shape, there is, of course, no decoration of any kind as none is allowed by the Moslem faith. After meeting up with some of the others, we gasped our way through the heat to the Red Fort but, like Lahore, we found it closed so were unable to see where so many of the terrible events had taken place during the Indian Mutiny in 1857.

We left Delhi fairly late that evening in order to arrive at Agra and get our first unforgettable glimpse of the Taj Mahal by moonlight. Eagerly we tumbled out of the bus and walked through the wide entrance gate and there, at the end of a series of pools, looking exactly as it ought to look from all the pictures we had seen of it, gleamed the familiar snow-white central dome, sentinelled by the four minarets. As we walked closer to it, I spared a thought for the 20,000 men it had taken 17 years to build this monument of beauty, dedicated by Shah Jehan to his favourite wife, Mumtaz Mahal who had died at an early age, giving birth to her fourteenth child. Shah Jehan outlived his wife by many years and was later imprisoned in the fort opposite, from where he could still see the monument to his wife, even if, as one story has it, only in the reflection of an emerald set in the wall of his prison.

We were stopped by a guide at the top of a long flight of steps at the side of the monument, who gave us cloth sacks to put over our shoes. This was so that we would not scratch the pristine surface of the marble floor. Then, lit only by the lamp he carried, the guide led us into the sanctum where lie the empty tombs of Shah Jehan and Mumtaz Mahal. Their actual remains lie in plain tombs in a vault immediately below the showpieces. The guide lifted his flickering lamp high over his head and we saw the marble screens of finest trelliswork surrounding the room, their lacy effect making them look deceptively fragile. More solid marble pillars supported them, each one inlaid with lapis lazuli, bloodstone, cornelian, agate and jasper to form flowers. In one flower alone, the guide told us, in an area one inch square, there are sixty different inlays, and so smooth you can run your finger over it and trace no roughness.

It was long past midnight when we dragged ourselves away from the moonlit magic. No Dak Bungalow was within reasonable distance, so we drove up a long driveway to Lauries Hotel but found it closed for the night. We carried on down the winding drive to the exit gate but it was bolted and barred. Since we could not back out in the dark, we had no choice but to put down our tarpaulins and mattresses in the driveway. The management must have been a trifle surprised when eighteen none-too-clean bodies requested breakfast some hours later but we were, nevertheless, cheerfully served with a large meal in the luxurious dining-room.

Peter and Robin were both preparing to leave us today, intending to catch a train

The Taj Mahal, Agra, India

across to Calcutta and thence a ship to Singapore. We dropped them at the station, where a series of porters lined up and loaded an assortment of luggage on to their heads, regardless of size or weight, only giving way to the next porter in the line when the load was about to topple off. The two boys seem to have accumulated a selection of weird shaped packages in addition to the suitcase they each had started with and which were soon overflowing. We did not envy them trying to keep track of all their parcels on the crowded train. We did not wait to wave them a fond farewell or see them scrambling for a seat but drove off, hoping that they would not have to cling on to the outside of the train – a very usual form of travel for those holding third-class tickets.

Scarcely thirty miles out of Agra, headed for Bombay, some important cog broke in the back axle of the bus and we came to a halt. Paddy diagnosed the trouble as a broken crown wheel and pinion and we sat disconsolately at the side of the dusty road while he organised a truck to tow the *Indiaman* back to Agra. Once again, we bedded down at Lauries Hotel but this time in fan-cooled suites, one of which I shared with Mildred. Mildred had the most amazing constitution, eating what she liked and drinking peculiar drinks from any available source without being any the worse for it. Fit and well-fed after an enforced two-day rest in Agra while the back axle was being repaired, we were eager to reach Bombay, our journey's end. Journey's end, that is to say, as far as we were concerned with the *Indiaman*. Some of us still had many miles to go before reaching base. Rene had persuaded me to come on to Sydney with her and it seemed an excellent idea to me as I had no plan to work in any particular city in Australia and liked the thought of being "among friends".

For the next three days, living mainly on curry and bananas, we travelled past fields of ripening cotton and dry jungle, and then over the Western Ghats, which gave way to lovely green country rolling into solid, untidy, rough-cut mountains which, silhouetted against the skyline at nightfall looked like a child's unsteady and unsuccessful attempt to cut jagged peak mountains out of cardboard. At last! Bombay, India. We were there. Around 8,000 miles and seven weeks by road from London, England. Just halfway to Sydney, Australia. But what was I really going to do? Besiege the shipping offices like my Aussie friends and get a passage onward with Rene as she had suggested? I was starting to have doubts. I had become so attached to the *Indiaman*, which now seemed like an anchor, a sort of home, that I was loath to leave it and go out in the cold, grey world. Cold world! It was hot. It was humid. It was oppressive in Bombay in October. We sweated through the day and at night I tried to sleep in a fanless room in the Y.W.C.A. Not for us the air-conditioned apartments of the famous Taj Mahal Hotel, that edifice so oddly built back to front because the builder had misread the plans of the architect.

Yet in spite of the heat, what fun it was to canter round the *maidan* before breakfast on a fat little pony; to stroll around the bazaars during the morning, sniffing the spicy smells and fingering beautifully worked shawls and saris, and wondering if our rupees would run to some of the fine carvings and brass trays; and to spend the afternoon in Breach Candy Swimming Pool, floating idly in its warm blue water, the churning brown Arabian Ocean a stone's throw away. Then, to have tea on the lawns, taking care to see that a choice sandwich was not too long in transit between covered up tea plate and open mouth, or a quick frightening rush of wings past your face and a huge bird would have carried it off, as happened to me. Quickly counting my fingers I mused how many fingers might be lost that way! To complete my thought a laughing neighbour told me the gruesome story of how a short while ago a vulture flying overhead had almost deposited in his lap the hand of a child which it had torn from a corpse placed on the nearby Towers of Silence. These Towers are the Parsee Burial Grounds, which are simply grids set high in a tower and on which bodies of the deceased are placed to be stripped of flesh by vultures, the clean-picked bones dropping through the grid to the Eternal Fire below. According to Zoroastrian worshippers, those who die may not be buried or cremated as this would sully the sacred earth or fire with the impurity of death.

In the days that followed some of us made an expedition across the six miles of water to the Isle of Elephants, once a mangrove swamp. Since becoming dried out, it is a favourite picnic haunt of the local Indian, who takes his carpet, his copper kettle, his hamper of food and his wife and family and settles down to a good day's eating. The local monkeys, mischievous little fellows, are all in favour of these outings and creep up on all sides to make sorties to carry off scraps of food when the Master of the Carpet has his back turned. The Island, however, was of more interest to us because of its fantastic cave temples dating back to the 8th century. These caves contain carved Hindu deities of immense proportions, topped by a nineteen-foot high three-headed bust hewn from a single rock.

Our evenings were generally enlivened by a visit to Qwality's where one or other of us was giving an ice cream farewell party. Bombay, being a dry city, we could not farewell on anything stronger. As the days went by, someone would depart for their destination. Ron was the first to go, most of us near to tears, closely followed by the others, all having found ships to their various destinations. I had still made no plans. For some reason I couldn't explain, I just didn't want to lose sight of the *Indiaman* and cut myself off from my last link with home. I felt very annoyed with myself for succumbing to such extraordinary weakness and allowing myself to be beaten by nothing more than mere depression and homesickness, but England was calling and weepily I made my decision. Thus it was that a week later, when Paddy turned the *Indiaman* for London and home, with a new set of passengers, I was one of them.

I was full of vague aches and pains. A complete disinterestedness in everything that went on kept me in the bus when I could have been sightseeing at the different places we called at on the return journey. Even when we reached Jaipur, the rose pink city with its romantic Palace of the Winds, I could not stir from my lethargy. That evening I was left alone in the Dak Bungalow while the others went out to "do the town". My thoughts turned to Norfolk. Beautiful, cool Norfolk. In June, the apple orchards glinting in the gold of a summer twilight, and a blackbird singing. In August, the fields of scarlet poppies swaying through the yellowing wheat, the larks trilling on high, the sudden whirr of partridge wings, the sweet-smelling cow-parsley edging the narrow lanes with a froth of lace. In November, the wild wet copper beech woods alive with rabbits, the evening flight of duck along the willow-sedged stream. And crowning everything, Norfolk's magic light which seems to shine like pale champagne over the flat fields just before it is blotted out by the blanket of night. Perhaps I would die in this hot, dusty country and never more see England, home and beauty.

I climbed into bed and gave myself up to paroxysms of tears. I found some pictures of Norfolk in my bag and squinted at them by the light of the moon streaming into the room, before throwing them on the floor and indulging in a further welter of tears. Suddenly I heard a thud as a Thing dropped through the open window and rasped its way over the coconut matting. With quivering ears, I followed the slight sound across the room and when I saw my pile of photographs move as the Thing insinuated itself under them, I took one leap out of bed and into the dining room next door. As I switched on the light, I realised I was clad in only the flimsiest of nightdresses, but nothing was going to induce me back to the bedroom to find more clothing. My immediate worry was finding a spot where no snake – for such I feared it was – could come after me. Resourcefully I wrapped myself in the snowy white tablecloth laid on the table and then sat on top of the table, defying any reptile to jump up at me or climb the single central leg.

In due course, the chowkidar came to make his rounds and became quite troubled to see the sick mem-sahib perched aloft, draped in the best table linen. He could not speak English and my Hindi consisted of counting from one to five, but by wavy patterns of my arm, I was able to indicate a snake in the bedroom. He shook his head and made squeaking noises, at the same time miming a creature very small and with a long tail. Mouse, indeed! I snorted and started waving my hands about again. Unarmed, the man braved the bedroom, where he shook the curtains, the matting and the blankets. He searched every possible snake's hide-out, but nothing showed itself to support my story and I had to retire to bed with ignominy. It wasn't until next morning that I noticed a grating in the wall by the bed where my snake had obviously lodged itself during all the pother.

A few days later we reached Zahedan. "Good grief," said Paddy to me over the morning cup of tea. "What's wrong with your face? You look like a Chinaman." He roared with laughter. "You've got jaundice, that's what." Immediately I felt better, but I regretted having shared that water and chicken mash lunch with the Persians when we had been stuck in the desert, as I suspected that might have been the time I had picked up the complaint. But at least a name could now be put to my affliction. I was heartened to realise that what I was suffering from was not Lack of Moral Fibre or fear to face a new country but simply an infection (Hepatitis A) which was notorious for giving one a poor-spirited attitude to life. In the circumstances I decided to leave the bus at the railhead of Erzincan in Turkey, and continue home more speedily by train or other means of transport. Travelling alone and feeling ill, the journey could have been a nightmare, but the kindness of the people in every country to help me on my way was heart-warming.

Low though I was feeling, I did not think it would put me off further travels. After all, I still had visions at the back of my mind of finding a sun-bronzed Aussie. A few months recovering in England and I'd be off again.

Returning across the Persian Desert.

Part Three – Back to the Bush

CHAPTER FOURTEEN

A Little Reminiscing

As the earlier chapters of this book show, I did recover from my jaundiced outlook on life and I did set off again and I did find that dinkum Aussie. And enjoyed some action packed years "setting up shop" in the place we called *Cooinda*. Now I was returning to England for a week or two of catching up with family members and reminiscing about the past, and hoping to discover whether I really was an Aussie or still a Pom.

March, 1974. A feeble sun dispersed the early morning mist as the *Himalaya* sailed into Southampton. Crowds of people were waiting at the dockside to meet friends and relatives. My brother-in-law, Anthony, was coming by train to meet me but I didn't suppose he would have got there that early. "I wonder if I'll recognise him," I thought. "It's been nearly 17 years since I saw him last." But he was there and of course I recognised him. He hadn't changed a bit. "Hi, Anthony," I screamed, jumping up and down to attract his attention. "Hi, Bonzo," he yelled back, as he spotted me on the crowded decks towering above him. To my chagrin, tears flowed down my cheeks at the use of the nickname. My dark glasses flew off as I continued jumping up and down with excitement, the tears continuing to flow. Oh, what the heck, I thought, it's probably a scene being enacted all over the ship by Pommies seeing England again. To me, it seemed as though I'd only been away a few months instead of an action-packed number of years in a country far across the sea.

Disembarkation began two hours later, but a further hour passed before I retrieved all my luggage from the hold, the albino buffalo horns proving elusive. Eventually the self-drive car I had organised at the Purser's Office was loaded up with suitcases and innumerable untidy parcels of steel pan, chess set, sewing basket, sombrero and odd carry bags full of smaller souvenirs. Then north to Norfolk along roads and motorways which were nearly all new to me. Occasionally, we drove along a road I remembered from my J. Davy driving days, and then it meandered off again and the new road system took over. All the towns with which I had hoped to make a passing acquaintance seemed to be by-passed. In between trying to enjoy the English countryside, I subjected Anthony to a barrage of questions on how all the family were. I had to adjust myself to a return to the family fold for a short time. I was finding it hard to realise that my youngest sister, Julia, was now a woman of forty and her first child, who had been only a few months old when I had left England, was a pretty, grown-up lass thinking of her first job. And there were three more boys I had yet to meet, plus the latest addition to their family, a tiny waif from Vietnam that Julia and Anthony had adopted.

I settled into their beautiful house in the village of Holt in Norfolk, and made it my base for catching up with the rest of the family and exploring England again. Elder sister, Gem, whose husband had recently died, now lived in a small house on the Norfolk coast a few miles away. I drove over to see her. She held me at arm's length after we had hugged each other. "Well, say something," she commanded, as I stood there, sniffing and gulping. "What's it like being home after all these years?"

"She'll be right, you'll find," I said.

"What does that mean, and where on earth did you get that extraordinary accent?" she cried. "Try something in English."

"Cor, stone the crows," I said.

"Hah," she said. "Now that's a bit more understandable, but it's still not quite the accent you went away with. Now come round and see my garden before it gets too cold and then we'll have a nice cuppa char."

A stinging wind was blowing straight off the North Sea and my face felt frozen, making it hard to appreciate the loving effort she had put into building up her garden. Fancy shaped flowerbeds and pathways, and a system of birdbaths and waterfalls (temporarily out of action lest the pump freeze up) showed the results of her endeavours. On a tour of her small greenhouse, I was able to take my icy hands out of my pockets for a moment and point at various plants that took my interest. "Prize lot of seedlings you have there," I commented, jabbing with a blue-tipped finger at a wooden box full of cardboard tubes sprouting greenery, "but what have you sown the seeds in?"

"Toilet paper rolls," she said. "You must have thousands of them in your motel. Don't tell me you throw yours away? Wicked waste if you do any gardening. Just fill them with potting mix and pop in a seed. No trauma at transplanting them then. Put the complete roll with its seedling in the prepared hole, slit down both sides, and Bob's your uncle."

Over a cup of tea we caught up with the past years of family happenings before branching out into general topics. "Australia seems to have done you good," said Gem, when I paused for breath after expounding dogmatically on some subject or other. "You seem to have got a bit of gumption. Not like the old days, eh? Remember how I always used to say you would run with the hare and hunt with the hounds with no mind of your own." I started to tell her of the ideas I had tumbled on that had liberated my mind. Ideas that had turned me from a helpless, negative being, swayed by the wind and a victim of circumstances, into the positive thinker I had now become, entirely because of Tom. But I got the feeling that I wasn't communicating with her on the same wavelength. Perhaps my blatherings were a lot of nonsense anyway. Maybe, as she said, I'd just matured a little. Only I could know that if I had not come to Australia and if Tom had not entered my life, I would probably never have matured.

A few days later, I visited my brother, John, with a wife and two children I had never seen. They lived in a charming old house on the Norfolk Broads that they had rehabilitated. Peacocks roamed freely in an olde worlde garden where green, velvety lawns stretched to the water's edge. They kept a few cows, hens, ducks, geese and innumerable rabbits and dogs. It seemed a wonderful atmosphere to bring up their two children. But John was unsettled. He didn't feel happy under the Labour Government in England and wasn't sure if his children were going to get the opportunities to expand themselves as they got older.

"What was Australia like for opportunities?" he asked. I spouted the glories of Australia to him. Land of opportunity. A sunny climate. Friendly people always ready to give a helping hand. I told him about the mateship, the pioneering spirit, the toughness of the battlers in carrying on the work of their forefathers in building up a new country. Although admitting no first-hand knowledge, I felt sure that educational facilities were excellent and I knew many new schools were under construction and new teaching methods being introduced. "Right," said John. "It sounds wonderful. We might come and join you."

I drove up to London to call at Australia House, wondering how I'd cope with all the new roads and the traffic in the city. I needn't have worried. There were road signs everywhere and a system of roundabouts which seemed simple, safe and effective and easily grasped by a complete stranger to the area. Although I would not have admitted it in England, I did feel that Australia's traffic system was sometimes lacking in a common-sense set-up. In Darwin, particularly, I had often felt confused with traffic coming at me from what felt like all points of the compass at certain intersections.

As I drove deeper in the heart of the city, making detours round suburbs well-known to me in the past, I became more and more shocked at London's state. As I remembered her, she had always looked slightly grimy, but it was the dirt of history clinging to her buildings, and any bomb-scarred buildings of the Second World War were an honourable eyesore. London may have exasperated at times, but one always had the feeling she was a city much loved by those who lived there. Now she looked tatty, unkempt and litter ridden, as though nobody cared about her any longer. Lovely old houses were abandoned, with broken windows roughly boarded up, and many of the large, elegant shops had closed down. Newspaper pages flew unhampered about the streets and a cheap and sometimes sordid atmosphere seemed to prevail. I wondered what my shipmates would be thinking of London, but questioning them later, I found most of them thought her quite a wonderful city. I was glad to reach Australia House at Kingsway and browse through Aussie papers and magazines and think about how lucky I was to live in such a country. I returned to Norfolk armed with brochures, pamphlets and forms for John to fill in, so that he too could live in a land of sunshine and opportunity.

A tour of both England and the Continent was included in the price of the Women's Weekly World Tour. There was little point in taking the English tour, but I decided it would be fun to re-visit the Continent without passport or accommodation hassles. I could then see at leisure the places I had missed on my previous visits when I was delivering cars all over the Continent to customers of the J. Davy Self-Drive Car Hire firm. We toured through nine countries in a 23-day tour, enjoying the sights, visiting museums, cathedrals, chateaux and schlosses. I collected more and more souvenirs, so that it was quite a struggle taking the various packages off the coach each night for safety. The wiser ones kept to small pieces of jewellery, cameos, and teaspoons, but I weighed myself down with a cuckoo clock from Lucerne, china plates from Vienna, glassware from Venice and all manner of other hard to pack items. I later found I could have bought most of the items in Sydney, and cheaper too!

Italy was enduring its highest rainfall period for forty years, and we spent our allotted three days in Rome seeing the Colosseum and the Forum in utter discomfort. The only time we were dry in our sightseeing was when we went underground to view the Catacombs. But rain or not, I sloshed my way through Venice, recalling the sunny couple of days I had spent there when a passenger on the *Indiaman* nearly twenty years before. It didn't seem to have changed, except the water line was gradually creeping up the buildings as the land sank in the sea.

The highlights of the tour for me were a boat trip down the Rhine, overlooked by gaunt castles perched on hills, the charm of Innsbruck in the snow, the beauty of the Black Forest, and seeing the graceful Lipizzaner horses performing at the Spanish Riding School in Vienna.

Back in England after the European tour, I still had a fortnight to go before the *Himalaya* sailed for Australia, and I spent it driving wherever the whim took me, reviving old memories, particularly of my WAAF days. The weather was warming up and the English countryside in sunny May was at its most beautiful. Colourful stands of rhododendrons, woods carpeted with bluebells, and stretches of daffodils in the gardens of old stone houses caught my eye as I drove slowly through the leafy lanes of Norfolk. Many of the villages looked much the same as I remembered them but Narborough, where my stepfather still lived, was changed. The chestnut tree over the village pond had disappeared, together with the pond, and so had most of the winding road and the old fashioned cottages that bordered it. Now a wide, straight road, lined with modern houses sporting TV antennae, carried a large volume of traffic. No longer did the villagers have to fetch their water in buckets from the stream, or make do with kerosene lights. Now electricity and water were laid on.

I parked in a lay-by near the crossroads, from where across a meadow, I could see Narborough Hall. I recalled the time my mother had requested me to return home from Chorley Wood, just after the war, when my interest in communism was mistakenly trying to develop. I looked across the fields to the empty flagpole on the Hall roof where I had hoisted up a piece of red bunting to my mother's horror. Now I called on my stepfather, Frank, and his new wife. They were keen to learn all about the motel which Frank had a hand in starting when, in 1963, he had "left" me the vital amount of money necessary to get a lease. We chatted away over afternoon tea of hot buttered toast, cucumber sandwiches and cake, in the gracious drawing room I had loved so well. It was rather a formal little reunion and I felt the raw colonial, boring them with my enthusiasm for my new homeland. But my days in England were numbered and the more I enthused over Australia, the less hard it would be to leave. Tea over, I found I could not bear to see the rest of the Hall again, conjuring up visions of every room quite vividly, even the vase cupboard under the stairs and what took place on the occasion of a Royal Visit. Full of memories of those happy days in Narborough, I said farewell to my stepfather who sadly was to die a few months later.

In a burst of interest at discovering some of England's prehistory, I drove one day to Grimes Graves, in Thetford Forest. These "graves" are a large number of depressions in the ground and have nothing do with burial graves. They are the partly filled shafts of flint mines dug by Neolithic man some 4,000 years ago. One of these shafts has been roofed over and preserved, and it was possible to go through a trapdoor in the roof and descend about 40 feet down a modern iron ladder to the base of the pit. It was an eerie experience climbing down into the clammy depths and fossicking about, imagining how the ancient Britons carved flint out of the chalk, using deer antlers as tools. The flints were then fashioned into arrowheads and other weapons. I couldn't help thinking of the Australian Aborigines, who used similar implements until the Europeans came along and, in a few short years, hurtled them into a totally different lifestyle. Perhaps the thoughts and experiences of those Aborigines, prior to colonialism, were on a par with some of those early Britons.

From Grimes Graves it was only a short drive to Weeting with its remains of a castle surrounded by a moat. William the Conqueror encamped at Weeting in 1066 when he was trying to wipe out the last resistance of the Saxons led by Hereward the Wake. Hereward followed William to Weeting to spy upon him, but the story goes that his disguise as a potter was useless as he had the misfortune to have one blue and one brown eye, so was soon detected and taken prisoner. He later escaped but his efforts were to no avail as England was shortly after conquered by William and his Normans.

I hadn't visited Weeting solely to see the Castle and think of the legends of history, but to look at the Church, part of which dates back to the Norman period of the 11th century. My own family history was tied up with a more recent period of the church. I sat in one of the pews, letting my eyes roam round the walls where tablets proclaimed that many Angerstein and Rowley bones were resting in peace in vaults beneath. John Julius Angerstein, known as the Father of Lloyd's of London, was an ancestor I held in the highest esteem from hearsay but knew little about. A certain mystery surrounded his parentage. As far as family gossip had it, he was born in St. Petersburg in 1735 and, supposedly was the natural son of a Russian merchant while his mother was Catherine the Great, Empress of Russia. But some doubt had recently been raised over this when some interested delver-into-dates realised that, if the year of his birth was correct, Catherine would have been only aged six. Here was a mystery which needed unravelling.

Outside in the churchyard, which smelt sweetly of new-mown grass, I found the huge stone-covered grave of Captain Richard Freeman Rowley, R.N., my great, great grandfather, who had married John Julius's (or J.J. as we always thought of him) grand-daughter, Julia. I knew that Captain Richard had died of cholera, too young to make the grade of admiral, which seemed to be the lot of most of the Rowley ancestors. From the picture in its silver frame, which always graced our family portrait table, he was quite the most handsomest of men in his naval uniform. I wished I had taken a deeper interest whilst I had lived in England, and visited Weeting Hall, the place where he had lived when not at sea. Now it was too late to visit the Hall. It had been pulled down in 1954 to make room for a modern housing estate. But at least the church and churchyard remained and had the capacity to provoke memory.

From Weeting I drove to Cockley Cley, the scene of my very first job in 1939, when I had so disgraced myself with my clerical ineptitude. Peter Roberts, my boss for the two days I worked before I got fired, was now Sir Peter Roberts. He had turned an actual part of his land where it had all happened so long ago, into a model village of the Iceni. The Iceni were a warlike tribe who roamed or settled in the area around 2,000 years ago, under their Queen Boadicea, until the Roman legions marched through Cockley Cley in 61 A.D., killing as they went. It was a fascinating dip into history to walk over the replica of the wooden drawbridge which would have protected the Iceni village from earlier incursions by other tribes. There was even the mock-up, lopped off head of some unfortunate enemy displayed as a sign of triumph on a pole outside the village. Nearby was the Snake Pit where prisoners were thrown to die from snakebite or from lack of food and water. It wasn't all war and nastiness, of course. Other figures dressed in the garb of the times were shown in the type of long house they would have lived in and how they occupied themselves in their daily lives.

From the tribal wars of long ago at Cockley Cley, I drove to Cambridge and on to Bourn to see the wartime aerodrome where I had been stationed in 1943 driving aircrew from Flight Offices to dispersal or wherever they needed to go. I had so often cycled along the road between Bourn and Cambridge in off duty moments, but now it seemed straighter and Madingly Hill less steep than I recalled. Many of the houses that had been friendly landmarks on the cycling trips had disappeared under new road works but, amazingly, a neat little bungalow called *Bonde Mteko*, a name that had always intrigued me as I cycled past, was still there.

There was very little left of the aerodrome I knew. I stood on the site of the 105 Squadron Flight Offices, now no more than a crumbling block of concrete, and imagined hearing again the scrabbling of bicycles against the outer walls as the Pathfinder crews reported for briefing. I "heard" the AFN radio playing Glenn Miller's signature tune *Moonlight Serenade* which usually coincided with briefing time, and the shuffling of the crews in their thick, lambswool-lined flying boots as they went up and down the passageway past our driver's rest room. And I remembered sitting in the vehicles on freezing winter nights waiting for the first faint sound of the returning Mosquito aircraft, so that we could dash to dispersal to pick up the crews.

The old WAAF quarters had vanished under a ploughed field, but I found the Sergeant's Mess and scrunched over broken glass, old teacups, papers and caved in walls, trying to imagine it as it had been. Another car drew up beside mine where I'd parked it on the roadway that used to run through the middle of the aerodrome. A young man with a red, fresh face came over with a brochure of some sort in his hand. A loose half-length tweed coat and muddy boots proclaimed him as a farmer. "Hello," he smiled. "Are you interested in this land too? It's not a bad piece but one would have to clear all those awful old buildings out of the way at once."

Blankly I mumbled "No, er, I'm just sort of looking, trying to remember a few things." "Oh, I thought you must have been interested in buying. It's for sale. Haven't you got this leaflet all about it? Jolly good farmland, you know." "No," I explained. "It's just that I've come over from Australia on holiday and I'm catching up on a few old memories. I was a WAAF stationed here in the last war." "Oh, that," he said, dismissing the war as inconsequential. "Well, cheerio, give my love to Down Under," and he got in his car and drove off with a friendly wave.

I got back into the car and sat there a moment as memories came flooding in. I thought of the Australian aircrew I had known – the crack Queensland pilot, Bill Blessing, who was later killed in ML 964 over Caen, Jimmy Malony, also of Queensland, and the oh-so-young Georgie Vance of Melbourne. I remembered dancing with English pilot George Whiffen at a NAAFI dance the night he joined the Squadron. He could talk of nothing but his new wife called Doreen. He went out in ML913 on his first raid a few days later and didn't come back. I remembered Pat Enderby's Mosquito MM134 swinging on take-off and crashing into a building next to the WAAF quarters, and how we'd had to make a chain of buckets to put out the fire – too late to save Pat.

And I recalled the time I was sent to RAF Manston to pick up a squadron crew whose aircraft, ML973, had been badly shot up and forced to land there in a hurry. Manston had one of the longest runways in England and was the nearest aerodrome on friendly territory for aircraft to land after a raid over Germany. Many aircraft would put down there, hanging together by prayer alone. On the occasion I was there, a threadbare looking Lancaster with most of its tail assembly missing, landed and lurched to a halt, slewing round with a broken leg and digging one wing in. An ambulance raced up and took away the wounded crew with the exception of the tail gunner whose remains would later be hosed out of the almost shot away rear turret. The stricken aircraft was towed hurriedly off the runway at the same time as a Lancaster and a Halifax approached from opposite ends, set on a collision course. As though it were actually happening again, I saw them heading to mutual destruction and then there was a blank and I could not remember whether they crashed or somehow swerved to avoid each other.

Shaking the grim thoughts of war from my mind, I saluted the past and drove off, heading for the Norfolk house of Anthony and Julia and my last few days in England. In the middle of May, I said my farewells to the family and drove to Southampton with Anthony. I took him round on a tour of inspection of the *Himalaya*. "It's your last chance," I said. "She's due for breaking up at the end of this year and this'll be her final time in England." There was still a couple of hours before sailing time and, after the inspection, we walked up and down the dockside. "Gee, it'll be good to get back home again," I said. "Just think of all that lovely sun." "Then what are you about to start bawling for?" asked Anthony. "I think you'd better whizz off while the going's good. Hooroo." "Yup. O.K. Toodlepip," I said, and turning my back, whizzed, whistling like mad. I wanted desperately to get home to Tom and yet England was still the land of my birth.

CHAPTER FIFTEEN

Where Do We Go from Here?

Our first port of call on the southbound trip was Lisbon, the city overlooked by an impressive statue of Christ with outstretched hands. The Portuguese weren't feeling very Christian-like, however, and with internal problems in the country, there was some doubt as to the safety of going ashore. But all appeared to be temporarily well and I took a tour which included the usual Castle. After visiting its treasures, we were shown over vast kitchens with their great cauldrons and heavy iron utensils. This made a change. After the European coach tour I had felt quite sated with castles and palaces, where each one seemed to have more treasures and paintings than the last. What interested me just as much as gazing at the magnificent gilt furniture and worn tapestries was wondering how they managed for cooking facilities and toilet amenities. We were never shown either. I had brought the question up at the Palace of Fontainebleau in France and was told the kitchens in such places were always kept far away. Footmen were supposed to dash at the double bearing silver dishes groaning with food to the dining apartments, and woe betide any footman if the food was cold when it got there. As for toilet facilities, well, the steps outside were generally used and an obliging, watching footman marked the spot and performed clearing up operations.

A day or two after leaving Lisbon, we sailed to Casablanca, but I was laid low with a mild case of shingles and missed going ashore. The next call at Dakar proved rather tiresome for the tourist. Dakar's bus system was unreliable, their taxi service even more so, and it was impossible to walk anywhere without being surrounded by hordes of itinerant sellers of silver bangles and other baubles. I bought a necklace made of nuts but later found it to be riddled with worms and it was confiscated by Customs.

At Capetown my sister, Billie, met me at the dockside. Billie had dedicated her life to the service of others and, after a spell in England caring for retarded children, had been sent to South Africa to a home at West Cape. She was very wrapped up in her selfless work. We chatted for an hour on the dockside, then I hugged her farewell and stepped on the tour bus to travel the Garden Route to Durban, where passengers would pick up the ship again. It was three days of sheer heaven and all too short a time to spend in the beautiful country of South Africa. I was saddened by the thought of the explosive situation she was facing with apartheid. We sailed out of Durban past the jetty where we were told the "Lady in White" had sung to all the troopships as they headed for battle during the Second World War.

In the middle of June, we steamed into Gages Roads in Fremantle. I'd been up early watching the dawn break over Rottnest Island. I thought of my first sight of Australia in 1958 when I'd watched the mist covered dunes trailing forlornly into the sea, and seen my first "dingo". Now, I tried to pick out the "dingo" with my field-glasses that had last spotted lion in Natal, and saw him still there, painted black on the yellow wall. Excitement reigned all over the ship but no-one could have been more excited than I, and I showed it, because of the 1,200 passengers aboard I was first in the queue that assembled for going ashore. "Won't be long now," I thought. But we seemed to have come to a halt in the Roads. There was a strike on and only a skeleton staff were working at the dock. It was rumoured we were sailing straight on to Adelaide. However, it was only a rumour and in due course the ship made fast at the dockside, and I disembarked with all my extraordinary collection of souvenirs and heavy bulging suitcases. A retinue of kind shipboard friends who were not disembarking at Fremantle, saw me safely ashore, but once through Customs I was on my own. Friends from Perth had come to meet me but I still had to get my luggage to them from the Customs Shed. I looked around for a porter. All on strike! I pushed and heaved and shoved my cases the required distance, my enthusiasm for my Aussie homecoming somewhat dampened.

After an overnight stay with friends in Perth, I flew to Darwin, hired a car and drove down the track to the South Alligator River, where I'd arranged by telegram to meet Tom. "Please bring beer and buff steak," I'd wired, "for reunion barbecue on river bank."

COMMONWEALTH OF AUSTRALIA DEPARTMENT OF CIVIL AVIATION	**AERODROME PAVEMENT CONCESSION**	CONCESSION NUMBER PC 4426 OPERATOR'S REFERENCE

This Pavement Concession is valid only for the operations specified below and shall not be varied or renewed without the authority of the Department. It covers approval from the aspects of pavement strengths and surface characteristics only and may be withdrawn at any time on short notice should significant pavement damage occur.

AERODROME	DATE AND TIME OF MOVEMENTS	NUMBER OF MOVEMENTS
COOINDA	21.6.74 ETA 1730 ETD 1745 22.6.74 ETA 0730 ETD 0830	4

OPERATOR	ROUTE	TYPE OF OPERATION
R.A.A.F.	Oenpelli – Cooinda – Darwin Darwin – Cooinda – Narbelek (A.L.A.)	Military (VIP flight)

TYPE OF AIRCRAFT	MAXIMUM A.U.W. (lbs)	TYRE PRESSURE (psi)
HS 748	39,000 lbs. (17,700 kg)	65 psi (450 kPa)

PAVEMENTS WHICH MAY BE USED
09/27 strip

LICENSEE (Name and Address:		LICENSEE APPROVAL OBTAINED
Opitz Cooinda Enterprise	Box 1090, P.O., DARWIN. N.T. 5794.	☐ YES ☐ NO

SPECIAL CONDITIONS

Conditions must be dry to depth.

NOTE: Where Licensee approval has not been obtained, it is the responsibility of the Operator to do so before operations take place	APPROVED D. McCARTHY FADG (GP) for Director-General of Civil Aviation	DATE OF APPROVAL 20.6.74

CA1539 (1970)

A special concession was needed for the large V.I.P. plane bringing Australia's Prime Minister to our air strip.

"Did you bring the steak? I'm jolly hungry," I asked Tom, after we'd enjoyed a welcome home beer. "Sorry, no time for dawdling," said Tom, "we've got to get back to the pub quicksmart. Big mobs of people in and the Prime Minister's coming to stay."

I had hoped we might have been able to enjoy our first evening together alone in the peace of the bush but Tom appeared agitated about leaving the pub for too long and I dutifully followed his dust along the track to the Jim Jim. Back at the pub, I sat on the right side of the bar after greeting all the staff and friends who were there. Something seemed to be wrong but I couldn't quite put a finger on the obvious tension. Then I realised what it was. Staff problems! Quite a few staff were working for us during the time I was away and there was an undercurrent of friction going on among them. And just when it was particularly necessary for operations to run smoothly! Gough Whitlam and his entourage of Federal politicians were due on a visit to the Northern Territory in a few days' time, and were scheduled to spend the night at Cooinda Motel. The motel was a handy stopover for a tour of the proposed, somewhat controversial, mining sites in the area then known as the Uranium Province.

Various government officials had been to-ing and fro-ing and bringing out special caravans for his party, till all was considered shipshape. Mr. and Mrs. Whitlam were to be accommodated in one of our demountables. However, a suitable bed had to be brought out for Mr. Whitlam as he was very tall and the beds in our demountable were just too short for a comfortable night's sleep for him.

At the appointed hour for the arrival of the V.I.P. plane, Tom and I and the officials due to greet the party lined up on the airstrip. I felt rather as though I were in one of those news films where royalty is met and hands shaken. Was I supposed to curtsey, I wondered. The tall figure of Mr. Whitlam unbent from the plane and I was introduced. He had evidently been primed that I was a Pom. "And what is an English rose like you doing in a place like this?" he asked, most memorably. Then I shook hands with Margaret Whitlam, a warm and sincere person. Their daughter, who was accompanying them, seemed a little cool but perhaps she was getting bored with visiting those wretched outback places which seldom had the mod cons she may

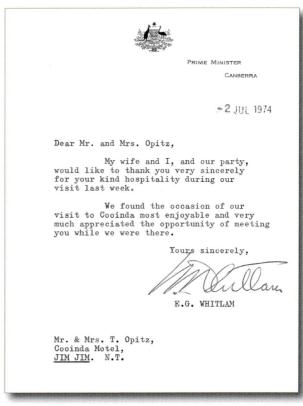

PRIME MINISTER

CANBERRA

2 JUL 1974

Dear Mr. and Mrs. Opitz,

My wife and I, and our party, would like to thank you very sincerely for your kind hospitality during our visit last week.

We found the occasion of our visit to Cooinda most enjoyable and very much appreciated the opportunity of meeting you while we were there.

Yours sincerely,

E.G. WHITLAM

Mr. & Mrs. T. Opitz,
Cooinda Motel,
JIM JIM. N.T.

Letter from Australia's Prime Minister, Gough Whitlam.

THE DIARY OF THE PRIME MINISTER'S WIFE

By MARGARET WHITLAM

CORROBOREE IN THE AFTERNOON

Jim Jim Motel, Arnhem Land.
NORTHERN TERRITORY
Friday, June 21

PERHAPS MORE of a camp than a motel but so welcome after a long day. Only 150 miles south-east of Darwin but we've come further than that today.

The proprietors of the Jim Jim motel, a dainty English woman married to former crocodile shooter and hunter Tom Opitz, have created a comfortable oasis providing accommodation and good food in a lushly vegetated area near the airstrip. I'm told tourist buses come here from Darwin, which is only about four to five hours' drive away.

The passengers stay for days and are taken out to fish in the Alligator River or to see the rock paintings, waterfalls or wildflowers. There's so much hidden in the bush.

We arrived at 2.30 pm via Darwin, having left Sydney at 8.15 am.

First stop on transferring to a smaller plane was Oenpelli Mission where the township was established 49 years ago by the Church of England Church Missionary Society. There are now nearly 600 people there, the majority

Directors of the relevant mining companies coincided their monthly visits with ours and in Jabiru we mixed social meals in the mess and club with discussions and inspections throughout the day.

We came first to Nabarlek this morning, 100 miles via Jim Jim Falls, which must be · magnificent when the water is really flowing. Difficult to see more than the confluence of waters at the top and the depth of the gorge.

Queensland Mines maintains a holding camp of three men at Nabarlek while the differences with the Aborigines over despoiling their sacred grounds are cleared up. Of all the uranium finds in Arnhem Land it would seem this has been the one giving most trouble.

En route to DARWIN,
Sunday, June 23

THE THIRD DAY of our visit took us to Maningrida which lies on the eastern bank of the estuary of the Liverpool River in northern Arnhem Land, 200 air miles from Darwin.

Here the population of 700 Aborigines

We hated to leave Jabiru (the word means stork and this splendid dark green, white-winged, red-legged bird is found all over the area) and its young pioneer men and women. There had been an excellent barbecue in the Jabiru social club. The young geologists, administrative officers and engineers and their families turned out in force and in finery, just as they would down south. Everyone has enormous pride in the place and the "camp" has the air of a good town.

Government House, Darwin,
Monday, June 24

SITTING HERE IN the warmest winter sun Australia offers there is time to think of our weekend in wonderland — of the memorable men and women, scenic beauty beyond description and the promise of activities which the world will envy.

My expectations of Arnhem Land were of a dry and yet grassed area, colourless almost. How wrong were the preconceptions. A national park of gigantic proportions is proposed — filled with billabongs and rivers, escarpments

cream) from the best shop in Australia. Must look at the new styles in bikinis and other bathers for nowhere in the world are they available in such quantity and such variety — well, that I know of, anyway.

★ ★ ★

Recently in Adelaide (Tuesday and Wednesday) a man of some importance from Sydney told me that he never eats in town in Sydney. When he wants to eat out he goes to the suburbs of Paddington, Redfern, Double Bay. And maybe he's right. Maybe the best restaurants are out of town (but not too far). Actually I gave him a few of my favourites in the city — Le Provencal is one — and he now promises to try them.

The South Australian Premier, Don Dunstan, is not so easily deterred. That same day he told me he now makes a habit of eating out and trying different places because he wants all restaurants in Adelaide to upgrade the quality of their food and the quality of their service.

I ate at two with him that day. The first was the Festival Centre Restaurant which really does have very good food and whose decor I enjoyed: white cloths,

Mention of the Jim Jim and Arnhem Land by Mrs Whitlam, July 1974

---

have been used to. But everyone had fun at the barbecue laid on for them, particularly Mr. Whitlam who kept coming back for more and more sausages, explaining that he never got any at the Lodge.

A week or two after the V.I.P. visit, four of the staff walked out. In one way I wasn't sorry. Wages had rocketed while I'd been away and on catching up with bookkeeping for that period, I found we were barely holding our own. Quite clearly, we couldn't afford to replace them and there was nothing for it but for me to be chief cook and bottle washer. A young couple who had not walked out stayed on, with the wife gallantly helping with domestic chores and being relief cook when I went to Darwin on business. Darwin trips were getting much easier now. The Arnhem Highway was opened with its bridge over the South Alligator River. To reach this new length of bitumen from the Jim Jim, we had to head first in the wrong direction and add a few extra miles, but what we lost in petrol we gained in time and comfort. The Highway from Darwin bypassed us by 40 miles and continued to Jabiru, a new work town that had grown to service the needs of the mining interests being developed in the area. Whether Jabiru would become the large town anticipated still appeared to be in the lap of the Gods, as Aboriginal Land Claims were being discussed, and the anti-uranium people were having their say, too.

Although I was feeling fit and full of vigour after the holiday, I knew that trying to sort out the financial problems of the motel and be cook at the same time could well undo all the good the holiday had done. I also found I was getting bored beyond belief with all the petty day to day worries that cropped up, and resentful of my tying responsibilities. We seemed to be getting no nearer to realising our dream. Perhaps putting in a working manager for a two or three year period would enable us to regain our vigour and carry on. Could we find such a man who might enjoy the challenge and not expect any great financial reward? Would an unusual life in the bush be sufficient inducement to make up for a high salary? We thought of a man we knew, full of *bon homie* and wit, who enjoyed a prestigious position in the tourist world. He was a frequent visitor, and had thoroughly enjoyed helping us out, quite freely, on many occasions behind the bar at busy moments. His wife loved cooking and had also helped us out on occasion just for the fun of it. They seemed ideal but whether what we could offer them for their more permanent services would be attractive to them, was another matter. Amazingly it was and, after long consultations, it was arranged they would join us, together with their children, at the start of the Dry Season 1975.

The future looked promising, not only for us but also to the company and the tourists to the area. With fresh blood and perhaps a new viewpoint, the motel could forge ahead and find new ways to please the visitors and make their stay a happy and comfortable one. Tom would be able to rest and get back his health which had been a trouble lately, and I could get down to writing my book and spend time and thoughts on songwriting.

On all my trips to Darwin over the years I would sing merrily above the roar of the motor and the jolting of the corrugations. When I had run out of all the musical comedy songs I knew, I had started to compose my own songs. I would stop on the side of the track at coffee break time, and jot down the words, and later pick out the tune on the electronic organ I had acquired but seldom found time to play. I put all my scraps of paper together, and found I had written about forty songs. Now perhaps at last I would be able to take them to Sydney, have them arranged professionally and get a backing tape made. Whilst I had no illusions about becoming some sort of pop star, I didn't see why I couldn't entertain guests in the pub by singing my own songs with proper accompaniment. The opportunity to do something about my ambition was at hand.

"It's almost too good to be true that you're coming to us," I told our prospective manager just before the Wet Season set in, "but I've got the most dreadful feeling you'll change your mind." "Don't you worry, I'll be there next April," he said, reassuringly, "I won't change my mind. There's nothing that could possibly make me change it." But something none of us could have foreseen did change his mind for him. Cyclone Tracy. All the world knows what happened to Darwin on the night of 24th December, 1974. I had been in Darwin myself on Christmas Eve, as the late rising of the rivers had permitted a few extra stores trips. Cyclone warnings were being played over and over on the radio before I headed back for the Jim Jim, but no-one took much notice. There had been a warning only a fortnight previously, and the cyclone had fizzled out. But this time there was to be a very different outcome.

A frightening sight greeted us at Cooinda at dawn on Christmas Day. Bearing down on us from the direction of Darwin was an ominous, boiling mass of sulphurous yellow clouds. But when it enveloped us, it brought only the slightest of breezes before

8—The NT News, Monday, April 28, 1975

Fisherman hooked

Reconstruction Commission PRO, Mr Roger East got well and truly hooked on barramundi fishing yesterday.

Roger went out to Jim Jim to try his luck and promptly landed a five pounder.

But when he tried to take the lure out of its mounth, the fish suddenly kicked and drove the hook into Roger's finger.

Unable to extract the hook, which had embedded itself in the bone, Roger contacted the Bush Missionary Society which arranged a plane to fly him to Darwin Hospital.

"It took six hours to get the hook out," said Roger, ruefully, this morning.

Darwin Star, 3rd February, 1976.

Roger East's body burned

A Radio Maubere message from Timor monitored in Darwin last night, gave more details of the death of Roger East.

A full account of his killing by Indonesian soldiers from eye-witnesses, was promised in today's broadcast.

Last night's message repeated that East has been executed, and added that his body had later been burned.

Poor reception made much of last night's message difficult to decipher.

The Darwin sub-branch of the Australian Journalists' Association, is expected to ask Telecom today for access to its facilities to hear the promised broadcast on East without interference.

passing on its way to dissipation. We turned on the radio. Nothing. And then faintly a voice could be heard reporting to someone that Darwin had been wiped out. We could not believe it. Some days later, when we were once more in two-way radio contact with Darwin, we offered to take some homeless families. The authorities, however, felt it would cause further hardship because of the problems of getting adequate supplies and medical requirements to us, and advised us it was more satisfactory to send the homeless south.

The man who had arranged to be our manager, had been on holiday in Adelaide with his family over Christmas when the cyclone struck. He returned alone to Darwin to find his home badly damaged. He seemed to lose heart. He wrote that he would now be keeping his family in the south. He suggested that as tourism was finished for some years to come, and there was little future for the motel, we wouldn't be needing him anyway. Actually, although tourists were banned from coming north, we were kept just as busy with construction workers who visited us from Darwin for some relaxing fishing.

One of our visitors during April was Roger East, the Public Relations Officer journalist for the Reconstruction Commission, who was writing up on the effects of the cyclone on Darwin. He came out to Cooinda to fish for barramundi one weekend but had the misfortune to have a hook driven into his finger when he tried to extract the lure from the fish's mouth. We contacted the Bush Missionary Society by radio on his behalf and a plane was arranged to fly him back to Darwin for treatment. He reported to us later with almost gleeful pride that it took a team of doctors nearly six hours to remove the hook without damaging the nerves in his hand. Sadly, Roger was to be the sixth journalist killed in East Timor by the invading Indonesian forces. When five journalists, now known as the Balibo Five, were killed by the Indonesians in October 1975, Roger went to Dili to investigate. But he, too, was killed on 8th December 1975.

At the end of June, we were besieged by caravanners and campers who based themselves at Cooinda and drove up to Darwin for a day to see the devastation. It was back to work as usual and my song recording had to be postponed, but only briefly. We worked through the season with the aid of the young couple who had helped us before, and then they kindly stayed on while I went to Sydney the following October. At last I was embarking on the first stage of trying my luck in the songwriting game. Allan Stewart of Nourlangie set me on the right track with his many contacts. I had no idea where to start but he opened a few doors and introduced me to Lal Kuring, a fine cellist in the Sydney Symphony Orchestra. Lal gave me tremendous encouragement and introduced me to David May, well known for his arrangements of Ted Egan's outback songs. Somehow David made sense of the poorly timed notes I had given him. With David at the piano, Lal on cello, a session guitarist and drummer, a backing track was put down at the Madrigal Studios. I was amazed at the sound that came out at the playback. The thrill of seeing for the first time something I had written in print was nothing like the thrill I experienced when I heard my music played by professionals. I couldn't believe I had written music like that. And, of course, I hadn't. All I'd done was think up a melody line and the wizardry of someone like David May had embellished it to sound like I hoped it would.

I decided I'd like to sing over the backing track myself for a final tape. Who knew? If I could sound as professional as the backing I had just heard, maybe there was a future as a recording artiste. Unfortunately one important detail put paid to that idea. My voice. It did precisely what it had done so many years ago at my last audition at the Coliseum in London. It broke. It cracked. It was soundless. It was completely uncontrollable. "You're nervous," said Lal. "Relax a bit." He made me a strong black coffee laced with a little something. Feeling on top of the world, I tried again. Same result. But why? I knew my voice needed brushing up at the edges to give it that professional finish, but this voice provided no basis for brushing up.

Back at Cooinda, over a quiet Wet Season, I practised in various ways with a head voice, a throat voice, a chest voice, a high voice, a low voice, but the only voice I could control was my speaking voice. Tom's opinion was that I was far too old to sing in public and I couldn't write songs, anyway. In the circumstances I didn't have the confidence to argue. I agreed I might as well forget the whole thing and settle down to attending to the well-being of the motel guests. Yet I couldn't help feelings of frustration and boredom with the continuing problems of running the motel on a shoestring occasionally getting the better of me. Fortunately, a year later, the man who was to have been our future manager before the cyclone hit, wrote from Adelaide to say that he was homesick for the north, and rarin' to get back to the Jim Jim. It was with a tremendous sigh of relief that, in April, 1976, we handed over the reins and Tom and

From Arnhem Land to Sydney with songs

13   The Sydney Morning Herald,

By JILL SYKES

The Vera Lynn of Arnhem Land has come to Sydney with 50 unpublished songs and a three-act musical.

Mrs Judy Opitz has had songs going around in her head for years as she shot crocodiles with her husband Tom and worked in their motel Jim Jim, 150 miles southeast of Darwin. But it is only in the past 12 months that she has recorded them.

Singing unaccompanied into a tape recorder she has put down a variety of gentle ballads, sexy cabaret-type songs and even a rock number.

She has taught herself to play electronic organ and guitar, but says she just can't manage to sing and play at the same time.

Her musical background goes back to post-war years in England where as third understudy she stepped into the starring role in Annie Get Your Gun on the opening night in the Liverpool Empire when her colleagues were sick.

"After that I did a bit of Noel Coward and some amateur shows, but in those days I was a bit shy. I suppose — just didn't push myself," she said.

"But I never lost my

Mrs Judy Opitz playing a rock song yesterday.

Sydney Morning Herald, *Wed., Oct 15, 1975.*

feeling for the theatre. Suddenly, in the past year or so, I felt I could do something about it.

"I composed most of the songs on trips to Darwin. It's four hours from home and you have to do something in an eight-hour drive.

"Coming down in the bus from Darwin to Sydney, I wrote four more." songs.

Shyly, and with a request that a musical backing should be imagined, Mrs Opitz set the tape recorder going in her Sydney hotel room:

"How I loved him,
How I kissed him,
But I never knew his
    name . . ."

Mr Opitz, who was hearing the tapes for the first time, encouraged her to play the rock number:
Rockin' is for oldies,
    yeah, yeah,
Oldies who were boldies,
    yeah, yeah . . .
Peggy Lee is fifty-three,
Dinah Shore is even
    more . . .
Even if you're fifty,
You can still be nifty —
Come on all you house-
    wives,
Do the Oldie Rock with
    me."

I shrugged off our responsibilities and retired from work, happy that our motel was in such competent hands.

We bought a Volkswagen Campmobile and planned a holiday around Australia, before settling back at our beloved Jim Jim. Once again, this time with belief that it was actually going to happen, I visualised Tom building us our little white house with the red front door deep in the paperbark glades. I saw Tom enjoying non-building moments in the company of his mates, but this time sitting on the right side of the bar. I saw myself practising the guitar and Yamaha organ, brushing up on my chess, taking up machine knitting, learning how to make more than just pillow cases on my Elna sewing machine, and most important of all, writing more songs and perhaps making a name for myself as a songwriter.

I had given up all thoughts of ever being able to sing my songs myself, but I couldn't get the songwriting bug out of my system. In May, I went to Sydney again, by Pioneer coach, to try my luck. I took with me the backing tracks that had been put down the previous October, as I had in mind making a souvenir cassette to sell in the pub. Lal Kuring was again most helpful and produced the cassette for me through E.M.I., with the lovely and talented Claire Poole Singers singing two of the numbers. The Claire Poole Singers were busy with the Perry Como Show and with Ginger Rogers who was appearing in Sydney, but they took the time to come to the studios and sing the songs of a nobody.

With an introduction from Allan Stewart, I called on Jack Argent, of Leeds Music Publishing Company. Tall, distinguished looking, dressed in black trousers and black polo-necked jumper, he ushered me into his sanctum. Over a cup of coffee he put me at ease and listened to the cassette of the E.M.I. produced songs, and also a cassette I had made at home of several more. He waved aside my apologies for the quality of the home-made cassette, and said he could judge well enough what I needed to know. Did I have any ability as a songwriter? That was the burning question. At last the unhurried verdict came. Yes, I could write songs. Yes. I could put a lyric together very nicely. Yes, they were pleasant and tuneful to listen to. I waited for the crunch. They were about thirty years out of date! They were early Vera Lynn type songs! Yes, he agreed, Vera Lynn's old songs were always popular but that was because they were part of a certain nostalgia. New songs written in the style of an earlier era meant nothing, and certainly had no

A rather fun publicity shot by the Sydney Morning Herald.

appeal to the present generation of record and cassette buyers. But, he said, if I could write a song in the modern idiom, he would see what he could do with it. I returned to the Jim Jim with new tunes buzzing round in my head. Unfortunately, none of them measured up to what I knew Jack Argent wanted! I finally gave up the struggle and consigned all ambition to become a songwriter to the pit of broken dreams. Tom had been right after all, as he usually was.

The season at Cooinda under its new management was going well. For the first time, I was able to sit back and chat to the guests if I was in the mood to do so, and without feeling I had to dash off to stir the soup or check on the roast. Tom was enjoying himself too, just sitting back with his mates over the odd beer or two without worrying about having to race down to the billabong to clear the footvalve if the waterpump suddenly stopped. Such responsibilities belonged to somebody else. We decided to put off our tour around Australia while we caught up on the relaxing pleasures to be found around the Jim Jim. It was as well we did. Our life of leisure was not to last. After a couple of months, our new manager opined that the salary the company was able to offer him was insufficient for the duties involved – and who could argue with him. A leasing arrangement was discussed which would have been an incentive for him to work above and beyond normal hours, but a

N.T. News, 8th July, 1976.

Sketch of Tom by well-known Australian artist, John Olsen.

rather large snag cropped up. He said our continued presence at Cooinda would cramp his style and, if he took over, he wanted us to go far, far, away! Naturally we weren't too keen on that idea.

Halfway through June, 1976, Tom and I came out of retirement and were back in harness again, ready for what the season would bring. Archaeological expeditions were starting to carry on serious work in Western Arnhem Land, which reminded me of Carmel Schrire's earlier work when she used to visit our store at the crossing. Now it was Rhys Jones, Harry Allen, John Kamminga and others. Personnel from the Departments of Wildlife, Water Resources, and Mines and Energy, as well as other Government workers, all made their calls for refreshment at the pub whilst engaged on work in the vicinity, and often stayed overnight or longer. One party of Wildlife Officers was accompanied by the artist John Olsen. During a convivial evening, he grabbed some paper from behind the bar and dashed off a few quick sketches

It's Jim Jim's best season yet for tourism

WHILE a shortage of caravan parks is seriously affecting the tourist season in Darwin, out at Jim Jim they're having their best season ever.

According to the owners of the Jim Jim motel, Judy and Tom Opitz, the season got off to a start in April, earlier than usual, and hasn't stopped.

More caravans than ever before are pouring in and hundreds of people have visited during the many long weekends.

The motel, with accommodation for 30 in twin rooms and unlimited space for caravans, is about four and a half hour's easy drive from Darwin along the new Arnhem Highway.

The major attractions in the area are fishing at Yellow Waters and Aboriginal cave paintings about half a day's drive away.

Water birds and animals also abound.

The season ends about November when parts of the highway are flooded.

But Judy and Tom are looking at ways to overcome this — probably a boat trip from the South Alligator river bridge to Jim Jim, which would take about four hours.

This would open up the area year-round.

Meanwhile, Judy is enjoying moderate success as a composer and is selling a tape Memories of Jim Jim at the rate of five a day.

The four songs on the tape, recorded by the Clare Poole Singers, are Coolinda, Jim Jim Rock, His Hat's Still Hanging on the Wall and Sunset at Yellow Water.

The tapes are on sale only at the motel as souvenirs.

Judy has composed about 60 songs which she describes as a cross between light pop, folk and country and western.

She hopes to interest a name singer in recording some of the songs.

Judy, a trained singer from England, had hoped to record them herself, but says she's "past it."

But whatever success her songs have in the future, Judy and Tom Opitz intend remaining at Jim Jim (or Cooinda as they named the area) for the rest of their lives...it's where they have always wanted to be — out in the bush.

N.T. News, 13ᵗʰ August, 1976.

of his party, including one of Tom.

Miraculously, I found I'd got my second wind and felt invigorated by the challenge and the exciting range of visitors. Instead of tearing my hair out in anger and frustration as I had so often done in the past when staff had left us for one reason or another, now I simply laughed like a drain at our staffless situation and tackled the hateful cooking with a zest. I must confess to a feeling of relief, however, when a few weeks later, Tom called me into the bar to meet some people who had just arrived to camp in the area. I went in and saw a handsome man with blue eyes and red beard, looking like a Viking, sitting at the bar with two beautiful, well-groomed girls. I thought the girls were sisters and undoubtedly models from their elegant appearance. We found out they were a Swedish family mother, father and daughter, who were on a camping holiday in the North after a few years spent in the southern half of Australia. They were shortly going home to Sweden.

Conversation touched upon our immediate staff shortfall and our new friends, Bruno, Margareta and Eva volunteered to stay a week or so and help us out until we could find new staff. The week or so stretched out and we put off looking for more staff. Our trio didn't mind the hard work, the odd hours, and they were willing and more than able to turn their hands to anything. They loved Cooinda and we loved them. And the customers loved them, too. Not every bush motel has a glamour girl looking like Doris Day cooking for them, or a beautiful blonde who should be gracing the pages of *Vogue*, waiting on them at table. Our Swedish family seemed to have identified with the place, so that it was not just a job to them but a way of life. Perhaps they might stay and take over management of the motel?

The Darwin Star, 4th November 1976.

MISSING HAT

IT WAS just a battered bushman's hat, but it carried some fond memories for the mob out Jim Jim way, particularly mine host of the Jim Jim Hotel, Tom Opitz and his wife, Judy. It belonged to John Barling, bushman and buffalo shooter, killed when his truck rolled during a buffalo chase about four years ago. Tom and Judy had been particularly close to John, and they hung his hat on over the bar as a simple memorial to a good bloke. The same hat has been celebrated in song in the ballad 'The Hat Hanging on the Wall', recorded in the south by the Claire Poole Singers. Last weekend, somebody stole it. If they don't know the story behind it, they'll probably return it, if they read this. If they did know, there's little use appealing to them.

The Darwin Star, 11th November 1976.

HAPPINESS IS

THEY'RE pretty happy out Jim Jim this week because the battered bushman's hat which had 'wandered' a couple of weekends ago has been returned with apologies. The hat, hung over the bar of Tom and Judy Opitz' popular watering spot, was a simple memorial to John Barling, bushman mate of the Opitz' who was killed hunting buffaloes four years ago. After last weeks story about the hat's disappearance, a sheepish bloke arrived saying he'd never taken the hat if he'd known the story. His heart was in the right place because he'd driven from Darwin to Jim Jim just to return it. Judy, who has already written one ballad about the hat, called 'The Hat Hanging on the Wall, is now considering another burst of bush verse called, of course, 'The Hat That Came Back'.

In February, 1977, we weren't sure if there would be any motel to manage or guests to cook for. Aboriginal Land Claims were in process of being dealt with by the Courts. An enormous area, in the midst of which our small lease fell, was now under claim. It was necessary to go to Court and put forward our case for remaining on the land we had physically strived for, and which was not being lived on by the Aborigines when our lease had been granted. Tom stayed to oversee the motel and pub while I flew into

Darwin. I attended the Hearings for several days until I was called before Mr. Justice Fox. A tall, stern man with silver hair and blue eyes, I had heard him devastatingly cut down to size anyone trying to be smart, but I also noticed he had a gentle and patient manner with those grasping for words. I was grateful for this as I am not an articulate person. I am one of those beings who cannot quickly formulate their thoughts into coherent speech. Perhaps I try to think too fast because words seem to come out back to front, and sentences get left in mid-air because I think I've already said what I meant to say.

Apart from seeking to keep the lease of our land, we also naturally sought to carry on the business with a liquor licence. There was some doubt as to whether we would be allowed to do so. Any restriction preventing us from serving liquor could jeopardise the viability of the business. Mr. Justice Fox had one final question for me which was quickly answered. "Could your business survive if your liquor licence was taken away?" he asked. "No, I don't think it could," I said. "And I don't think your guests could survive either," quipped the learned Judge, with a twinkle in his eye. The outcome of the Hearings so far as we were concerned, was that although the land around us was to be claimed, we were to be permitted to stay on our lease and carry on the business, complete with liquor licence.

The Land Claim Hearings were concluded and we still had the land and our business. And we were still trapped in the running of it. Our wonderful Swedish trio felt they wanted to return to Sweden soon. This time I didn't laugh like a drain at being left staffless. Coping with any further staff hassles, and the problems of trying to run a bush pub without adequate finance but in the manner guests expected, was by now completely beyond my patience or desire, not to mention my capabilities. Both Tom and I felt that with our present way of thinking, we simply could not give the tourists what they wanted. Since we were no longer an isolated oasis catering for the adventurous traveller, city facilities were expected. Air-conditioning, electric jugs, refrigerators, T.V. and other niceties were sought by the motel guests, as well as icecream, daily papers, fresh bread, a la carte menus and fancy cocktails.

Apart from the lack of finance needed to provide better facilities, Tom and I were starting to realise we were not really geared for the type of operation it was expected to be. We would have to change into a higher gear and approach the operation with a different level of thinking entirely. Did we want to? We were losing heart. Tourists were enjoying themselves immensely in the peaceful bush surroundings but we certainly weren't. This wasn't turning out to be the way of life we had dreamed about. How could we escape the way of life it had become? If we sold, the buyers might not want us to remain on the land? What if we leased? Yet if that was going to be anything like the last experience, we'd still find ourselves exiled from the Jim Jim. It might, however, be possible to ease our load by leasing the motel only, while retaining the pub operations. This would, at least, halve the problems and would permit of our continued living at Cooinda.

A go-ahead couple, John and Chris Bell-Booth, who operated a venture called Boothy's Safariland Tours proved to be the answer. They called at our motel regularly for accommodation, in between the regular weekly Pioneer Arnhemlander tours. We got on well with them. We couldn't imagine them being the slightest bit interested in getting embroiled in the task of running a bush motel, but there was no harm in asking. "It's probably a silly question, but would you like to lease the motel, ha ha?" we asked. "Tell us more," they replied and, shortly after, the paperwork was finalised and they moved in.

Our worries were indeed satisfactorily halved by not having the responsibility of running the motel but, after a while, we still felt the need for a much-needed holiday together. We got on so well with the Boothy's that we now considered leasing the pub to them as well as the motel. Their personalities were large enough to permit all of us living in close contact so we did not think there was any danger of them turning us off the Jim Jim. They knew how much the place meant to us, as it was also beginning to mean the same thing to them. They leapt at the idea when we put it to them, and, at the beginning of February, 1978, they leased the whole business for six years. Their youth, their boundless enthusiasm for hard work, and their up-to-date ideas could make Cooinda an even more exciting place for the tourist to visit.

Tom and I would live at Cooinda, not quite in our house with the red front door, but at first in a caravan. We would get a tractor and launch into agricultural work on the land outside the portion we had sub-leased to the Boothy's. We'd put in more fruit trees, particularly grapefruit and lemon trees which thrived so well, and perhaps supply the mining camps with fruit and vegies. It would be almost a return to Tom's dream back in 1960 when I had first met him, and he had wanted to start a vegie venture but had lost the wherewithal.

But first that holiday together. Tom suggested a trip to England, and plans were made to board the P & O ship *Canberra* in Sydney at the end of February. The ports of call en route sounded exotic – Port Moresby, Hong Kong with two days in China itself, Singapore, Columbo, Port Victoria, Mombasa and a side trip to the Tsavo Game Park, through the Suez Canal with an overland tour to visit the Pyramids and the Sphynx, Naples and finally disembarking at Southampton in mid-April. Could anything be more romantic than England in the Spring? I forgot our trials over the past few years at the thought of showing Tom the bluebell woods, the rhododendron forests, the white puffy cloud in the clear blue sky with larks trilling merrily. "Sounds delightful," said Tom, "but I hope we're going to visit a few little olde English pubs as well." There was to be a coach trip through most of the European countries and then the plan was to leave England in June, after a last stroll down a Norfolk country lane, heady with the scent of honeysuckle and wild roses. Then home to Cooinda.

CHAPTER SIXTEEN

End of the Fairy Story – Tom's Death

Tom and I on our holiday.

The holiday didn't work out quite the way we'd planned. The unseasonably cold, raw weather England was experiencing that April was too much for Tom. He had caught a cold in Naples, after walking round the ruins of Pompeii in the rain, and couldn't shake it off. He pined for the warmth of the Northern Territory. The bright lights of London didn't appeal to him and the only thing he enjoyed was a visit to the Imperial War Museum and feeding the squirrels in Kensington Gardens: the squirrels played games with him and cheekily untied his shoelaces. Our European Coach Tour was out of the question with Tom feeling so poorly, and after five chilling, rainy days in London, he boarded a Qantas plane back to Darwin. Our five month holiday was over in five weeks!

I stayed in England for a further week as I was on the Angerstein trail again. In the few days we had spent in Sydney before boarding the *Canberra*, I had spent hours in the Mitchell Library pouring over the Farington Diaries and other contemporary writings, in an effort to solve the mystery of who was John Julius Angerstein's mother. Everything pointed to the Empress Anne of Russia, not Catherine. Historically, Anne appears to have been a much-maligned personality and finding more on her background could prove an interesting adventure later. Once again I visited Weeting Church in Norfolk, checking more closely on the burial tablets. I was particularly seeking some further point of reference and the name of Woodlands, Blackheath, sprung out at me from most of the tablets as an alternative residence for many of the Angerstein family.

Back in London, I took a southbound bus to Greenwich and Blackheath. I had no idea where I was going and decided to leave it to chance, which had so often led me in certain directions. As luck would have it, as they say, I looked up from perusing my notes as I travelled on the top deck of the bus, in time to see a signpost pointing to "Woodlands". I leapt out at the next request stop, backtracked and followed the sign to a lovely old Georgian house. So this was J. J.'s. town house where he had entertained his guests who had included King George III, Dr. Samuel Johnson, Sir Joshua Reynolds and Sir Thomas Lawrence. The Angerstein family had sold the house in 1876, some 50 years after J. J.'s death in 1823. The tablet to his memory is in St. Alphege Church, Greenwich. The Greenwich Borough Council acquired the house in 1967 and, after restoration, opened it as a Local History Centre and Art Gallery in 1972.

In 1974, the year I had visited England on the *Himalaya*, they had held a bicentenary exhibition celebrating the building of Woodlands by John Julius Angerstein. Had I only known it then, I could have saved myself a lot of delving through records as other interested parties had already solved the mystery of the identity of his mother, and it was all written up in a booklet put out by the Gallery. John Bunston, Keeper of the Art Gallery, was most helpful and permitted me to go over the house with him, to parts where visitors are not normally allowed. I had the feeling I would like to sit alone in an alcove in the drawing room, gazing out into the garden and wait for thoughts to come into my head. But time was pressing and I couldn't permit myself to indulge in fantasies. Perhaps one day I might return and pick up the atmosphere enough to write a book on the Angerstein family. There was certainly enough exciting material, but I rather doubted whether my style would do the subject justice.

I left London the next day and flew back to Australia. Tom was staying with friends in Darwin who had mollycoddled him until he had shaken off his cold. Together we returned to Cooinda. But the smooth sailing we had hoped for was still not yet to be. There were too many debts owed by the company before we could hope to be recompensed for our past labours. The debts were being paid off by the incoming lease rental but we had very little ready cash money for ourselves. I was willing to do any

April 1979. In order to have an interest and an income, we opened the Bush Boutique in a shed behind the motel on the main site. Due to the small range of goods we could sell that didn't compete with the Bell-Booth's range, the business could not prosper.

job in the motel but our lessees did not want to employ us, saying it would not look right. We had the idea of re-opening the old store over at the crossing. It was looking tumbledown and deserted but a quick redecoration soon had it spick and span again and we turned it into a small bush boutique.

This proved hardly lucrative as all callers – and there was no shortage of them – wanted cool soft drinks and snacks, not shorts, shirts, hats and sundresses. The Boothy's, with an understandable and proper business-like attitude, naturally objected to us selling anything which may have been in competition with them. The store was once more closed and we returned to the main motel site. I tried the Bush Boutique idea in a shed behind the motel, again selling sundresses I made myself, sarongs, sunhats and such like. In this location, it went quite well, but not well enough.

Tom was not unduly worried. After the cares and tribulations of the past few years, he had relaxed completely, and now enjoyed nothing better than to sit under his favourite mango tree, chatting to his mates. His sense of humour, his generosity, his one-of-the-boys outlook had made him a very popular figure over the years when he had served in the pub. During that pub time, he appeared to have a very strong head and beer had had no noticeable effect on him. This was as well as he was the recipient of many shouts from his friends but, when they had had enough, they could leave the pub and go and sleep it off. Tom always chose to remain on duty to serve whoever was in the bar. Drinking sessions went on far into the night. Any pleas I made, when I woke up around 3.00 a.m. and went groggily back to the bar suggesting it was time to close up, fell on deaf ears.

There was still no shortage of mates who wanted to drink with him. From 6.00 a.m. onwards, they would roll up with their 6-pack of beer. This, along with Tom's shout exhausted, they would leave to go fishing, or whatever their plans for the day were. A few minutes later, another set of mates with 6-packs would roll up. Beer in such liberal quantities must try anyone's constitution, and I was starting to see signs of the damage it was doing to Tom. I had the terrible feeling his mates could ruin his health and hasten his death, but "What of it?" said Tom, blithely. "They'll give me a bloody good funeral." I mentioned my fears for his health to a close friend of his, but my fears were laughed away with the friend merely saying, "What a way to go, eh?" and "Tom's happy, so what are you worrying about?"

I wished I could relax like Tom but money problems continued to haunt me, and entertainment under the mango tree did not come cheaply. Two things could happen. We would have to cut our expenses drastically or increase our income. To curb Tom's carefree happiness after his years of slogging, seemed unkind. There had to be a way to increase the income. On a shopping trip to Darwin, I happened to stroll around the Jape Shopping Centre. In the window of Elaine's Uniform Shop, I saw a sign reading "This Shop for Sale". "Oh, well, in for a penny, in for a pound," I thought, and called on the Bank Manager to see if I could borrow some money to buy it.

A couple of weeks later the shop was mine. A girl who had worked in the motel managed it for me while I visited Melbourne to call on wholesalers, and tried to find my feet in the shop proprietor world. I was amazed at the range of uniforms available. I had thought a uniform meant a rather shapeless garment worn over one's ordinary clothes, and was astonished to find the trim tailoring which went into business girls' uniforms. Elaine, from whom I had bought the shop, retired to have her baby and Judy's Uniform Shop came into being. It set the scene for our personal financial recovery, but it meant I had to work it myself as wages paid for someone else to run it would not have made it worthwhile.

I found a bed-sitter in Darwin and only got home at weekends. So much for our home life together at Cooinda! I didn't like being away from Tom, but there was no way we could live there without an income. Tom's fruit trees, which were his pride and joy, would hopefully be a source of income later, but that day seemed a long way off. When it did finally come, perhaps I could sell the shop and rejoin him at Cooinda. In the meantime, perhaps there was a way of earning money and living at the Jim Jim. We would buy a suitable safari vehicle and Tom and I could operate day tours in the area. I would also keep on the Uniform Shop, but put in a girl to run it. The vehicle was acquired, the business name *Cooinda Land and Water Tours* duly registered and painted on the side of the vehicle, and brochures put out. We would not ourselves operate the boat cruise part of it but make use of the services of our lessees, John and Chris Bell-Booth who were now operating such tours. We would however, be doing the road content.

Unfortunately I had underestimated the extent of Tom's health problems. Lacking the fitness he had always prided himself on having, he suddenly lost heart and momentum for any further personal involvement in the tours. After a couple of trips with a stand-in driver, the tours folded but I still had the Uniform Shop to run, and our weekly separation continued. By now the thought was beginning to creep into our minds as to whether we still wanted to live at Cooinda.

It was no longer the place we had loved so much. The earlier ambience of the bush that had so appealed to us had disappeared. It had lost what it once had, with so many people about, new bitumen roads cutting across the land and constant traffic. And yet wasn't that part of what we had planned – to make it easier to bring the beauty of the area to the notice of visitors? In this we had certainly succeeded but Tom was now beset with guilt and believed he had destroyed the very thing he wanted above all to cherish. He didn't seem to realise that if he had had no hand in it, there would have been someone else who would have brought about such change. All he saw was that we had quite successfully killed a place of peace and beauty by seeking to share it with others.

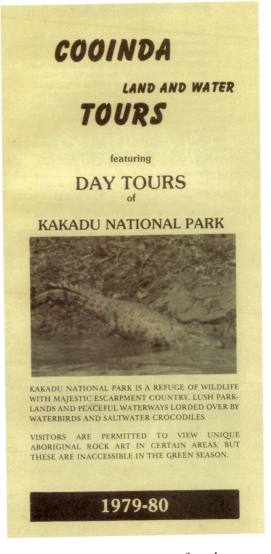

COOINDA

LAND AND WATER

TOURS

featuring

DAY TOURS
of

KAKADU NATIONAL PARK

KAKADU NATIONAL PARK IS A REFUGE OF WILDLIFE WITH MAJESTIC ESCARPMENT COUNTRY, LUSH PARK-LANDS AND PEACEFUL WATERWAYS LORDED OVER BY WATERBIRDS AND SALTWATER CROCODILES.

VISITORS ARE PERMITTED TO VIEW UNIQUE ABORIGINAL ROCK ART IN CERTAIN AREAS, BUT THESE ARE INACCESSIBLE IN THE GREEN SEASON.

1979-80

It was a sad fact of life that so many of those others were not after the same feeling of relationship to the land that we felt. The majority of pub visitors merely saw it as another convivial watering hole, where they could clink their tinnies (cans of beer) and discuss the state of their particular worlds. To others, it was a good camping spot, where they crowded themselves together, turned their trannies (transistors) up to cover the raucous cries of the cockatoos, and zoomed up the billabong in high-powered motor boats. To some, it was one of the best places to stock up the deep freezers with barramundi. Only a very few caught the magical mystery of the place. And, sadly, we were starting to find that the aura of magic which had captivated us enough to make us want to live at the Jim Jim "for ever," completely at one with nature, had been swamped by the pressures involved in trying to attain our goal.

The country surrounding Cooinda was changed too. The opening of the uranium mines meant the narrow, winding, rain-rutted tracks had now become wide, straight,

Cooinda Land and Water Tours. By December 1979, hiring a casual driver for the tours makes it unprofitable and it is reluctantly decided to sell the vehicle and venture. There are no takers.

usually corrugated dirt roads. A trip to the East Alligator River was no longer an adventure along a track so unworn that now you saw it, then you didn't, with buffaloes snorting in your path. The track no longer skirted a forest thick with wallabies peering out from the long grass, past lagoons seething with water bird life. A new road had been cut through the forest and the only adventure was in trying to avoid getting covered in dust when heavy trucks passed at great speed about their lawful business to one mine or another.

It was, of course, true that you could still see wildlife at selected places, but you were no longer a part of it, just an onlooker. To most tourists this was an insignificant difference and a visit to the area was a highlight of many of their tours. Disillusioned, Tom now thought it might be best to sell motel and pub and make a complete break with the area. So it was that we came to the reluctant conclusion that it might be better to sell the motel, and leave the Jim Jim. With the money gained, we would head off for pastures new, and try and forget our earlier dreams. Accordingly, arrangements for an auction were put in hand by a real estate agent. These plans came to naught as the Traditional Owners of the land surrounding our lease were not in favour of an "outsider" coming in. The Traditional Owners, who later formed themselves into the Gagudju Association, made an offer which, as there was no reasonable alternative, was accepted. They also bought the interests of our lessees, John and Chris Bell-Booth.

The Opitz "Cooinda" Enterprises Company was wound up and we duly received

our share of the proceeds. The Traditional Owners, who included Mick Alderson, son of Yorky Billy who had died only recently and for whom we had had such high regard, gave us a present of a quarter acre of land at Cooinda. There we could build a house and live there for our lifetimes if we so chose. It was an unexpected and gracious gesture which we treasured: it was like a lifebuoy thrown to us which could perhaps have the capacity to bring us back to our dreams. However, our plans had advanced to the point where we felt that first we should try an entirely new life in North Queensland.

Judy's Uniform Shop was sold for a happy price, our few belongings were packed up and in November, 1980, Tom and I set off for Queensland. Tom drove the diesel one-ton Toyota ute we had bought from the Company and I followed in a recently purchased Toyota Land Cruiser. Mine was going to be a far more comfortable ride as I had a radio, cassette player and an air-conditioner. November is not the best time of year to travel the Barkly Highway with its scorching dry heat. Both vehicles were well loaded. Mine included Hobo, the dog. Hobo was not, of course, the same animal who had first accompanied us to the Jim Jim but was a stray who had been dumped in the bush by his owner and left to fend for himself. He had been a faithful friend to us over the last few years.

A week or so later we pulled into the San Remo Motel at Holloways Beach, a few kilometres north of Cairns, which was to be our base until we decided where to settle. We parked the diesel Toyota and toured in the Land Cruiser up to Cooktown, to Daintree, Cape Tribulation, and Port Douglas with its old world charm. We drove to Innisfail, Mission Beach and Etty Bay. We travelled the narrow, winding Palmerston Highway, dodging the milk trucks taking milk from Malanda to Darwin, the Kennedy

Titles to land handed over

MEN   N.T. News   11/8/80

TITLES to land claimed under the Land Rights Act were handed to Aboriginal land trust officials in separate ceremonies at Kakadu and Delissaville on Friday.

The handover comes after a protracted dispute between the Northern Land Council and the Federal and Territory Governments.

The Territory Government refused to register the land titles until it was given control of "public" roads across Aboriginal land.

NLC representatives demanded that the Government specify the roads considered to be public roads, but were thwarted when the Federal Government amended the Land Rights Act.

(From right) Senator Bernie Kilgariff hands copies of the Kakadu title to traditional owner Toby Gangali and land trust chairman, Mick Aoderson, while Mick's wife, Stephanie looks on.

Northern Territory News, 11th August, 1980.

Highway to Kuranda with its picturesque railway station, up the corkscrewing Gillies Highway and down the Rex Highway with its fabulous views from the top. We visited most of the beaches, each one more inviting than the last. The mountains were green and beautiful, the sea was blue and beautiful, the sand was golden and beautiful.

It was totally different to the Jim Jim but the staggering variety of scenery had us spellbound. The mystique of the mountains in the early morning mist, the lush rolling hill pastures grazed by fat Friesian or Jersey cows, the fantastic world of coral and strangely marked tropical fish viewed from a glass-bottomed boat, compelled us to agree with the tourist brochures that North Queensland is truly a paradise. We were ready to settle down.

In January, 1981, we found ourselves 80 acres of green hills and rainforest nestling at the foot of Mount Bellenden Kerr, just outside Babinda. The Queensland-style

● **Tom and Judy Opitz prepare to leave Darwin after pioneering at Jim Ji**

house needed some renovations but it was just what we wanted, set well back from the road and completely hidden by the tall sugar cane in season. A small tributary of Frenchman's Creek ran sparkling through the property. Just outside the property we could climb a hill, which had been cut through the rainforest to accommodate a water pipe line, up to a series of waterfalls tumbling furiously over huge boulders into fuming spray. Staghorn and birdsnest ferns and orchids grew in profusion in the trees which rose nearly a hundred feet in the air, and lawyer vines twisted their way through the heavy undergrowth where cassowary and wild pigs lived.

We moved in and Tom set to work pulling out old cupboards, putting in new ones, and organising a new roof on the house. We bought a tractor and Tom cleared the ground to take a few bananas and a variety of vegetables, with the idea of establishing a market garden. Enormous blue-winged butterflies flitted about as he toiled but there was a peculiar dearth of birds. In other gardens we had noticed the ubiquitous willy wagtail, and peaceful doves, plovers, and ibis, but they seemed to give our place

Opitz saga at an end

By DICK MUDDIMER

OM and Judy Opitz are ving the Top End to draw a close one of the great neering sagas of the last years.

ey went out to the Jim Jim crossing e Alligator Rivers country in 1964 a tent, brickmaking machine, elbarrow and a dog and a cat.

ey finished up with $300,000 dev- ments at the Jim Jim store and the nda motel.

ogether, they spanned an era of natic change and an awakening e timeless bush.

e Opitz team landed in the Top End widely different backgrounds.

m was production executive for Hoist company in Adelaide,

N.T. News, 4th November, 1980.

quitting modern industrial pressures as a deliberate act.

Judy came from a gentler English background. One grandfather was Viscount Molesworth and another forebear was Julius Angerstein, a reversed figure in the history of insur- ers, Lloyds of London.

The turning point came when they both worked in 1960 with "Great White Hunter" Alan Stewart at his safari camp a Nourlangie.

Alan Stewart, sometime journalist, advertising man and politician, always had a vision that the Alligator Rivers country would become a tourist drawcard.

Tom and Judy Opitz caught the Stewart enthusiasm and joined pioneers in the region including aviator Frank Muir of Murella Park and Don McGregor of Patonga.

They started on their own in 1964, with the wheelbarrow more important than anything else.

One can of beer has to last six months and they saved it to have half a can each one Christmas Day.

On Hunting trips, Judy swam across croc- odile infested lagoons after game, otherwise they did not eat.

They preserved, and opened the Jim Jim store in 1965 for travellers on the old Oenpelli track.

They battled on to build the Cooinda hotel- motel.

This was leased to Booth's tours in 1978, and last year sold at auction to the Gagudja Aboriginal Association, representing the area's traditional owners.

It was time for the Opitz couple to move on, and they left Jim Jim for the last time yesterday.

At farewells, traditional owner, Toby Gungali and the Gagudja Assoc- iation presented them with some land for life.

The block, which includes a cabin and Tom's mago tree, was a mark that the Aborig- ines considered it was Opitz country as well as theirs.

Tom and Judy Opitz now turn their backs on Jim Jim, leaving Darwin tomorrow to start a new life at Port Douglas in North Queensland.

---

a miss. We wondered if some chemical had been sprayed on the sugar cane in the adjacent paddock, and that this had killed the bugs which the birds ate. Nevertheless, Tom's garden flourished. Tomato bushes grew thick and green in the infant state, while cucumbers, zucchinis, melon and pumpkin, rows of carnations and sweet peas pushed their way through the earth and healthily put a great spurt of growth on.

Meantime, partly to augment the income, partly for fun and partly because I was flushed with the success of my Uniform Shop in Darwin, I decided I'd like to own another shop business of some sort in Cairns. It would be my intention to run it for a

Our Babinda property, north Queensland. Tom missed the Territory, so we returned after eighteen months.

couple of weeks, get the feel of it, and then employ a girl. A haberdashery and materials shop which attracted me was being sold for a bargain price, or so I thought. The stock alone was worth more than the purchase price. Foolishly, I did not seek the advice of an expert and bought the business and signed on for two years to lease the premises from which the business operated. After a month of working in the shop myself, travelling daily to and from Frenchman's Creek, I realised I had made a bad mistake. The shop was entirely in the wrong location for the lines it was selling. It barely made the rent to which I was committed for the next two years.

I got chatting to one of my customers, Nell McKay. Big, blonde Nell, with an ever-present infectious smile, was a Cairns resident and knew the problems of a wrongly located shop. There was really only one guaranteed successful location, apart from the big shopping complexes outside the city area, she said, and that was in what they called the Golden Square, an area bounded by Lake Street, Spence Street, Shields Street and Grafton Street. "If haberdashery isn't a goer here, why don't you try another line of goods," said Nell, "perhaps something

more in the tourist line. A lot of tourists get down this way in their wanderings. What about a souvenir shop? Maybe you could include Aboriginal artefacts? And why not sell seashells too?" "It could be an idea," I said, "but I don't know much about shells," immediately starting to mull over the thought that now could be a good time to brush up my knowledge. All I knew was that they were objects in which crabs sometimes lived, and that you picked them up on the beach.

With the increasing indications that my haberdashery business was an economically hopeless proposition, I decided to cut my losses. I reduced the stock drastically and quickly sold all the materials, patterns, braids and laces, ribbons, zips, elastic, needles and thread. Two small ads in the *Cairns Post* brought an onslaught of eager women out for a bargain. Nell came in to help me in the mad rush and then gave helpful suggestions for re-organising the shop. A few weeks later, after acquiring totally different stock, I was back in business, this time selling souvenirs, artefacts, and seashells. With all my happy memories of the Jim Jim, I called the shop "Cooinda Connection". It wasn't a particularly helpful name as it meant nothing to the customer, but it meant the world to me.

Nell offered her services and I was able to leave her to run the shop, probably far better than I when it came to shell selling. Seashells were her particular hobby. She and her husband, Maurice, went collecting whenever they could, and corresponded and exchanged shells with people from all over the world. Their own private collection of cones, cowries and murex that they showed me, I later came to realise was an enviable

one. At that time I didn't know the difference between a cone and a cowrie – they were all certainly beautiful objects but at first they all looked rather the same to me. After handling a few shells I couldn't help coming under the spell of their infinite variety of shapes, patterns and colours and I pored over books describing the different species and their habitats.

With Nell running the shop, I could be at home at Frenchman's Creek all day with Tom, helping him in the garden. The earlier signs of healthy growth which we had been so excited about, had somehow disappeared. Daily, now, we watched the promising young plants wither and die, or keel over with a wilt or virus with which Tom wasn't familiar. We dug up some wilted remains and took a boxful to the Department of Primary Industries at Kamerunga, just outside Cairns. "Ah, yes," said the helpful man we saw, as he examined the pitiful contents of the box, "you would have had more success growing fruit and vegies in the Territory than you will ever have at Babinda. You are in one of the wettest spots in Australia and the viruses in the soil there will put paid to all your dreams of a market garden. Of course, you could always try up in the Tablelands if you want a market garden. Good soil, there, it'll grow anything."

Tom shuddered at the thought of the cold winters on the Tablelands. He'd been based near Kairi during the war, when he was on training exercises before heading for the jungles of New Guinea, and he knew just what to expect weather-wise. What we didn't expect, weatherwise, was how cold Babinda could be in winter. Friendly neighbours said it wasn't cold at all, just a seasonal mildness, but after the Territory warmth, to us it was definitely cold. With Tom's garden failing, my shop not really showing signs of being anything like the good little money-earner I had hoped for, even in its new guise, the cold weather getting into our bones, and the fact that we both missed Cooinda, we considered returning to the Territory. Perhaps we should never have left there, although it had seemed there was no alternative at the time. Now we were beginning to realise that although the magic appeal of untouched wilderness might vanish, one could not deny that the encroachment of civilisation could also bring comforts which in some ways could enhance one's enjoyment of a place. And, if we went back and sometimes became overwhelmed by the modern Cooinda, well, we could always escape for a while to one of the remaining pockets of peace, like the Place of the Whispering Shadows. Surely that could never change.

We decided to take up the offer of a plot of land to live on for our lifetime, made so generously by the Gagudju Association at the time of the sale of the motel. We shut up the house for a fortnight and made a quick trip back to the Jim Jim to ensure that such a move was still in order with the Traditional Owners. Indeed, it was. It was heartwarming to find they would make us very welcome. Not only could we live on our little plot, but I would be permitted to have a small seashell shop, which perhaps could be an additional tourist attraction to their business. Tom's own idea was to grow a few vegies, which the Motel might buy. Thus both of us would have interests we enjoyed, a small income from our labours and, at last, be living in the land of our dreams.

The property at Frenchman's creek was put on the market, the souvenir stock disposed of to other shops, and my seashell stock carefully packed into boxes for the journey north. I was looking forward to having them on display once more in a kiosk type shop at Cooinda. Leaving most of our furniture behind for sale with the house, once more we loaded our goods and chattels onto the two Toyotas and set off in convoy. This time, we had no dog to accompany us. Our faithful Hobo had sadly succumbed to heartworm complications.

The weather in July, 1982, as we crossed the Barkly Tablelands, was pleasantly cool, unlike the searing heat we had experienced on our earlier November crossing. On the final run in to Cooinda, on the dirt track leading from Pine Creek to the Jim Jim, we made very slow time. At each creek crossing we stopped and sat for a while recalling how the track used to be, how it was now wider and straighter, and how it would soon be bitumen. We remembered the places where old so-and-so had taken the corner a bit too fast and ended up in the scrub, and wasn't that where we had been bogged for two nights, and wasn't this where some other little adventure had occurred? We stopped at the old store. The piers, with the bricks Tom had made in the two-brick-making machine, were as good as new, but the wooden steps had rotted away, the flywire hung in tatters, and the double front doors swung in the breeze on broken hinges.

We boiled the billy under the same tree we had boiled it so many years ago, in 1964, when I had danced around feeling like John Superman. I reminded Tom of my words "one day we'll live somewhere round here in a little white house with a red front door" and of how he had told me to keep it in the back of my mind as a fairy story for the time being. Now the fairy story was about to come true. We met some of our Aboriginal friends on the way in to the motel. They expressed happiness at our return to their country. It made us feel we were coming home to the place where we belonged. Full of elation, we drove the last few miles. We were to be guests of the motel for one night until we could pitch our tents and make plans for a house on our piece of land.

We found the motel had recently changed white managers. The new managers were a couple we had known since early Cooinda days. Whilst not being close friends, we had shared the camaraderie of the bush. The camaraderie was over. We were made to feel the part we had played in putting Cooinda on the map was history, and that our turning up out of the past with the idea of living there as though we belonged, was something they did not welcome. We felt they might be a little out of kilter with the environment but that was none of our business. They had been picked to do the job of running the motel, and we certainly didn't want to tread on anyone's toes or make things difficult. We were quite entitled to stay, with the full approval of the Traditional Owners, but we did not feel the hostile atmosphere our presence would apparently generate with the new white staff, would make for happy living. We left next day and headed up the Arnhem Highway to Darwin. The fairy story was finally over and I believe it broke Tom's heart.

Tom didn't feel he could live in Darwin itself. I was too benumbed to have any particular thoughts on the matter. We looked around outside Darwin for a piece of land, large enough to grow a few vegies, but with power and water laid on as Tom was no longer in the mood for wrestling with generators and waterpumps. We found an acre of land at Howard Springs and settled into the Caravan Park there whilst organising the

FROM SHANTY STORE TO THRIVING TOURIST MOTEL ‖‖‖

● Tom Opitz

Tom loves 23-year 'holiday'

A SHANTY store set among virgin bushland has become a thriving motel catering for up to 20,000 tourists every dry season.

The place is Jim Jim and the man who did it is Tom Opitz, pictured left, a Territorian of 23 years standing.

"I came up for a holiday in the 50s," said Tom, "and I never left."

He is 62 now and as he relaxed in the idyllic surroundings of the Cooinda Motel, he talked about his early days in the Jim Jim area.

Tom started off carting tourists around the country for the Nourlangie Camp Safari, but when the organisation went broke after a few years, he found himself out of work.

He joined the Public Service and slogged it out with Forestry Branch until 1963.

There was no Arnhem Highway then and the only road to Jim Jim, Oenpelli and Mudginberri was a dirt track via Pine Creek.

It was along this track at a river crossing that he built the Jim Jim store, taking out a special purpose lease in 1963.

Undeterred by the fact the store was under three metres of water every wet season, Tom opened up shop and did a roaring trade from the start.

HIGHER

"We had to clear out the store and move to higher ground for four months of every year," he explained.

"But as the track was impassable, we wouldn't have done much business anyway."

It was the only store within 100km on a track which was much frequented during the dry.

The store became a well-known watering hole. People passing through the district seldom failed to drop in for a few tinnies.

"Public servants did a lot of work there," one member of the company equipped.

Tom married Judy that year.

Opening night, 17 years before, was fondly remembered by all.

It ended in a wild brawl with members of the company fighting underneath a Volkswagen. Judy Opitz flogged the offenders over the head with a torch to restore order.

"Everyone started off friends and ended up enemies, so the success of the establishment was assured," someone remarked.

The same thing happened when the motel opened six years later.

All the reasonable people went home early, but the brawlers were invited to stay on for a

get-together afterwards.

One member of the company fell asleep in his car and it rolled into Yellow Waters. It had to be lifted out by crane.

He was later beaten to death and robbed after a win at the races.

Tom said he could see the potential in the Jim Jim area from the start.

The country is lush and abounds with wildlife. Visitors are attracted to the picturesque Jim Jim falls and many operators bring tourists through.

The river route is at least as popular as the road. During the wet it is the only access, apart from the air.

Many people visit from Jabiru and the numbers can only increase as the township grows.

LAND

Although Tom is in his 60s, he is not planning on retiring. "I'll play it by ear," he said.

"I've got a block of land at Port Douglas but I don't want to live at Port Douglas."

He wants to live in the Jim Jim area which has become his home.

He devoted years to creating his niche in the Kakadu bush and he is not giving it up for an easy retirement in southern climes.

Northern Territory News, 15th January, 1979.

building of a house. We found Frank Wards' Transportable Homes to be the answer. These transportable homes, which are hardly distinguishable from any other type of home, were built on premises owned by Frank Ward and then transported to their final site. Within a month the bare shell of a three-bedroom house was put on our land, but there was still a lot of internal work to be done before we could move in. Wiring, plumbing, and carpeting all took time. "But I promise you you'll be in before Christmas and can have your Christmas turkey there," said Frank.

Meanwhile, I looked around for suitable premises to open a seashell shop. I had nearly $10,000 worth of seashells, shellcraft and shell jewellery, and wanted to do something with it. I walked around Jape Arcade and found an empty shop right opposite where I had had my Uniform Shop. Tom helped me set up shelves in the new shop, but was not really interested. The shop, which I called Darwin Seashell Centre, soon began to show a most promising trend, but I was getting desperately worried about Tom. He made a game try at pretending interest and planning the garden he could make on the Howard Springs block, but he seemed to have lost heart in everything. Even eating was a bore to be avoided if possible. He enjoyed drinking with his mates in the local pub but was finding he couldn't keep up with them drink for drink without ill effect. He tried saying "No," but mateship is very strong and to be a piker was quite repugnant to Tom. He could avoid going to places where they drank, but he couldn't avoid drinking with them if they came with a carton to visit him in our caravan in the Caravan Park. I hoped the problem would get better after we'd moved into our new house and, with

My Darwin Seashell Centre, in the Jape Arcade in Darwin.

Tom occupied in his garden, drink would hopefully not flow quite so freely with any visiting mates.

True to his word, Frank Ward completed the house at Howard Springs for us just one week before Christmas. We moved in. We were looking forward to having some of Tom's special friends in for Christmas drinks in our new house. Then, five days before Christmas, Tom complained of feeling ill with chest pains. On the advice of the sister-in-charge of the Howard Springs Clinic, I drove him to Darwin Hospital. After many tests, he was put to bed with what I understood was a chest infection and nothing to be unduly concerned about. I stayed all day with him and he appeared to get a little brighter from the effects of the drugs he had been given.

Nevertheless, I couldn't help feeling all was not well as I left that evening. I approached the ward sister, thinking to reassure myself over my silly thoughts. Realising I was being a bit ridiculous about it all I asked, almost in a tone of jocularity, if there was any chance of Tom's popping off in the night and me finding the police on my doorstep at some ungodly hour to tell me the news. In the spirit of Christmas goodwill, I was assured all was well and I happily went home chiding myself for being such an imaginative idiot. A couple of days in hospital, I thought, and he may miss out on those Christmas drinks with his mates, but we'll make up for that at a New Year party, I told myself.

I spent much of next day with him. Before I left after visiting hours that night, again I asked about any possible disastrous downturn in his condition. As we weren't on the phone at Howard Springs, I told them I wouldn't be able to get to the hospital quickly if I were needed, and I reiterated I didn't want the police banging on my door. Again I was reassured. I went back once more to Tom's bedside. "Baw baw, old man," I said, using an Aboriginal form of goodbye, "see ya tomorrow." Tom raised a weak hand. "Baw, baw, old woman," he answered.

At about 5.00 a.m. next morning, a police car drew up at the front door and hammered on it. Tom had died around 4.00 a.m. One could not complain about his funeral. As Tom had predicted, his mates gave him a "bloody good one".

CHAPTER SEVENTEEN

Life Begins Again

I sat on the short, sweet grass at the edge of a billabong. Unseasonable blue skies, fleecy white clouds and the paperbark forest which frilled the billabong, were reflected in the placid waters. An occasional ripple stirred the surface where a barramundi lurked. I heard a sea eagle cry as he flew over, snowy-breasted and graceful, followed by a vee of wild geese honking mournfully. A wallaby hopped to a clearing at the far side of the water bent on a quick drink, then propped and turned back to the forest. But no movement of mine had startled him. I sat motionless, deep in thought, the past, the present and future pressing themselves upon me.

Tom had been buried the previous day. I had been puzzled by his sudden and seemingly inexplicable death and I did not then know its cause. I later was to learn the result of the autopsy. The death certificate stated the cause as bronchopneumonia, septicemia and pulmonary fibrosis. I had raised the question with the hospital of why I wasn't given just an inkling of his dangerous state of health and its possible outcome, so that I could have stayed by his bedside. The matter was officially examined and I was eventually advised that he had NOT been in a state of impending death when I had left the hospital. He had suffered a totally sudden, unexpected and unforeseeable deterioration some time later.

At that particular moment I still could not believe it. I had felt the need to be alone in a piece of the bush at the Jim Jim, a place which had seen so many of our failures and small triumphs. At my request, Ken Couzens, Tom's nephew, and his wife, Betty, who lived in Darwin, had driven me to the Jim Jim and dropped me off from their vehicle along the track leading to Cooinda Motel. They were scheduled to pick me up at a certain point a little later. I had waved them off and followed a tree line through the scrub to the place Tom and I called The Place of the Whispering Shadows. It was a magical place where we would, when time had infrequently permitted, sit on a log and absorb the peace of the place, and think deep thoughts of our eventual future together.

Now I was sitting alone. No, not quite alone! I realised what had disturbed the wallaby as the wet nose of a dog pushed into my shoulder. Perhaps he belonged to someone at the motel and had gone walkabout. He was just the friend I needed, and I put an arm around him and buried my face in his furry neck. He didn't appear to mind his coat getting sodden with tears for a moment before he licked my face in companionship and settled down peaceably by my side. "What am I going to do?" I asked the dog. He looked at me with limpid, brown eyes which told me nothing. It was evidently my problem and only I could solve it.

I thought of my past twenty-two years with Tom and how we had been a close-knit pair forging a life together in the bush. Before I met Tom in 1959, I'd been a useless wanderer on the face of the earth, seeing much, getting nowhere. I tried Australia as a Pommie migrant but still couldn't settle, and after two years arranged my passage home to England. On a last holiday in Darwin before sailing, I met crocodile hunter, Tom Opitz, and knew it was time to stop travelling. With the looks of a Peter Finch in his heyday, Tom was a dinky-di Aussie and, as I was to learn, a rugged individualist, a bushman, a hard drinker, a man's man, and yet with a softness and gentleness about him that made tears come to his eyes if he found an injured wallaby by the roadside. I'd cancelled my sailing and turned to a life of outback adventure with him.

Now there was no Tom. Did I have the courage to stay in Australia without him or was it better to go back to England and try to take up the threads of life there once more? "What do you think?" I asked the dog. "Should I return to England?" He wagged his tail energetically. "Or stay?" The dog wagged his tail even more enthusiastically. "Would you like a walk?" That really got a response. He leapt to his feet and wagged his tail until I thought it would fly off. At least a decision seemed to have been made and we ambled off, skirting the edge of the chain of billabongs before reaching the milkwood tree where Ken and Betty were to meet me. My friend, the dog, sat at my side in the shade of the tree and waited patiently until the rendezvous was made, then trotted off happily in the direction of the motel, satisfied he had done his good deed for the day.

"Any decisions?" asked Ken. "No," I said. "I just can't think clearly and I don't want to make any rash moves like selling the house and business and heading for England if that's not going to be the right answer." "Then why don't you fly over for just a few weeks?" suggested Betty. "We'll look after the house and business while you're away. If you find you really want to go back there to live, you can sell up here later. But don't make any decisions now about going for good, or you may regret them." Betty was undoubtedly right. How could I leave Australia and the bush that I loved

This large milkwood tree was another landmark when we commenced the Cooinda Motel, still standing amongst modern units in 2008.

so much, and never see Cooinda, the Happy Place, again? Cooinda, the place Tom and I had actually put on the map by having a dream and trying to make it come true. My English family connections may have been pulling me in my immediate moment of grief but my Cooinda connections would be an everlasting memory of Tom.

So Tom's life had ended. He used to say that life is a simple matter of individuals who are here today and gone tomorrow. He seemed to consider that life is for the now and should be lived accordingly, neither bowing to the past nor looking at the blank wall of the future. I didn't share his sentiments in that direction. Life is both the past and the future, each having an inescapable bearing on the other. But if Tom wanted to be a part of the nothingness of tomorrow, I would respect his wishes. Tom had had children by his previous marriage who could carry on his name, but he and I had had no children. Now it was time to put my years with him into the limbo of nowhereness and forge a new life on my own. I didn't know it would take some eight years to come to grips with the future and release myself from Cooinda.

I made several visits to Cooinda over those years, watching it change managers every so often whilst the facilities were remodelled and expanded and finally settling down to a high grade motel in the heart of the bush. Yellow Water boat tours were winning renown and becoming one of the main attractions for visitors. I was thrilled and gratified when I found one of the boats plying the waters was named *Tom Opitz* and even more so when I found one had also been named after me. It may not have been

The Judy Opitz, *one of the Yellow Water Cruise boats.*

quite on a par with having a frigate named after one for stirring deeds at sea, like one of my ancestors being remembered by *H.M.S. Rowley*, but I found the gesture of those who had arranged it, to be very warming. Now, every time I see the boat, I acknowledge the gesture with a salute.

The immediate problem was to start picking up the threads that would once more give meaning to my life. But where to start? Was a return to England the answer? With a friend taking care of my shop, I flew off. On the Qantas plane that was taking me to London, I decided not to force any answers but wait and see where my inclinations might draw me. The plane landed at Heath Row (now "Heathrow") Airport on a bitterly cold English March morning. My brother-in-law, Anthony, was there to meet me with a bag of warm, woollen underwear and strict instructions from my sister, Julia, to put them on. It was, of course, wonderful to see the family again in Cambridge, but I no longer felt a vital part of them. Neither did I immediately find I had any particular feelings for England. London, with its thick, petrol-fumed atmosphere had me gasping for clean fresh air, and the motorways completely baffled me.

I had been given the use of the family car to go where I chose. To explore English country roads by car had so often been a pleasure in the past, but now it was a nightmare. I soon gave up the struggle of trying to find my way out of Cambridge on memory trips to places I had known and loved. I made a couple of trips to Norfolk along the new motorways. The journey was fast, but boring. Yet there was no fun in finding a narrow lane to potter along, because any other drivers using it seemed to think they were still on the motorway and drove at an according speed.

It seemed pointless to make any further trips to Norfolk. Even a trip to Weeting

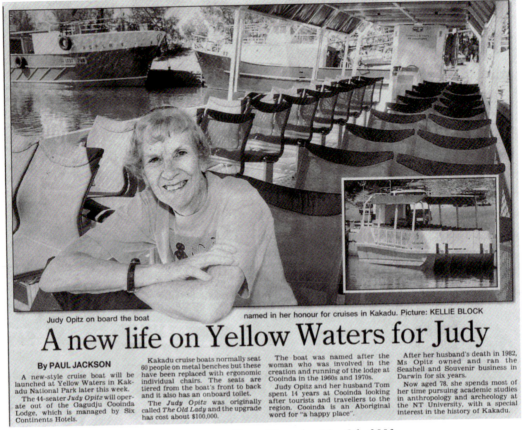

Judy Opitz on board the boat named in her honour for cruises in Kakadu. Picture: KELLIE BLOCK

A new life on Yellow Waters for Judy

By PAUL JACKSON

A new-style cruise boat will be launched at Yellow Waters in Kakadu National Park later this week.

The 44-seater *Judy Opitz* will operate out of the Gagudju Cooinda Lodge, which is managed by Six Continents Hotels.

Kakadu cruise boats normally seat 60 people on metal benches but these have been replaced with ergonomic individual chairs. The seats are tiered from the boat's front to back and it also has an onboard toilet.

The *Judy Opitz* was originally called *The Old Lady* and the upgrade has cost about $100,000.

The boat was named after the woman who was involved in the creation and running of the lodge at Cooinda in the 1960s and 1970s.

Judy Opitz and her husband Tom spent 14 years at Cooinda looking after tourists and travellers to the region. Cooinda is an Aboriginal word for "a happy place".

After her husband's death in 1982, Ms Opitz owned and ran the Seashell and Souvenir business in Darwin for six years.

Now aged 78, she spends most of her time pursuing academic studies in anthropology and archeology at the NT University, with a special interest in the history of Kakadu.

Northern Territory News, Thursday May 8th, 2003.

Church to see if I could dredge up some feeling of interest for the Angersteins proved fruitless. What did ancestors matter, after all. Although I used to feel that he was missing out by having no interest in trying to bond with his roots, Tom was unconcerned about any previous family history. All I could ever glean from him was that his grandfather, Carl Otto, had inadvertently killed someone in a duel and had had to flee Prussia in a hurry, ending up in Australia. Now I began to feel that perhaps he was right that life was simply a matter of here today, and gone tomorrow, and what had gone on in the past was irrelevant. Live for the day, that was all that was necessary. Let circumstances take their course, painful or otherwise. Grin and bear it. All I wanted to do was return to Australia, the country I believed I now loved beyond all others. I was proud of my Australian citizenship.

I cut a week off my planned month's stay and flew back, leaving Heath Row on a soggy, misty raw afternoon. I landed at Darwin Airport where a warm, seasonal morning shower was just finishing and took a taxi back to our new house at Howard Springs. The sun shone through clean, sweet air and birds were singing in the stretch of wild forest behind the house. I believed my English connection had been laid to rest. But what next? The Cooinda connection was pulling strongly. I was tempted to go out there and live a hermit's life in the bush that had meant so much to Tom and me, but realised this was hardly practicable. I also doubted whether I would be able to live such a quiet life with the influx of tourists to the area. With the finance available to the Traditional Owners, the motel was having the sort of face-lift our small company had been unable to give it. A new bar and dining-room complex, and more units, all air-conditioned, were being built. It was now surely destined to become one of the great attractions for tourists to Kakadu National Park but could it prove to be sufficiently attractive to me?

Still not knowing in which direction to head, I threw a series of ideas to the four winds to see what eventuated. Perhaps a social life and meeting new people would lead somewhere? I went on a luxury cruise to Fiji and the Pacific Islands – but somehow couldn't find the mood to join in the fun. I drove across to Cairns and found great solace in the glorious North Queensland scenery – but couldn't quite make the break to go and live there permanently. Back in the Territory, I sold the house at Howard Springs and rented a flat nearer town, so that I could have easier access to my shop. I pretended there was no great change in my life and it would be "business as usual". Business was brisk and kept me sane as I drifted on in meaningless fashion.

Indeed, business was proving to be so brisk that Ann Fox, a neighbour during the brief Howard Springs sojourn, came in to the shop to help out occasionally. She also took complete charge when I found it necessary to drive over to Cairns in order to bring back full loads of stock from my contacts there. It was safer to fetch them myself, I found, after one consignment by truck had arrived in very poor shape. My trips to Cairns meant I could indulge in seashell talk with my friends, Nell and Maurice Mackay, who now owned their own stall, Nell's Shells, in Rusty's Bazaar, Grafton Street. I also met up with John and Chris Bell-Booth, the couple to whom we had leased the motel in 1978 who also now lived in Cairns. They ran a very successful souvenir shop, called Boothy's Souvenirs, in Lake Street, the Golden Square location, where they couldn't miss.

Agatha, as I called my new diesel Toyota Hi-Lux 4-wheel drive utility, purchased partly in exchange for Tom's 4-wheel drive Toyota and his Kubota tractor we'd brought back from Queensland with us, was ideal for the Cairns supply trips. I also found that, driving entirely on my own where no-one could see or hear my grief, I was able to weep, rage, shout, curse and howl until I succeeded in expunging it in sheer noise. After that, on all future trips, I found I could speed across the vast empty spaces of the Barkly Tablelands, revelling in the joy of the electrifying nothingness. At times, along the many dead straight stretches of road, where the heat shimmered on the tarmac cutting off the horizon ahead, it was almost like driving lickety-split into eternity. In the euphoria this engendered, I found I could almost become one with the nothingness, absorbed into a part of the cosmos where earthbound tribulations were irrelevant and insignificant.

Immediate grieving done, I threw myself wholeheartedly into my shop business. Seashells, shellcraft and shell jewellery were enjoying great popularity at that time, and when the shop next to mine was vacated, I took over that one also, knocking down the intervening wall and refurbishing. Colourful coral on glass shelves, striking jewellery hanging on black velvet-lined walls, long dangling shell chandeliers, unusual oystershell craft, and glass-fronted, internally lit, mirror-backed cabinets displaying exotic shells in pleasing arrangements attracted my customers, and gave me enormous personal, visual pleasure. When the nature of Jape Arcade changed a year or so later, other businesses began to move as customer traffic lessened. I did not renew my lease either, but transferred into a tiny shop in Anthony Plaza in the Mall itself, in the tourist heartland.

While my Darwin shop was a pleasure and an interest and continued to run smoothly, with Ann helping out where necessary, it presented no challenge. I began to find my brain was screaming for something to munch on. I bought a Kawai piano and took up my music studies where I had dropped them in my teens. I bought a guitar. I applied for a course in Real Estate with the Darwin Community College but soon decided it was not a career for me. I bought an Apple IIe computer, with appropriate hardware, and completely absorbed myself in word processing and transferring the parts of my life story I had been writing at various times in various notebooks on to discs. I even considered learning computer programming but this idea was somewhat shattered when I realised the extent of maths knowledge I would need. I thumbed through some books on maths in a bookshop and discovered my knowledge of maths was around Year 4!

Not to be deterred, I bought a suitable text book and some discs on algebra put out by Apple, determined to prove myself to be more than the silly cuckoo my algebra teacher had pronounced me to be in my schooldays. Finding algebra to be really rather fun and most satisfying when quadratic equations were successfully brought to their conclusion, I took a higher course in maths with the Northern Territory Secondary Correspondence School. Then I added courses with Stott's Correspondence College and took basic Geology and Biology, Ancient History, Classical History, and Australian Social History.

This happy occupation, which at first took place in evening leisure hours, helped to appease an extraordinary burning desire which had surfaced. Clearly I was trying to make up for an education which I had missed out on many years ago when World War II had interrupted my schooling. Dabbling my feet in the heady waters of acquiring knowledge, I began to spend more time in wanting to pore over textbooks in my shop than taking an interest in my customers. I was hooked on learning! But to what end?

By 1987, seashells and shell craft were declining in popularity and it became clear I would have to diversify if I wanted to remain afloat. Yet every idea offering potential seemed to clash with the other trading occupants of the Plaza putting me in unacceptable competition with them. Apart from these problems, I was finding staleness and boredom were creeping into my efforts at customer service. More and more I was burying my head in my text books during shop hours when I should have been taking an interest in my customers. Did I really want to continue in shop business? A combination of factors, including an Australia-wide tightening of the economy, soon made it vitally necessary that I rethink where I wanted to head.

In 1988 I finally closed my seashell business. The thought now occurred to me that

I could retire to the piece of land granted to us by the Traditional Owners and end my days there. I could bury my head in books which would teach me about the far away past of Kakadu. Remembering how entranced I'd been by the work of Carmel Schrire when she had called at our store at the crossing in the sixties, perhaps now that I had the time and the enthusiasm, I could volunteer as helper on the more recent excavations in the region. Yet it was hardly likely that I would get any such chance without some training but how would I get that?

While I was winding down the business and mulling over my next move, my sister Julia phoned from Sydney with an offer. Julia and Anthony who now lived in Cambridge, were presently staying with their son and his family at Bilgola Plateau. The unit they owned at Newport as an investment was standing vacant, in between tenant occupation. "Come down here and live a life of easy retirement," she said, "you're welcome to make use of our unit in Newport for as long as you like." I loved Sydney from various visits I had made over the years, and could easily envisage embarking on a different but exciting lifestyle amid its bright lights and hustle and bustle. Far from any idea of retirement, which certainly didn't appeal, I could see myself recharged to run a little souvenir and gift shop in Newport, or Avalon, perhaps.

In October, 1988, with *Agatha* crammed full of bits and pieces that weren't being sent south with a carrier, I left Darwin in cheerful mood and headed off down the Stuart Highway. East across the well-loved Barkly Highway, then south once more before becoming embroiled in the horror stretches of the Bruce Highway. Severe traffic stress began taking its toll on me soon after skirting Brisbane. At my last overnight stop at Gosford, I tried to memorise a route to the Northern Beaches to little advantageous effect. Navigating a lone course in dense traffic, without advance advice as to which lane to get into for the next turn is not a joyful experience to anyone accustomed to the rather quieter thoroughfares around Darwin. When I finally arrived in Sydney my nerves were in tatters.

Family greetings soon smoothed away jagged edges and I settled into the neat, second-floor unit overlooking Pittwater and the yachting scene. Full of enthusiasm and relishing the thought of an exciting new business, I soon started looking around for something favourably priced, and found the very thing I wanted in a tiny shop in a Dee Why shopping mall. At which point reality struck! Even at the low price being asked, my financial position was too shaky to strike out without a bank loan which I had anticipated. This, however, was in no way forthcoming. Obviously, as the family cynically pointed out, the business was only being sold because it was no longer viable and the owners were only waiting for a mug like me to come along and relieve them of it. I realised that it was just as well, perhaps, that I hadn't had the immediate asking price available or I would have been throwing good money away, yet I'd been so sure I was on to a "good thing". I began to doubt my business ability. Clearly, I just didn't have financial acumen. Looking back on my shop ventures, it appeared I had nothing material to show for any of them. All they had been were self-indulgent amusements rather than profit-makers. My self-esteem plummeted. I lost heart. I panicked. What capabilities did I have to get me satisfyingly through the rest of my life?

"Relax," chorused the family. "Retire, do nothing, sit back and enjoy your life." But on what basis was I to enjoy so many idle hours? I loved travelling but that takes money and I was now reduced to living on a pension from Veteran's Affairs, for which I was eligible as Tom's widow. While such a pension certainly kept food hunger at bay, it didn't seem to offer any particular dimension to living. Then I brightened up at the thought of all the learning I could do in endless free time. But this was quickly followed by gloom. What would be the point of all that wonderful learning if there was to be no end product to it. Passion without purpose holds no deep fulfilment for the mind. Self-pity set in and, hard on its heels, guilty thoughts that there was always someone worse off than oneself. Surely I could perform useful works for the truly disadvantaged, or visit the old and tired of life and those dispirited souls hidden away in nursing homes. But in the state I had by now worked myself into, I too had become one of the old and dispirited and tired of life, and it was all I could do not to ring "Life Line" with a cry for "Help".

Sydney and its environs offered nothing I could relate to. Much as I loved it as a tourist destination, the city was proving too overwhelming for any length of time. I knew I had to escape to the solace of the bush to think for a while. Thoughts of Kakadu and of Cooinda sprang to mind. A visit there might clarify my thinking. Perhaps I could, after all, even live on that quarter acre allowed us by the Traditional Owners. Yes, it was a very appealing idea but maybe not just yet. Once again, I loaded up my trusty Agatha and, gritting my teeth, headed north through the hated traffic melee, not knowing quite what was going to eventuate. I had the cheerful feeling that I was not yet destined to stagnate and that there could be more "adventures" left in me which had to surface before I could settle down to Cooinda's peace.

Back in Darwin, in the New Year, 1989, my first "adventure" was to lease a barrow in Casuarina Shopping Square, calling it Lotus Lily Gifts and selling Egyptian jewellery. A few weeks later my old shop in Anthony Plaza became vacant and I couldn't resist moving back there once more to try and make a go of it with stock which in no way competed with other traders there. The business was short-lived. For some reason, I could not maintain my earlier enthusiasm for shopkeeping and, after being offered a job in Darwin's most prestigious bookstore, I disposed of my stock and shut up shop, this time I felt for good. I was going to join the paid work force, and could think of nothing nicer than being surrounded by books. I lasted barely a week! A state-of-the-art computerised till interlocked with a stock system was beyond my capabilities to master in a few minute's tuition, and after messing up the system several times to the exasperation of the proprietor, I left under rather an undignified cloud.

Now what? Perhaps seek employment at Cooinda if I didn't feel I was ready to sit back and do nothing there? I phoned the manager of the motel – not, of course, the same manager Tom and I had had the misfortune to encounter on our return from Queensland in 1982. I found out that work was slowing down for the season but, yes, there would be various casual positions available at the start of the next season. Casual work could always lead to something more permanent and congenial but that left a Wet Season to get through. Once again Julia and Anthony fortuitously came to the rescue. "How would you like to look after our house in Cambridge for six months," they phoned, "while we're away for six months of sunshine in Sydney?"

I arrived in England in late October, as the trees were shedding their last autumnal leaves of russet, a sight never seen in Darwin. After the heat of the tropics I revelled in crisp, icy cold days with bare branches limned against a clear, blue sky. Certainly I had to contend with storms and sleet and fog and drizzle but the house was warm in cold, inclement weather and the cat would purr gently on my chest as I stretched out with a book on such days. In January came the early sprinkling of snowdrops, aconite, then golden celandine, poking through the frost covered ground, followed by a burgeoning of new shoots in a faint flush of green on the trees, the froth of white blackthorn, catkins drooping their tails; a sea of daffodils, primroses and bluebells. This was the England I knew and loved.

In May, Julia and Anthony returned from Sydney and it was time for me to return to Australia. My most precious moments had been spent in King's College Chapel, with its jewelled, sun-streamed stained-glass windows beaming down on me, while I listened to the organ practice, the notes soaring and swelling, the sound contained and returned by the high, exquisite fan vaulting of the roof. Temptation now said stay in England, but a holiday in someone else's house with all its mod cons was not the same as living permanently in one's own abode on inadequate means, and even the non-costing pleasure of listening to organ music might have palled after a while.

Back in Australia, I wasted no time in contacting the management of Cooinda Motel, and shortly thereafter presented myself for work in some capacity to be decided, perhaps even as shopkeeper. I had not quite foreseen the immensity of the improvements which confronted me. For a start, the shop, which I had visualised along the lines of our old original store where I had easily kept track of stock in several cheap notebooks, was now an efficient, totally modernised business. Stock ordering was now all fully computerised, a very necessary procedure to cater for the enormous number of tourists it had to serve. As I was taken on a tour of inspection it became clear to me that shopkeeping was out and neither did I seem to have the ability or training to help out in any position other than kitchenmaid or housemaid. À la carte waitressing or cocktail mixing behind the bar would certainly be beyond me. As for working in the tours department, well, one glance at the formidable barrage of telephones and computers in the Booking Office was enough to make me feel my inadequacy in that department also. It was no longer a case of chatting to intrepid travellers and pointing out places of interest on a Mud Map. It meant handing out expensive looking coloured brochures followed by the processing of a ticketing operation on a computer. Remembering my disastrous sallies with the computer in my brief bookshop employment, it seemed any placement in the tours department was also likely to end in ignominy.

Gratefully, I thanked management for so kindly considering me as a prospective employee, and returned to Darwin to consider options. I could, of course, enrol in a Tourism and Hospitality and/or Business Computer Course of some sort and then, with proficiency achieved, contact Cooinda again. But did I really want to work there with all those Rules and Regulations for Staff I'd seen posted on an office wall? The laid-back atmosphere of our bush motel had vanished. Cooinda Motel was now an up-market establishment providing high quality service. Whilst I would enjoy the comfort as a guest of the place, I didn't think I wanted to be an employed part of an establishment that made such comfort possible.

On a different tack, I made another trip to Cooinda, this time seeking out Mick Alderson, one of the Traditional Owners of the land, who had been such a part of Tom's and my life in the early days. He now lived near the old Jim Jim Crossing and had a position of some eminence concerned with the running of Kakadu National Park. He told me of plans that were in the pipeline for an Aboriginal Cultural Centre, and suggested that could be of interest to me for employment possibilities. There would be some time before the Centre was a *fait accompli* so there was no need for an immediate decision. This was as well as, although I had spent some years on their land, I realised I actually knew very little of Aboriginal culture and Australia's past which I could authentically share with visitors to such a Centre. The interim period could be most profitably used in educating myself on the subject, but where was I to begin?

David M. Welch

"Where the wild geese flew, there my happiness would lie." Magpie Geese above Yellow Water and Cooinda, Kakadu National Park.

CHAPTER EIGHTEEN

Uni. Student – Studying the Aboriginal Past

Receiving my Batchelor of Arts in 1996.

Before I even attempted to look at Aboriginal culture in any depth, I decided my first studies should be to find out where the Aborigines had originally come from, when, and by what means. The story of Australia certainly didn't begin with the arrival of Captain Cook or with the first settlement of New South Wales under Governor Arthur Phillip in 1788. It was now being said that Aboriginal populations colonised Australia at least 40,000 years ago, which should be when the story of humans in Australia really began. But how and when did those first Australians get here? To find the answer to these questions, and with rather a haphazard plan in my quest for knowledge, I turned initially to newspaper and magazine articles.

A "Newsmag" article in the *Northern Territory News*, 1ˢᵗ November, 1980, had as its headline "The Day the Nomads Crossed a Land Bridge". The journalist stated the "nomads had walked down through the islands to the north of Australia and across the flat plains that today lie beneath the shallow tropical waters of the Timor and Arafura Seas". That theory was refuted by another journalist, Frank Alcorta, who said in an article a week later in the *N.T. News*, that not only was there no land bridge and that migration into Australia required a "rather formidable expanse of water," but that in any event "Aboriginal man, quite a distinct species, is not the product of migration but originated and developed in Australia itself".

What was one to believe? Other newspaper and magazine articles appeared to verge on the fanciful though for all I knew could well have been true. Did the Aboriginal people walk or make the sea crossing and, if so, how? And where did they come from? Perhaps books written by historians or anthropologists could tell me and I read several of these with their conflicting stories.

Charles Duguid in his book *No Dying Race* (published in 1978) wrote that it was in the southern part of India that the aborigines of Australia were first specialised as a race, and from there migrated eastward and southward. He believed they may have reached Australia at the end of the last Ice Age, somewhere about ten thousand years ago. They travelled by land except, perhaps, when they arrived at the very deep water which the aborigines and their dingos almost certainly crossed on rafts or canoes.

Geoffrey Blainey, in his 1983 book *Triumph of the Nomads*, suggested that one possible way to Australia was to cross the deep water to Lombok, then follow the chain of islands to the east, and then perhaps cross from the mountainous island of Flores to Timor. However, he noted that the gap of deep sea could still have been 70 to 100 miles wide so the voyage would certainly have been hazardous.

John Molony, in his 1988 book *The Penguin History of Australia: the First 200 Years*, wrote that the Aborigines have lived on the Australian continent for over 60,000 years and many of them still insist that they had their origins as a people in its soil.

With the dates varying from ten to sixty thousand years before the present, and the differing thoughts on the manner of arrival, or indeed, if the Aborigines had ever been anywhere else, I was totally confused. Russel Ward's book, *Finding Australia*, written in 1987, made partial sense of my confusion. He suggested that until about 1950, those few writers who were interested supposed that the ancestors of the Aborigines came here, with their semi-domesticated hunting dogs, not very much earlier than 10,000 years ago. This was because until the mid-point of the twentieth century, there could have been no certain way of adducing evidence to the contrary because radiocarbon dating, pollen analysis and other modern means of determining the age of organic matter were not available in Australia. Archaeological discoveries in the 1960s, using these means of dating, pushed back the date way beyond 10,000 years BP (before the present), but this information did not necessarily seep through to all writers. Further selective reading on my part revealed that new knowledge was continually coming to light, with each new discovery adding a piece to the jigsaw puzzle or creating a debatable problem.

In 1962, D.J. Mulvaney excavated a cave in the Great Dividing Range of southern Queensland which yielded a radio carbon date of 16,130 B.P. from the bottom layer of occupation. After this breakthrough, still earlier dates were established for human presence in Australia. Carmel Schrire noted in her 1967 PhD dissertation how she unearthed from three rock shelters in Western Arnhem Land what appeared to be the oldest axeheads, sharpened and polished by grinding, dating back some 20,000 years.

Josephine Flood, in her 1989 book, *Archaeology of the Dreamtime* commented that the quest for the origins of the first Australians is one of the most difficult and challenging tasks for archaeologists. She went on to say that Arnhem Land has great potential for archaeological research, since traces of prehistoric culture are preserved both in the floors and on the walls of rock shelters from early times to the present. Moreover, she believed it was likely that still older sites would be discovered, for only a handful of excavations had been carried out.

In a later book, *The Riches of Ancient Australia* (1990), Flood said that the most important discovery so far in Arnhem Land was the find by Rhys Jones and Michael Smith of stone tools dating to 50,000 years BP in the rock shelter of Malakunanja 2.

During our early Cooinda days, Tom and I had enjoyed the passing through of many parties of archaeologists, biologists, botanists and artists. Casting my mind back I well remembered John Mulvaney, Rhys Jones and especially Carmel Schrire, who had often called in to our store at the Jim Jim Crossing in the 1960s, when she was finding those edge-ground axes. With my curiosity now thoroughly aroused by all I was reading, I dreamed very, very briefly of becoming an archaeologist! There was hardly any chance of that! At my stage in life all I could probably do would be just to enjoy knowledge from books on the subject and hope that this might assuage my growing curiosity.

As I slowly tried to get a grip on all I had read, it occurred to me that visitors to the proposed Aboriginal Cultural Centre could be interested not only in acquiring a more in-depth appreciation of Aboriginal history and culture but learning, as I was, about the archaeological aspect also. Unfortunately, I felt it was hardly likely that my necessarily superficial knowledge would qualify me to say anything with the slightest modicum of authority and, in any event, the Centre itself would probably be the source of all information for visitors, with the traditional owners themselves doing any talking required. My role would doubtless be no more than serving customers in the Centre's shop and chatting enthusiastically about the area to them but it might be just enough to keep my still hammering brain quiescent.

To fill in more of my time before the Centre was established, I decided to learn T-shirt printing. Perhaps I could use the knowledge for a possible range of designs I could sell at some of the markets around Darwin. Courses were being offered in the subject at the Darwin Community College at Casuarina and on what I thought was the appointed sign-on day, I fronted up with my application form and joined a queue. A friendly girl in front of me asked "What are you hoping to major in?" I looked blank. "Major in?" I asked. "Yes, aren't you here to enrol for a Degree Course, Batchelor of Arts, or something? I'm hoping to major in Anthropology myself," said the girl. "Degree! Me!" I squeaked in astonishment at the enormity of the thought. I explained that I thought I was a bit ancient for that and doubted if the necessary grey matter was there. I was obviously in the wrong queue! I turned and scurried off but had barely gone a few paces before an inner voice screamed at me "Don't be such a wretched wimp! Go for it! What was all that swotting for in the shop when you should have been serving customers, if not for just such a chance as this?" I thought again about Carmel Schrire and the exciting and challenging work she was doing when I had first met her in earlier Cooinda days. I turned back and practically flew to the Enquiry Desk to find out how to enrol in a degree course in archaeology/anthropology.

Armed with the necessary papers I strolled off and sat under a shady tree in the campus grounds and was immediately assailed by doubts. How could I possibly sit in a classroom with a lot of just-left-school bright young teenagers who would probably be considering me a silly old coot who should be pushing up the daisies? How could I compete knowledge-wise with those students? My own early schooling had been interrupted by the Second World War, leaving me with educational gaps and hardly up to University standards for entry. But perhaps the correspondence courses I had recently taken would stand me in good stead. They certainly did.

Thus it was that in July 1990, at the age of 66, I found to my acute joy that I would be accepted as a Mature Age Student in the recently formed Northern Territory University based at Myilly Point. I was hoping to major in Anthropology. Because it is the study of humankind, telling the story of its very beginnings, I felt this would give me the necessary basis for all the answers I was seeking on where the Aborigines came from and how they got to Australia. I would certainly need to know all this if I was going to work in an Aboriginal Cultural Centre. My acceptance into the University was to herald the most enthralling and satisfying period of my life as my brain was to slowly fill with academic knowledge.

I was about to find out how humankind began. I learnt that present evidence suggests that humans evolved from small, apelike creatures which lived about 12 million years ago, long, long after dinosaurs roamed the earth. About eight million years ago, these apelike creatures had become fully adapted for moving about on their hind legs in a distinctive human manner. Two and a half million years ago, with the evolution of a better brain, stone tools began to be made by these early examples of true humankind. Then, rather than having to rely on their physical attributes for survival, which conjured up mental pictures of hefty, large-jawed cavemen beating each other with clubs to get what they wanted in the way of food, the new humans came to rely on learned behaviour as an effective way of adapting to their environment and their fellow humans. They began to move about, probably from their birth place in Africa, and populate the whole world. Gradually, over the millennia, they refined their thinking and instead of using lumps of stone with the odd piece bashed off to give a sharp edge for hacking away at raw meat, they started, by more delicate touching up, to manufacture the stone into definite shapes for definite purposes, even artistic purposes. They began to organise themselves into social units which made hunting and gathering more proficient and they learned to preserve their traditions and knowledge to bridge the past and present, by the use of symbols. In other words, humankind had now acquired the ability to produce culture, with all their learned behaviours being capable of being passed from one generation to another. And so humanity was born.

Studying wasn't easy at first, and headaches were the order of the day, accompanied at times by quite extraordinary little pings felt in my head. Someone suggested the pings were the result of neurones in the brain firing off while they were being stimulated by use after lying dormant for so long. But whatever it was, the headaches and pings soon disappeared and study became total pleasure. It wasn't all poring over books though, as the occasional field trip was involved. The only fairly big field trip which I had the opportunity to join, took a group of us out on the South Alligator River plains where we were supposed to walk in a long spread-out line over a five kilometre stretch, looking for any artefacts on the surface. The area should have been burnt off but for some reason most of this section had been spared. Struggling and straggling through the fallen and well-tangled high grass didn't help the search. One also had to keep an eye out for wild snuffling black pigs which might have come charging out of the undergrowth.

At a small clearing around a large tree, I stepped over a thick broken-off branch to be confronted, not by an angry boar, but a king brown snake rearing up as though poised to strike. I stepped back very, very quickly, but I'd forgotten the fallen branch I'd just stepped over and, naturally enough, fell back over it. I hit the ground with a tremendous thump, my legs left exposed on the snake side, the rest of me on the other. "That's it, curtains," I thought, as I lay there helpless, only to see the snake's tail disappearing behind the tree. And that was the last I saw of him. Whether the thump as I fell distracted him or whether he simply lost sight of what he supposed was an enemy as I suddenly disappeared out of his range of vision, I don't know. Whatever the reason, I was able to safely pick myself up only to realise I had by now lost the rest of the party. This gave me the chance to do something I'd always wanted to do but been inhibited about for lack of a real reason to indulge myself. Now was the moment. I let fly with a resounding, full throated, yodelling "coo-ee" and got a far-away answering call. That's probably about the only time I've felt really, really Australian!

For my lecturers I was lucky to have eminent scholars in their field such as Ian Walters and Peter Hiscock for the Archaeological subjects, David Mearns, Chris Healey for Anthropology, and David Carment and Alan Powell for History. By 1994 I was ready for my first "Independent Study" under Peter Hiscock. I decided I'd like to examine the 20,000 year old edge-ground axes I knew Carmel Schrire had excavated from a rock shelter near the East Alligator River in the mid 1960s. Now, perhaps, I was about to get the most extraordinary chance to look at some of the very artefacts she had unearthed. I supposed all this material was housed at the Museum in Darwin.

However, when I enquired at the Museum for permission to look at the axes, I was told by the Archaeology Curator, Norma Richardson, that Schrire's collection contained in 53 large boxes, had only just been returned to the Northern Territory from Sydney, where it had been reposing in their Museum, seemingly unloved, for nearly 30 years. But there was a snag. As it was impossible to know in which of those 53 large boxes, containing innumerable smaller boxes, the axes lay, there didn't appear to be much hope of putting my hands on them. But, said Norma, half-jokingly, if I'd like to sort the lot out and rebag and rebox the collection I should be able to find what I was after.

What a challenge! What an opportunity! The timing of events was almost uncanny. By some amazing coincidence, here I was, having the chance to do what I'd dreamed of doing back in 1965, except that here I'd be messing about with the stones in a nice, air-conditioned store-room instead of slaving away under a hot sun: I must confess I now found this rather more appealing. Handling the artefacts with their 20,000 year old background with all the respect they deserved and getting some small idea of the lifestyle of the early inhabitants of the Alligator Rivers Region proved to be both an enriching and humbling experience. I experienced a certain *frisson* of excitement at such a link with the human past. Suffice it to say, I was able to turn in an essay on the axes. At the same time I was able to get Schrire's entire Arnhem Land collection in order. I felt quite proud of myself and hoped that by this I'd achieved something that would enable any future researcher to put their hands on any one particular artefact they may wish to examine.

During the course of the rebagging exercise, I came across several boxes of material from Schrire's very first excavation near the Oenpelli township, in Arnhem Land, which she called Malakunanja I. This excavation had been abandoned after a week's work on what she calls in her dissertation a hot and uncomfortable site, because it did not offer the research possibilities she sought at the time. When I came across them, the artefacts were still in their original, now disintegrating, bags in which she had placed them. A little ochre-filled paint brush, the base of a firemaking stick, a hairball pendant and other treasures of material culture were all crushed together with shells and burnt bones. I hoped to further analyse this material in an Honours dissertation after I graduated.

Of the total of 24 units taken over the years, in my exams I managed 3 Passes, 8 Credits and, amazingly enough, 13 Distinctions. I didn't rise to any High Distinctions but at least my marks were enough for me to receive the award of Bachelor of Arts on 2nd May, 1996. I was now able to turn my attention to my Honours thesis with Ian Walters as my Supervisor. His never-ending patience, encouragement and availability for discussion guaranteed an outcome I could only ever have dreamed of as a Very Senior Student. I called my thesis *Malakunanja I, a Rockshelter in Arnhemland, North Australia: an Interpretation of Site Use.*

The bags of material were finely picked over with their soil residue and sorted into bone, stone, shell and miscellaneous material, before each element was counted, weighed and measured where practicable. The final results of my examination clearly showed the similarity to Schrire's other plains sites in that all could be considered shell middens, mixed with human bone. A feature common to all sites was the human bone deposit, much of it broken and charred, mixed with the food and occupational debris.

Whilst waiting for the results of my Honours thesis, I did further volunteer work at the Museum by rebagging and reboxing the actual material from the Ngarradj Warde Djobkeng site which had been excavated by Harry Allen in 1977.

By the end of 1998 I was deemed to have completed the requirements for the award of Bachelor of Arts (Honours) with Second Class Honours, Division A, and duly graduated as B.A. (Hons). Any thoughts I may have had about acquainting myself briefly with Aboriginal culture and then working in the proposed Cultural Centre being set up at Cooinda, were now forgotten. I had become totally academically hooked and was suffering from a kind of learn-even-more bug. Perhaps the results of some specific research in a PhD capacity could equip me to share what I'd learnt with visitors to the Territory – but I would try to share it in less complex fashion than the formalities of academia sometimes dictated. It might also make good copy to add to the chapters of my life story so that it could reach the wider reading public, even of the world. I may have been carried away and was fantasising as I enrolled for a PhD. But why not! My life suddenly seemed to have become all go, go, go.

CHAPTER NINETEEN

Post Grad. Student and Whither Away? – To the Stars

Before I enrolled for a PhD, there were certain hurdles to be overcome. Was my mind racing ahead of my capabilities? (I was now 74 years old.) The first burning question was could I do it? Did I have the necessary staying power for another gruelling few years of study, let alone the ability to write a 100,000-word thesis in a truly academic manner? In chatting with friends and acquaintances, I was also plagued with the few doomsayers who wanted to know what I was going to do with a doctorate at my age – IF I got it – and wasn't I taking up a younger person's place whose successful result could probably provide greater value to the community? I felt that time alone would answer the precise question of what I was going to do with a doctorate, but the immediate answer was perhaps that the seeking of it would keep me sparking along. Otherwise I would probably be bound for a nursing home and in need of care as I withered[6] away. And that would be of very negative value to the community!

Then sheer passion in what I was about to embark on came to the rescue. Because I found myself so earnestly believing in the value of archaeology in aiding the search for an understanding of humanity, I wanted to slant my doctoral thesis towards the fact that archaeology, and its importance, must be understood not only by academics, but by non-academics. Archaeology's ultimate goal – if it is to have any meaning or justification – must surely be to convey its findings, not only to students and colleagues in the academic world, but above all to the public.

While most Australians are well aware of such archaeological places as Troy, or Stonehenge, or Angkor Wat, and other treasures of Europe and Asia, are they also aware of the richness of the archaeological material of another kind to be found within Australia? My object, then, in doing this research included trying to find out what the public already know about archaeology, what they think they know, and particularly what they are being encouraged to know.

I had one big advantage over the usual students in the work I was about to undertake: I would not have to suffer the situation where a lack of finance forced me back into the workforce before I had completed my thesis. Unlike younger students who might have obligations of family or working pressures just to get food on the table, I was lucky enough to be "kept" by Welfare. I lived in a Housing Commission unit and

---

6 Note Judy's subtle use of "whither" and "wither". To "wither away" is to fade away and die. "Whither away" is like "Whither goest thou?" meaning heading off on a journey somewhere. Very opposite meanings. [Ed.]

received an Old Age Pension. This pension covered an adequate intake of food, since I had developed quite a partiality for baked beans on toast and "two-minute" noodles. So unless I was struck down by some entirely unforeseen event, I had no doubt I could stay the course I would be embarking on with such passion.

That just left the question of my mental ability. I boosted up my ego by re-reading some of the nicer comments made by the examiners of my Honours thesis. One of the examiners wrote:

> The candidate has produced a readable and excellently produced thesis. It is clear that considerable amount of effort has gone into the analysis of the data upon which the candidate's arguments are based. The fact that this work has been produced in the absence of detailed published information, radiocarbon dates, field notes, and even a basic catalogue of artefact provenance is testimony to the candidate's perseverance and dedication. The inclusion of an extensive bibliography reflects the large amount of background research that the candidate has obviously undertaken. . . . The candidate has made a bold attempt to present her arguments within a sophisticated theoretical framework. It is refreshing to see a researcher engage with archaeological evidence above the level of economic or technological issues.

My other examiner noted that:

> The honours thesis is very well written and organised. . . . The tables and information show a high standard of research potential and organisation. . . . The thesis is an interesting and thought provoking one.

I was certainly pleased with these encouraging comments but there was also some adverse criticism. I took the less cheering remarks to heart and learnt from them. The idea that it was considered I had high research potential – even if my thoughts had led me astray on some issues – bolstered my esteem. My imagination obviously needed curbing but I hoped the "research potential" would stand me in good stead for any PhD attempt. Now all I had to do was write a suitable research proposal and have my candidature accepted, then write my thesis and hopefully have that accepted, and I would at last be on my way to the next step – whatever and whenever that was. I didn't have any definite idea of where I was heading for my future, but the thought of being at least in transit was incredibly elevating.

In November, 1998, I set out to draft my proposal. My idea for the thesis was to compare two very different archaeological sites in order to find out how the general public both understood and appreciated them from an archaeological point of view. The two sites I chose could not have been more different. One was an Aboriginal rock shelter in Kakadu National Park which had been home for the Aborigines for some 20,000 years. Archaeological excavations had revealed stone artefacts indicating the prehistoric use of the shelter. It also contains an extensive gallery of rock art. The other site was the nineteenth century European convict site at Port Arthur in Tasmania, now undergoing continual archaeological digs in which the public are sometimes invited to join. Artefacts found here relate to a more modern historical era than the rock shelter. Apart from my proposal indicating the theoretical side of the research, I would also need to show a general design for questionnaires which would indicate visitor reaction to the sites on which I would be working.

In the New Year, 1999, my proposal was accepted and I began my Post Graduate Research at the Northern Territory University. This had now moved from Myilly Point to a redeveloped site of the Darwin Community College at Casuarina, and on 1st January was to change its name to Charles Darwin University.

Charles Darwin, the British naturalist, never actually visited the area, but it was named after him by his friends on the *HMS Beagle*. There were three voyages of *HMS Beagle*. The first (1826-1830) made a hydrographic survey of Patagonia and Tierra del Fuego and never touched Australia. The second voyage (1831-1836) carried Charles Darwin as naturalist, when it visited South America and the Galapagos Islands, returning to England via New Zealand and Australia. In 1837, once again the *Beagle* left England on its third voyage, under the command of John Clements Wickham, with assistant surveyor Lieutenant John Lort Stokes in the party. This time it surveyed large parts of the Australian coast and Wickham named Beagle Gulf and Port Darwin. When the area was settled, the town was originally named Palmerston, but later changed its name to Darwin, after the port.

Charles Darwin University, with which I was now being closely associated, meant I certainly had something to live up to if I was to get anywhere near the intellectual thinking of the great man himself. It was a name which should inspire all students of the University. I was very gratified when I was awarded an APA scholarship. These Australian Postgraduate Awards are for students who enrol in a higher degree of research as full-time students and have reached the necessary level of attainment. The annual stipend of nearly $18,000 available for three years, together with additional grants, greatly helped with expenses incurred travelling to my chosen sites and to conferences.

I started off in a wave of supreme enthusiasm and hope, blissfully unaware of any traumas which might accompany my efforts. After my first supervisor, Ian Walters, left the University I had a wonderful supervisor, Clayton Fredericksen, who had been one of the examiners for my Honours thesis. Clayton, tall, with an Elizabethan style beard and an old fashioned elegance and charm so that you almost expected him to throw his cloak in your path if the road was wet, was bound to have many of the younger students in a flutter at his lectures. Had I been sixty years younger I would undoubtedly have been in a flutter too! As it was, I had the greatest admiration for him and hoped I would not let him down in any flounderings for the achievement of a PhD.

Initially I was assigned a carpeted office with the use of a computer, telephone, printer and photocopier. Although such luxury was not to last, I also enjoyed ample shelf space, two desks on which to spread out, two filing cabinets and, to crown it all, a comfortable armchair to sink into while I perused the necessary literature. All enviable accoutrements, indeed. I could hardly believe my luck. I was to share this office with another PhD student, Dan Dwyer, whose robust sense of humour and love of Shakespeare made sharing a total pleasure in non-thesis moments. Dan was engaged in research on Indonesian fishing practices off the northern coast of Australia and his knowledge on maritime matters was clearly profound. A big burly man with the tang of the salt sea air about him, his commanding presence often made me think of my ancestors striding the quarterdeck of a ship of Nelson's navy. I used to delight in giving him a navy salute as we went our ways at the end of a day's study.

My first chats with Clayton set me on the right course as I prepared the questionnaires and discussed what I should be looking out for on my visits to the two chosen sites. Before the questionnaires could be distributed, however, they had to be written and then approved by an Ethics Clearance Committee. This created somewhat of a dilemma because I didn't know exactly what questions I wanted to ask until I had got ideas from the sites themselves. But I couldn't do any research at the sites until I had the Ethics Clearance!

Over the next two years I made several visits to both Kakadu and Port Arthur, delivering and collecting completed questionnaires, and making on-site notes. I also attended conferences in various cities and the presentation of papers at these conferences was encouraged, but I felt I needed to first try out my wings by giving several talks at the *University of the Third Age* in Darwin. This organisation, known as U3A, began in France in 1972 with the idea that universities should be required to provide more community education. It quickly spread to Europe and North America, and when it reached England various changes were made to the French model, so that it became more of a community based organisation not tied to universities. The British model was introduced into Australia in 1984 and the term "university" is still used, but only in the original sense of the word which is "a coming together of like-minded people with a common interest in learning".

After giving talks at the U3A, I gave my first academic paper at the joint AIMA/ ASHA (Australasian Institute of Maritime Archaeology / Australasian Society for Historical Archaeology) Conference held at Adelaide University in 2000 when I spoke about my research in progress. At the conclusion, someone asked me a question, and lacking experience in this situation, my mind went blank, I gave a terrible answer, and I felt abysmal shame. I felt I hadn't prepared adequately and began to lose self-confidence.

On my return to Darwin, this worsened and I felt I'd lost the plot completely. As I appraised the results of the returned questionnaires I realised that the questions were too broad to make the answers much more than a sort of rather innocuous tourist survey, and hardly PhD stuff. I now needed to change the main thrust of the thesis more towards showing how each site was presented to the public, rather than specifically noting the perceptions of the public.

By 2002, I considered I was ready to submit the first draft of one of the thesis chapters to Clayton. The draft came back with lots of red writing. Above all I needed to "deconstruct" more positively what previous writers had said about the sites. Panic set in on reading the dreaded word "deconstruct". I'd often heard this word, but always thrust it to the back of my mind. What does the word mean? How does one "deconstruct?" Is there a formula? From the Internet I had downloaded pages and pages of mostly, to my ignorant mind, gobbledegook, but which I knew must mean something important if only I could fathom what learned French philosophers, such as Derrida or Foucault, were talking about.

After my awkward Adelaide presentation I attended other conferences although I did not give any more papers. A conference held at the Port Arthur Historic Site in 2003 had its amusing moments. My supervisor, Clayton, was also attending. I had flown down some days in advance of the conference, as I wanted to do some more research on-site as well as touring in a hire car around the beautiful Tasmanian countryside so reminiscent of my beloved England. I had volunteered to meet Clayton at Hobart Airport and transport him to Port Arthur and the on-site hotel where I always stayed. This time it was full of conference people instead of the usual tourists. I was looking forward to showing him round the site. On one of the walkabouts through the Interpretation Centre he consented, with great panache and holiday style humour, to being attached to a convict style ball and chain and having his photo taken. The result was a picture I had great pride in showing to my family

Clayton with ball and chain attached to his legs. Port Arthur had been a penal settlement.

later as evidence that supervisors are really quite human people and can join in a joke with their students.

A later incident at Hobart Airport on Clayton's departure was not quite so well received by him. At the conclusion of the conference he accompanied me back to the airport when I returned the hire car. I parked the car and walked into the depot to hand in the keys, leaving Clayton to get the luggage out. I completed the necessary paperwork with the pretty young girl at the depot counter who then said she had to check the car over to make sure I hadn't damaged it in any way. As we walked to the car she chatted politely, but in those slightly condescending tones sometimes used by the young who believe they have everything going for them, to a senior customer who, they imagine, is way past the joys of life. Then we reached the vehicle and she saw the luggage spread out on the ground and Clayton in attendance. I could almost feel her thoughts: "How on earth did that old bird manage to get herself a gorgeous hunk like that?" would no doubt have been fluttering through her mind. I was tickled pink at the almost deferential tone she used as she continued talking to me while business was concluded. "Good grief," I said to Clayton after she had departed, "she thinks you're my toyboy." I thought it was rather hilarious but poor Clayton didn't seem to know quite how to react.

Back in Darwin hilarity went out the window as I tried to knuckle down to the demands of thesis writing. The next draft chapter I showed Clayton, although acceptably written in thesis-like language, purposely contained gaps where I felt I needed guidance and clarification on what I was trying to say. I wanted to thrash out my ideas, discard some, get new ones to play with, learn from someone with more experience and knowledge than I possessed. I was told, however, that a properly finished draft with nothing but my own thoughts was what was needed, not a half completed one. What I felt I really needed was more time with my supervisor but this did not seem to be on the cards. It seemed that modern day bureaucracy in universities ties up the time of lecturers and supervisors so that they are no longer able to have the one-to-one chats on philosophy and other matters with their students. I had always imagined such chats were a part of university life.

I felt if only I could talk at length with my supervisor, bring my muddled thinking out into the open, discuss and be given direction, I would be able to blossom and produce something academically acceptable. But it now appeared that that was a pampering too far and not the way PhD students were expected to achieve their goals. Clayton, echoing what was apparently the now accepted formula for student work, told me, "It's *your* thesis, *you* must write it." Stunned, I thought I might as well work on the entire thesis and then give it to him *in toto* instead of chapter by chapter. This idea seemed to be quite acceptable. I still had meetings with my supervisor every month but these now tended to be brief enquiries as to how I was progressing to which I replied, "Oh, getting there slowly," and made some general reference to a particular chapter I was working on.

In March 2004 I handed in a complete 100,000 odd words thesis, with added voluminous tables, references, plates and appendices. It was a stupendous and monumental effort. But unfortunately, as an academic study it turned out to be far too imaginative, with ideas irrelevant to the main aim but which, in my ignorance, I thought gave it a rather pleasing body. I had even brought in Shakespeare and Henry V at one point! If only I had been able to chat over each chapter with my supervisor, I could have discussed all these extraneous ideas before wasting precious time putting them down on paper.

My thesis was returned to me in May, having been pulled to pieces and comments made on my shortcomings. As Clayton said, he had to be stern and even harsh in his comments if the examiners were going to accept it. I submitted several of my new chapters but they met with only slightly more approval and I seemed to have misunderstood Clayton's suggestions for a new approach and gone off once again at an unnecessary tangent. Then Clayton moved to Canberra to take up a new position and advancement in his own career. He intimated he would continue as my supervisor if I wished, but clearly he had enough on his plate.

And then a quite amazing and uncanny thing happened. I received an email from Harry Allen, an Associate Professor presently lecturing at Auckland University, New Zealand, asking if I might like his help with my thesis. Tall and fair haired, I always remembered Harry as a charming and kindly man from the time when he used to call in at the pub at the Jim Jim when he was engaged in archaeological investigation in the area in the 1970s. I had also had the enormous pleasure in my Museum days of boxing and bagging the artefacts he had excavated from the western Arnhem Land site of Narradj Warde Djobkeng. Perhaps because of all this, Harry never failed to give me a brief and friendly, "And how are you, Judy?" greeting at the various conferences we both happened to attend, whereas I noticed other well-known academics were inclined to ignore undergrads at such gatherings.

Harry had also been one of the examiners for my Honours thesis. Perhaps he had seen some glimmering of my academic potential for research, which he also recognised needed some guidance. But how did he know I so desperately needed guidance now? Perhaps some academic contact between Clayton and Harry had mentioned my name as one of Clayton's students needing help.

With communication by email, Harry suggested papers I should read which gave me new ideas for integration into my work. I was learning. I was expanding my thinking. I really felt I was getting somewhere with my thesis and I was enjoying every single minute of it.

The thesis was finally called *The Interpretation of Australian Heritage Sites: Kakadu and Port Arthur* and by the end of June, 2007, the total product of my efforts, amounting to some 490 pages, was despatched by the Research Department of the University to three examiners. The results would not be known for at least a couple of months.

With my thesis in the hands of the examiners for their approval and my study days over for the moment, I had time to sit back and consider my next step through life and also reflect on past moves. I realise how fortunate I have been to have had all those opportunities to experience so much, with each experience – whether good or bad – expanded into another. I am very conscious of the fact that I have been lucky in that so much of my life has been blessed with good health and good fortune. Whilst it is true that at one point I felt I was about to wither away from lack of purpose, now it was a case of "Whither away?" The answer, I felt, was "To the Stars," whatever that meant. I was simply full of elation at future prospects which I felt sure would come my way. Chance is a funny thing. Had I chosen the right path which might lead me to those stars when I decided to emigrate in 1958?

Did I have any particular regrets in my life? Briefly I wondered how I would have fared if my voice had not played up on me and kept me from a life on the stage. Would I have made it in musical comedy? Who knows? I do sometimes feel regret at not having been able to extend such a career to find out. And yes, I regret that circumstances were not in my favour for having those seven children I had dreamed of as a teenager – or indeed, any children at all – and therefore never knowing the joys of motherhood. But do I now miss waves of visiting grandchildren? Or feel lonely without some form of live-in companionship? Am I envious when most of my friends have partners? No! I feel totally liberated! Selfishly perhaps, I find a single life in my senior years rather enjoyable in being able to do what I want to do, when I want to do it.

As I no longer enjoy the social "whirl" I can, without being churlish to a partner particularly "after hours," spend my evenings in silence reading a book if I wish, change TV channels to suit my taste, or nod off to sleep without warning. I am tied to no one person but at the same time, in the daytime hours, have the joy of many friends and acquaintances who keep me in the swim of life. The companionship of marriage has become a thing of the past. The good, bad and fun times I had with Tom have now mingled into a kaleidoscope memory of adventure with that true-blue Aussie.

I thought about my parents who gave me such a stable early childhood filled with love, and an education which instilled into me those essential basics of literacy. That gift was to be a start-up point for those later unimagined explorations of the mind, since it provided me with the capacity to read my way to higher thought – always assuming that I had the ability and sense of purpose to use it. University then provided me with the best environment to set me on the right path for academic knowledge with its insistence on theoretical underpinnings and proven processes to support any research.

For a time, when writing my thesis, I enjoyed the mind-tugging and constant self-discipline I had to employ – it was very necessary to choose words and reasoning of a standard acceptable to my supervisors and the examiners. But at this stage of my University career I was beginning to realise that perhaps such self-discipline wasn't really me. I wondered whether it might be time to acknowledge the fact that I was a dreamer rather than a scholar! It seemed the astrological split personality of a Gemini was taking me away from academia and my desire to climb its giddy heights. Was it time to seek an alternative direction for my life – but what direction could that be? Perhaps my dreaming soul was destined to search for the meaning of life by connecting in some way with nature.

I have related in earlier chapters of my love of the Kakadu area and the idea of living there "for ever and ever" at the place Tom and I called *Cooinda*, "The Happy Place". That dream was not to be when circumstances beyond our control forced a change of direction for us and we had to sell, but it was by no means the end of Cooinda. Under the guidance of the new owners, the Gagudju Association, Cooinda was forging ahead as the kind of tourist destination we had envisaged. Always known for its natural beauty, now Aboriginal culture and spirituality were also becoming part of its image.

Was such a spiritual connection with nature a path I should now travel? Was it finally time to settle down in that little shack on the piece of land our Aboriginal friends had promised us? I could just spend my days sitting and meditating on the banks of the billabong at the spot Tom and I called the *Place of the Whispering Shadows*. Yet I didn't feel as though I could sever myself quite so drastically from the world of practical learning.

As I tried to sort myself out, I decided to make a quick trip to Kakadu to see if the idea really appealed to make a more permanent location there. In the meantime, on a website relating to the Territory Wildlife Park at Berry Springs, which was only some 40 kilometres from my Palmerston home, I read that a six kilometre easily walked path meanders through natural bushland immersing visitors in a variety of typical Top End habitats. In fact, it said, visitors could be forgiven for thinking they were in the middle of Kakadu. That sounded rather promising so, instead, I made my first visit to the Territory Wildlife Park and became hooked. I found that, as a Friend of the Park, I could make free visits whenever I wished.

My first port of call in the Park came to be what was called the *Woollybutts and Wallabies Enclosure* where a mock rock shelter had been constructed of huge slabs of rock. I started to knock idly on these rocks as I went by in a sort of gesture of greeting until on a visit around one Christmas time I gave it several hearty knocks and noticed the

With Trevor Le Lievre, who helped me at university, and Emma, the tour guide, aboard the Judy Opitz, *on Yellow Water, 2008.*

different sounds that were produced from various points on the rock. In frivolous spirit I gaily knocked away until I achieved a passable rendition of "Good King Wenceslas," followed by "Three Blind Mice," and "Camptown Races". I ended with "Advance Australia Fair" as a group of other visitors to the Park approached. I explained what I was doing and left them knocking away at tunes of their choice. Meeting people in such a milieu as this Wildlife Park is a friendly affair. The brief greetings exchanged, with a cheery "G'day" as one passes on the track, always brighten my day.

Apart from such pleasantries with other visitors, what was I getting out of these visits to the Park? Was I connecting with nature? I liked to think I was. Strolling the leafy pathways which link the exhibits, I experience that deep peace of mind akin to that spiritual connection with nature which is so much a part of the Kakadu scene. At my call at the rock shelter on each visit, I no longer tap out a tune but do always give a particular rock a greeting tap before placing my full palm against one of the configurations in its natural form. I have found these configurations neatly accommodate my fingers and thumb in the slight grooves.

CDU celebrates students' achievements

Hundreds don robes for graduation

MORE than 250 graduands robed up to receive formal recognition of the successful completion of their studies at Charles Darwin University during last night's end-of-year graduation ceremony at the Darwin Convention Centre.

Some 1000 students officially graduated as part of the ceremony which recognised the academic achievements of students from both the higher education and vocational education and training sectors.

A total of nine PhDs were awarded, along with an Emeritus Professorship.

Professor MaryAnn Bin-Sallik received an Emeritus Professorship in recognition for her commitment and contribution in advancing education and equity policies for Indigenous Australians.

PhD graduands Bernadine Atkinson, Janet Whitehead, Rodney Nixon, Gao Yu, Azmah Abdul Manaf, Linda Jan Rice, Fay Johnston, Tricia Nagel and Judy Opitz were all present on the evening. Mikiko Kawano received a Doctor of Teaching.

The night also saw Dr Len Notaras, General Manager of Royal Darwin Hospital, and the late Australian paediatrician, Dr Alan Walker, recognised with Honorary Doctorates.

A determined and well-respected paediatrician both in the Territory and in many renowned organisations in Australia and overseas, Dr Walker had a major impact on both his patients and the medical profession. Through his pioneering efforts, the Royal Darwin Hospital was recognised nationally for work on improving the health and lives of Aboriginal children.

Following his Honorary Doctorate presentation, Dr Len Notaras gave the Occasional Address. High-profile Bachelor of Nursing

Judy gains PhD at 84

By RAQUEL DUBOIS

AT age 84, PhD graduate Judy Opitz has combined her two passions – learning and Kakadu – and steered a straight course for the highest academic honour.

After 18 consecutive years of university study, she received a Doctorate of Philosophy at Charles Darwin University's graduation ceremony last night.

In 1990 Dr Opitz started an Arts degree at CDU's predecessor institution, Northern Territory University (NTU), majoring in archaeology and anthropology. she said her days as an undergraduate were the happiest of her life, and she wholeheartedly embraced student life and the opportunities for learning.

Immediately after finishing her first degree, she enrolled in an Honours course and was awarded BA (Hons) from NTU in 1998. But with her appetite for learning yet to be satisfied, she decided to begin a PhD.

Her thesis compares the archaeological significance of two Australian Heritage sites – Port Arthur Penal Colony (in Tasmania) and Kakadu National Park – and examines the different ways each site's archaeological history is presented for visitors.

She said that visitors to Kakadu were seeking a more in-depth knowledge of Indigenous culture, and wanted to know about the use and significance of the site to prehistoric peoples, not just about its present-day significance.

At the same time as working on her thesis, Dr Opitz wrote her autobiography entitled "An English Rose in Kakadu", which has been accepted by a local publisher.

The book recounts her childhood in England where she was raised by nannies and governesses, to her

POM" in 1959, and eventually to meeting her future husband and crocodile hunter hero, Tom Opitz, in the famous Darwin Hotel.

Tom worked at the Nourlangie Safari Camp as a guide, leading hunting and shooting parties for well-heeled American tourists.

In 1964 the couple built a store in Kakadu, which later became the Gagudju Lodge Cooinda, renowned for its Yellow Water boat cruises. After her husband died in 1982, Judy opened a shop in Darwin's CBD, selling seashells and jewellery.

To satisfy a seemingly unquenchable desire for learning, Dr Opitz enrolled in correspondence and short courses in Egyptology, literature and mathematics.

READY AND RARING: Judy Opitz in her early days in the Territory. INSET: Dr Judy Opitz is preparing for further study.

Research probes Kakadu and Port Arthur

something I wanted to try out," she said, "just to see if I could do them."

She submitted the first complete draft of her thesis to her supervisor in 2004, but it was rejected as not meeting academic standards required to be offered for examination. However, she wasn't easily discouraged, and she began re-writing.

And after another four years' work, her determination finally paid off.

philosophy. Her study ambitions, however, will have to fit in with promoting tourism in the Top End and publishing her autobiography. The proceeds of her book will go towards Indigenous educational programs in the Territory.

Dr Opitz said education would always be important to her, and helping people access education was her current passion. She said getting a degree was never her primary focus, but rather she set out to acquire knowledge and discovered the personal rewards education offered.

"I see education as tremendous exercise for the brain, and I feel particularly rewarded in knowing I've

---

On one of the rocks towards the back of the shelter, a hand stencil has been blown, similar to those found in many genuine Aboriginal rock shelters. These stencils are made by the artist holding a solution of colour in his mouth and spraying it over his hand which is held spread out over the rock. Unlike those hand stencils, my hand stencil is only illusory, but nevertheless briefly connects me in some way – or so I imagine – to the rock itself. I often wonder if such a connection is what the Aborigines were doing when they made those marks on the living rock. As I "connect" through my own hand touching the rock, I look upward through the swaying branches of the tallest trees to a blue, blue sky. I hear the birds singing and the thud, thud of wallabies hopping about their business through the undergrowth. I hear the muted voices of visitors in the distance and the excited cry of a child. It is a special moment of peace and happiness for me before I continue on what I have come to call my Meditation Trail around the Park. This Trail provides me with what I need to keep me in harmony with humanity.

These moments of peace with the world extended to life outside the Park and calmed me as I waited and waited for the Examiner's Reports. When they came at last I found I was required to make some minor changes at the request of two of the examiners; however, some fairly extensive changes were required by the third examiner. It was a relief when my final offering was accepted by the governing board and I had my doctorate. My status would be confirmed officially at the October 2008 Graduation Ceremony to be held at the new Darwin Convention Centre.

David M. Welch

Our old store still stands at the Jim Jim Crossing and the high water mark from each Wet Season can be seen on Tom's brick piers. Termites have eaten away the stairs, but the sandpalm cladding remains. 2008.

Then what? What would be the answer to my query "Whither away?" if I did not think I was going to be motivated enough to use my thesis as the basis for any future work in academia, nor settle on the banks of the Jim Jim Creek and meditate in solitude? The realisation came that my time spent during my research at the Anbangbang rock shelter was now offering to lead me in another, less academic, direction. During my informal chats to tourists on the site I had achieved a certain rapport with them and learnt of their interest in what Kakadu could offer them spiritually as well as visually. They were beginning to understand that humanity is a part of the infinite world of nature and the two must go hand in hand if humanity is to survive. For the wellbeing of a world whose inhabitants seem at times to have lost direction, perhaps this message could be passed on by tourists as they tread the globe in their vast numbers, by communicating with each other and the peoples of the countries they visit.

Who better to initiate such a message and start it on its journey round the globe than visitors to Kakadu? And in involving myself in some way in such a journey, I believed I would be led to the starry sanctum that I sought.

Acknowledgments

Firstly, my thanks to David and Annie Welch, who evidently saw worth in bringing one woman's story before the public gaze and helped in every way to bring it to fruition.

Secondly, in alphabetical order, I would also like to thank the following: for their interest and encouragement in getting this book off the ground, I would particularly like to thank historians Baiba Berzins, Mickey Dewar, and Peter and Sheila Forrest; for giving me inspiration and help in ways of which they may not be aware, I thank CDU lecturers David Carment, Clayton Fredericksen, David Mearns, Alan Powell and Dennis Shoesmith. I am similarly grateful to CDU staff members Judith Austin and Linda Cuttriss. Museum professionals George Chaloupka, Christopher Chippindale, Mike and Anne Eastman, and Pina Giuliani, instilled in me a more percipient depth of feeling for rock art and understanding of Aboriginal culture for which I thank them. Thanks to Yvonne Forrest and members of U3A, Darwin, who bore with my talks about the early days of Cooinda and other adventures and spurred me on to get it all down on paper. Grateful thanks to my Uni colleagues, Julie Mastin and Ron Ninnis, for their help in proof-reading and suggestions to clarify meanings of certain wartime terms which they believed were unfamiliar to modern day readers. Special thanks to Jeff Gillies and all the staff at Gagudju Lodge, Cooinda, for their hospitality during my recent visits to the area. Thanks likewise to Helen Rysavy of Storm Front Web Design for her valued assistance in setting up my Web Page. I would also like to pay tribute to my dear wartime companion, the late Kay Watts, and her family, for helping me keep alive so many memories of those WW2 days.

I must especially note and give thanks to the staff at the Territory Wildlife Park. Their more recent kindness and consideration in permitting me access to the Rock Shelter site – part of my Meditation Trail – during the period of a reconstruction program of the area was much appreciated.

My deepest thanks, of course, to my own dear sister, Julia, and brother-in-law, Anthony, who have always been there for me.

I must not fail to mention the three men in my life who have offered me, in my Uni days and beyond, so much in terms of the helping hand of friendship, in both academic support and later assistance in the publication of my book.

My never-ending thanks go to Associate Professor Harry Allen of Auckland University who pulled me out of the doldrums when I began to think I was an academic failure and who, by his wisdom and encouragement, succeeded in getting me back on track.

Enormously grateful thanks must go to Dan Dwyer, my one time office mate, whose friendship I hope will continue far into the future. He could be relied upon to lighten the load of life with a good giggle at some gag or other, and was always ready to verbally spar with one on more abstruse ideas – such as the purpose of life!

And thanks indeed to Trevor Le Lievre, a fellow PhD candidate, for not only steering me through the intricacies of the electronic preparation of my thesis for publication – a task somewhat beyond a typewriter mentality, but also for his contribution to the readability of my autobiography. His interest, encouragement and friendship were indispensable in producing this book.

Judy Optiz
Darwin, December 2008